D0900748

WEST ACADEMIC PUBLISHING'S
LAW SCHOOL ADVISORY BOARD

JESSE H. CHOPER
Professor of Law and Dean Emeritus,
University of California, Berkeley

JOSHUA DRESSLER
Distinguished University Professor, Frank R. Strong Chair in Law
Michael E. Moritz College of Law, The Ohio State University

YALE KAMISAR
Professor of Law Emeritus, University of San Diego
Professor of Law Emeritus, University of Michigan

MARY KAY KANE
Professor of Law, Chancellor and Dean Emeritus,
University of California, Hastings College of the Law

LARRY D. KRAMER
President, William and Flora Hewlett Foundation

JONATHAN R. MACEY
Professor of Law, Yale Law School

ARTHUR R. MILLER
University Professor, New York University
Formerly Bruce Bromley Professor of Law, Harvard University

GRANT S. NELSON
Professor of Law Emeritus, Pepperdine University
Professor of Law Emeritus, University of California, Los Angeles

A. BENJAMIN SPENCER
Justice Thurgood Marshall Distinguished Professor of Law
University of Virginia School of Law

JAMES J. WHITE
Robert A. Sullivan Professor of Law Emeritus,
University of Michigan

PRINCIPLES OF SECURED TRANSACTIONS

Second Edition

James J. White
Robert A. Sullivan Professor of Law Emeritus
Member, Michigan Bar
University of Michigan Law School

Robert S. Summers
William G. McRoberts Research Professor in
Administration of the Law, Emeritus
Member, Oregon and New York Bars
Cornell Law School

Daniel D. Barnhizer
Professor of Law and The Bradford Stone Faculty Scholar
Michigan State University College of Law

Wayne Barnes
Professor of Law
Texas A&M University School of Law

Franklin G. Snyder
Professor of Law
Texas A&M University School of Law

CONCISE HORNBOOK SERIES™

WEST ACADEMIC PUBLISHING

The publisher is not engaged in rendering legal or other professional advice, and this publication is not a substitute for the advice of an attorney. If you require legal or other expert advice, you should seek the services of a competent attorney or other professional.

© 2007 Thomson/West
© 2018 LEG, Inc. d/b/a West Academic
    444 Cedar Street, Suite 700
    St. Paul, MN 55101
    1-877-888-1330

Printed in the United States of America

ISBN: 978-1-68328-517-5

Preface

With the addition of three new co-authors, this new edition updates prior versions to include new caselaw developments, substantive discussions of law and policy, and references to current UCC revisions and amendments.

Acknowledgments

Professors Barnes, Barnhizer, and Snyder, in taking on this project, uniformly agreed that "we are standing on the shoulders of giants." The contributions of Professor White and Professor Summers to the development of understanding of the UCC by students, practitioners, judges, legislators, and scholars simply cannot be overstated. We are honored to have the privilege of continuing this work.

Summary of Contents

Table of Contents

PRINCIPLES OF SECURED TRANSACTIONS

Second Edition

Chapter 1

SCOPE OF ARTICLE 9

Analysis

1–1   INTRODUCTION

a.   The History of Article 9

Article 9 was the most innovative of the original Code articles. Unlike other articles, which tended to conserve and improve much existing law, Article 9 marked a substantial departure. Those most responsible for the new law—Grant Gilmore, Allison Dunham, and

1

Karl Llewellyn[1]—found themselves faced with a large body of separate pre-Code personal property security regimes that varied widely among the states. Each of these regimes had in mind the same basic situation: A debtor owes money to a creditor, and gives the creditor the right to take and sell the debtor's personal property if the debt is not paid. These situations can range from the very simple (e.g., a consumer's pledge of a gold necklace at a pawn shop) to the relatively complex (e.g., a firm providing inventory financing to a retailer.) Sometimes the creditor's interest is based on money lent to purchase the item, like an automobile; sometimes it is taken on property unrelated to the debt. The number of different situations in which creditors take and execute on such interests is limited chiefly by the imagination of business people and commercial lawyers, and both groups often can be *very* imaginative.

In pre-Code days, lawyers for creditors and debtors had to work with a whole range of different legal methods for securing repayment, each governed by its own distinct body of law. These were many and varied, including such things as pledges, chattel mortgages, conditional sales, trust receipts, and factor's liens. What made things even more difficult was that laws varied widely from state to state. What was a statutory device in one state would be found only in the common law of a second, and might be wholly absent in a third. Moreover, the requirements of a particular device in one state might be different in another which ostensibly had the same device available. This was not, perhaps, a serious problem in the 19th century, when lending was largely local, but by the middle of the 20th, it was increasingly difficult for nationwide lenders to get the loan protections they sought, which made loans both more expensive and harder to get.

The grand innovation of Article 9 in 1962 was the introduction of a "unitary" security device. In place of the dizzying array of prior terminology, Article 9 substituted one device and one set of basic terms: "security agreement," "secured party," "debtor," "collateral," "security interest," and so on. In place of the various bodies of substantive law governing the various pre-Code security devices, Article 9 provided a single body of law. There are, to be sure, a few pre-Code legal distinctions that were carried over into the new law,[2] but these generally reflect either different types of collateral that

---

[1]   All three seem to have come upon the idea of a unitary security device at about the same time. G. Gilmore, Security Interests in Personal Property § 9.2 at 290 n. 2 (1965). The most important early general discussion of Article 9 is Gilmore, The Secured Transactions Article of the Commercial Code, 16 Law and Contemp. Prob. 27 (1951).

[2]   The best index to these appears in the lengthy official comment to § 9–102 of the 1972 Code.

require somewhat different treatment (e.g., goods or accounts), or to functionally different types of security interests in such collateral (e.g., possessory or non-possessory,[3] purchase-money or non-purchase-money[4]). Instead of multiple security devices, however, there is only a single "security interest" even though the requirements for particular types of collateral or different interests may be treated differently.

Article 9 was promulgated in 1962, and it was adopted in all the states. The 1962 Official Text of Article 9, however, was the victim of more state non-uniform amendments than other Articles. Partly for this reason, a committee constituted by the Code's Permanent Editorial Board completed a new version of the Article in 1971.[5] This version was embodied in the 1972 Official Text and is sometimes referred to as the 1972 Code.

The 1972 version also had its defects, particularly a lack of clarity in several key areas. These problems led to a new round of amendments. A Revised Article 9 was adopted by the National Conference of Commissioners on Uniform State Laws in the summer of 1998. Acceptance from the American Law Institute came in 1999, and the act carried an effective date of 2001. While sources variously use the 1998 and 1999 dates—they are used interchangeably—for convenience we will use the 1999 date for the revisions.

The 1999 Article 9 is more comprehensive than the 1972 revision. Dealing with the ambiguities in the earlier version made the new one longer and more certain, but also more complex. These changes made the job of sophisticated commercial lawyers much easier, but made it more difficult for a casual student to understand. It is important to note that the 1999 revision required a substantial reorganization. Many sections were renumbered, while others were dismembered and had their parts strewn among other provisions. Because of this, one must be careful when reading older cases because the references may well have changed.

Another set of amendments to Article 9 were approved by NCCUSL in 2010, and went into effect in 2013. (We in this text will use the 2010 date.) Most are relatively technical changes aimed at fixing issues issues—particularly those regarding filing—that arose in practice under the 1999 version. Many of the specific 2010 amendments were designed to make the filing system more reliable for users. They have been adopted in all U.S. states, along with the District of Columbia and Puerto Rico. Except where specifically

---

[3]   See, e.g., §§ 9–203; 9–207.

[4]   See, e.g., §§ 9–103; 9–309(1); 9–317(e); 9–324.

[5]   See Perm. Ed. Bd. UCC Rev.Comm. Art. 9, Final Report (1971).

noted, the references in what follows will be to the 1999 version as amended in 2010.

b. Important Definitions and Concepts in Article 9

Article 9 is filled with important and intricate definitions and concepts. Subtle differences in the law under Article 9 depend upon what seem to be subtle differences in definitions. It is important to remember that the terms used in Article 9 have very specific definitions to which lawyers (and law students) must pay careful attention. When article 9 uses words like "attach," "perfect," "proceeds," and even "debtor" and "creditor," these do not always mean (and may often be very different from) what they mean in common usage and even in other legal contexts.

The most basic concept is that of the "security interest," the term that replaces all of those older forms. A security interest, as defined in 1–201(b)(35), is (1) "an interest in personal property or fixtures" that (2) "secures payment or performance of an obligation." Assume, for example, that A borrows money from B to purchase a sailboat and grants B a right to seize and dispose of the boat if A does not pay. The contract between A and B is called the "security agreement," and the boat (which "secures" the repayment) is the "collateral." Because B gets an "interest" in the "collateral" that "secures repayment" by A, B has a "security interest."

Code definitions in this situation tell us that B is the "secured party" under the agreement, and A, the owner of the collateral, is the "debtor." Because A also owes B money, A is also the "obligor." (While the debtor and obligor tend to be the same party in most transactions, there are some in which the person who owes the money grants an interest in property owned by someone else.) Students should understand that the security agreement, typically a written or electronic form provided by the creditor, is both a contract and a deed—a conveyance of a present interest in property.

With these basics set, the first concept a student should understand is "attachment" of a security interest. A security interest "attaches" to the collateral when it "becomes enforceable against the debtor." Usually that requires three things: (1) that the debtor sign or electronically authenticate a security agreement; (2) that the debtor have rights in the collateral in which it is conveying an interest; and (3) that value has been given for the security interest. In our example above, the security interest attaches when A signs the agreement, B makes the loan, and A gets ownership of the boat—whichever comes last. Once the security interest has "attached," it is effective between the debtor and the creditor. (Whether it will be effective against third parties will depend on whether it has been "perfected," which we discuss below.)

Attachment is the building block on which all of the secured party's Article 9 rights. When the security interest has "attached" there is a conveyance of a property interest from the debtor to the creditor just as if the parties had used a deed. Unlike a simple deed, however, the security agreement will also contain many promises by the debtor, including such things as making payments, insuring and protecting the collateral, making periodic financial reports to the creditor, and various representations and warranties. Although a security agreement in complex transactions may be an elaborate document negotiated between the debtor and creditor, it can be as small as a single page. There is no magic form.

After attachment, the next step is "perfection." Attachment alone is enough to protect the secured party's rights against the debtor, but it is a melancholy fact that debtors who have stopped paying one creditor have often stopped paying others, and thus the party with the security interest may find a number of other creditors (or a bankruptcy trustee) clamoring to seize and dispose of the collateral. The key to protecting the secured party against other creditors of the debtor is perfection.

A perfected secured creditor defeats most other claimants to the collateral in which the creditor holds a security interest if the competitors' claims arose after the secured creditor's perfection. For example, an unperfected secured creditor loses to a lien creditor (e.g., someone who got a judgment and then had a sheriff seize the debtor's property) and also to any secured creditor whose interest attached later but who perfected first. By far the most ubiquitous lien creditor is the trustee in bankruptcy who, under federal law, is treated as having a judicial lien on all of a bankrupt's assets on the date the bankruptcy petition is filed. This means that every creditor who does not properly perfect will be treated as an unsecured creditor in its debtor's bankruptcy.

How does one "perfect"? In the large majority of cases, the secured party perfects by filing a document called a "financing statement"—generally referred to in practice as a "UCC–1" form—in the government office specifically designated by the state for that purpose. In most cases, that will be the office of the state secretary of state, but in some instances and for some types of collateral filing may be required in a particular county.

A financing statement (described in 9–304) is a sparse document, even with the changes made in the 2010 amendments. Its primary job is to identify the debtor and the creditor, and describe the collateral against which the creditor has a claim. The theory is that by searching the files under the debtor's name, those who subsequently seek to deal with the debtor can learn of outstanding security interests it has granted before they lend money.

Filing is not always required, however. Sections 9–308 through 9–316 set out the rules for perfection. In some cases, a secured creditor will perfect by taking possession of the collateral. In a pawn shop transaction, for example, the debtor hands the pawned item over to the shop to be held until the debt is paid. Such possession amounts to a perfected security interest. In other transactions, such as certain consumer purchases, perfection is automatic and occurs at the same time as attachment. There are also unusual cases in which perfection is attained by a process called "control." For now, we ignore the intricacies of automatic perfection and control.

"Collateral" is the generic term for any tangible or intangible asset belonging to the debtor in which the debtor grants a security interest. In our simple example above, we noted that the boat was collateral for the loan. But article 9 contains a set of devilishly intricate definitions of types of collateral. For example, goods are broken down into four categories: inventory (9–102(a)(48)), farm products (9–102(a)(34)), consumer goods (9–102(a)(23)), and equipment (9–102(a)(33)). Intangibles have even more complicated subdivisions (often with even more complex definitions: accounts (9–102(a)(2)), chattel paper (9–102(a)(11)), deposit accounts (9–102(a)(29)), documents (9–102(a)(30)), instruments (9–102(a)(48)), investment property (9–102(a)(49)), letter of credit rights (9–102(a)(51)), general intangibles (9–102(a)(42)) and even money.

Understanding these categories is important, because perfection rules vary depending on the category of collateral. A mode of perfection that is permitted—even required—for one kind of collateral may not be permitted for other kinds of collateral. One can, for example, perfect a security interest in a deposit account only by having "control," but one can only perfect a security interest in a general intangible (like a partnership interest) by filing. Careful reading of the definitions is important. Suppose, for example, a farmer raises chickens both for meat and for eggs. He grants a security interest in all of his "farm products" to a secured creditor and the creditor files a financing statement that identifies "farm products" as the collateral. The farmer goes bankrupt and the issue is whether the lender perfected its security interest. Are the eggs "inventory" because they are held for sale? Are some chickens "equipment" because they are capital assets used to produce eggs? Are some of the chickens equipment, while others (the ones being sold for meat) inventory? Or are they all "farm products"? Their correct classification will be critical, because if the filing was wrong the creditor's security interest is invalid and the creditor goes from having rights to the specific property to being an unsecured creditor likely to get pennies on the dollar.

In addition, the rights of third parties, such as bona fide purchasers of assets from the debtor, sometimes depend upon the nature of the collateral. In general, a bona fide purchaser of "inventory" from a debtor takes free even of a prior perfected security interest, but that is not true of a bona fide purchaser who buys "equipment."

A final concept, the meaning of which is not obvious, is "proceeds." In cases and in the Chapters that follow, students will see many references to "proceeds." According to 9–102(a)(64), proceeds are what is "acquired upon the sale . . . or other disposition of collateral . . . ." Assume a secured creditor has a security interest in a car dealer's inventory of automobiles. Assume further that the car dealer sells an automobile to a consumer in return for the consumer's promise to pay, accompanied by a new security interest between the consumer and the car dealer to ensure the consumer's payment. The consumer's promise and security agreement, added together, constitute "chattel paper"—a different kind of intangible—and the chattel paper is now "proceeds" of the automobile. The person who loaned money to the car dealer no longer has a perfected security interest in the car (which the debtor no longer owns) but will now own a perfected security interest in that chattel paper as "proceeds" of the car in which it had a security interest. If instead, the consumer had paid with a check, that check in the hands of the dealer would be "proceeds" of the car.

Learning Article 9 requires persistent and careful attention to the definitions in section 9–102. When you work on a problem or read a case, you should keep one finger in 9–102 and, at the slightest doubt, should turn there. Eventually you will be able to carry some of the definitions in their heads but it is foolish to attempt to memorize the meaning of every single word and concept; it is far better simply to return to 9–102.

PROBLEM

Assume a debtor, Local Mortgage Co, wishes to borrow against its body of real estate mortgages and their accompanying notes. Big Bank is willing to lend, but it wants to be sure that it has a perfected security interest. One lawyer has suggested that a filing listing "mortgages" would be the way to perfect. A second lawyer suggests that nothing need be done because Bank is going to take the "sale of a promissory note," and those security interests are perfected upon attachment under section 9–309. A third lawyer agrees that the collateral is promissory notes, not mortgages, but maintains that a filing needs to be done because the transaction contemplated is not a "sale."

The third lawyer is correct. The real estate mortgages are not the primary collateral; the real collateral is the notes that promise repayment. They thus are properly classified as "promissory notes," while the mortgages are regarded in this transaction as "supporting obligations" (see 9–203(f)). Nor is the transaction a "sale," for Bank is not buying the instruments outright but rather plans to hold Local Mortgage liable in the event of a default. The principal difference between a sale and a conventional security interest is that in the sale the party acquiring the interest can look only to the asset sold, and has no right to get a deficiency or to satisfy that deficiency out of the debtor's other property.

The example shows the danger of ignoring the definitions. To answer the bank's legal issue, one needs to understand that the collateral is promissory notes and that the transaction is not a sale. It also shows that many, but far from all, of the definitions are found in 9–102.

1–2   BASIC ARTICLE 9 SCOPE PROVISIONS, SECTION 9–109(a)

A major theme in Article 9 is that substance governs over form. This is important, because particular economic transactions can often be structured in different ways to achieve different ends. Suppose, for example, A wants to acquire $24,000 worth of computers from B, and wants to pay for them in 12 monthly payments of $2,000. If this were a sale on credit, B would use a security agreement and would have to file a financing statement to protect itself in the event A fails to pay. But leases of goods do not fall under Article 9, because the creditor retains ownership. So if the parties call the transaction a 12-month "lease" with a $1 option to buy at the end, B can argue that it is a lessor and not a secured creditor, and therefore did not have to file to protect its interest. There is nothing inherently illegal in doing things like this. Structuring transactions as leases instead of sales (or vice versa) is a common practice for a variety of reasons noted below. But Article 9 is intended to be a unified national system that creditors can rely on, so allowing creative lawyers to escape it by artful language in their particular agreements would defeat the purpose.

Thus, if Article 9 otherwise applies, parties who are engaged in ordinary financing transactions cannot render it inapplicable merely by casting their arrangement in the language of a lease or some particular pre-Code device. The drafters of the 1962 Code provided in the basic scope section of the Article that it applied to security interests "created by contract including 'pledge, assignment, chattel mortgage' . . . ."[6] The terms pledge and chattel mortgage, as well as several others (such as conditional sale) are now archaic, yet courts and parties sometimes still use that terminology. Each of these is a label for a separate kind of transaction that would have created something equivalent to a security interest under law prior to Article 9. Although, as noted above, vestiges of all of these transactions can be found in Article 9, today each is merely a particular form of Article 9 security interest. To decide whether Article 9 governs a transaction, the student and lawyer must usually turn at least to sections 1–201(b)(35) ("security interests"), 9–109 ("scope"), and perhaps to 9–102 ("definitions"). Each bristles with problems.

Section 9–109 emphasizes that all security interests, "regardless of . . . form," are included within the scope of Article 9. It even sweeps in certain financing transactions even though they are not conventional security interests. Section 9–109(a) reads in full as follows:

Except as otherwise provided in subsections (c) and (d), this Article applies to:

(1) a transaction, regardless of its form, that creates a security interest in personal property or fixtures by contract;

(2) an agricultural lien;

(3) a sale of accounts, chattel paper, payment intangibles, or promissory notes;

(4) a consignment;

(5) a security interest arising under section 2–401, 2–505, 2–711(3), or 2A–508(5), as provided in section 9–110; and

(6) a security interest arising under section 4–210 or 5–118.

Section 1–201(b)(35), as noted above, defines "security interest" broadly. Because it applies to any transaction that "regardless of its form" creates a security interest, parties will find it difficult or impossible to create a transaction that has the economic characteristics of a security interest but is treated under the law as something else.

---

[6] Section 9–102(2) (the scope provision in the 1972 Code) read: "This Article applies to security interests created by contract including pledge, assignment, chattel mortgage, chattel trust, trust deed, factor's lien, equipment trust, conditional sale, trust receipt, other lien or title retention contract and lease or consignment intended as security. This Article does not apply to statutory liens except as provided in § 9–310."

Article 9 also governs certain security interests arising under other provisions of the Code. These are brought into Article 9 by 9–109(a)(5) and (6). The "agricultural liens" of subsection (2) are 1999 additions to Article 9. The coverage of "sales" of accounts and other intangibles were enlarged by the 1999 revision. The "factoring" or "sale" of rights to payments by the person entitled to those payments to a third person has long been regarded as a financing transaction. As such, they have most of the economic characteristics of a personal property financing transaction and are now covered more fully by Article 9 than was true prior to 1999.

Article 9 covers all consignments, at least as that term is defined in 9–102). But be careful here; the definition of "consignment" excludes certain transactions a lay person would recognize as consignments, such as consignments of used clothing or furniture to a resale shop.[7]

Clear cases of consensual security interests to which Article 9 applies are easy to imagine. Perhaps the simplest are what were once called the "pledge," the "conditional" sale (in which the seller extends credit and reserves a security interest), and the "chattel mortgage." But it also applies to sophisticated forms of business finance, including inventory "floor planning" and accounts receivable financing. It governs the rights of the so-called "financing buyer" who advances money to the seller and acquires an interest in the goods to be supplied, which secures the supplier's duty to deliver the goods. Thus, an Article 9 security interest can also secure the performance of non-monetary obligations. Section 9–102(a)(42)'s "catch-all" provision for general intangibles also allows for the attachment of security interests to a wide range of property interests.[8]

Section 1–201(b)(35) defines "security interest" to mean an "interest in personal property or fixtures which secures payment or

---

[7]   § 9–102(a)(20) defines "consignment" as follows: "Consignment" means a transaction, regardless of its form, in which a person delivers goods to a merchant for the purpose of sale and:

      A. the merchant:

           a. deals in goods of that kind under a name other than the name of the person making delivery;

           b. is not an auctioneer; and

           c. is not generally known by its creditors to be substantially engaged in selling the goods of others;

      B. with respect to each delivery, the aggregate value of the goods is $1,000 or more at the time of delivery;

      C. the goods are not consumer goods immediately before delivery; and

      D. the transaction does not create a security interest that secures an obligation.

[8]   See, e.g., In re Scheidmantel Olds-Cadillac, Inc., 144 B.R. 296, 18 UCC2d 1222 (Bankr. W.D. Pa. 1992).

performance of an obligation," a definition broad enough to include *any* distinctive claim to assets of a debtor that a creditor might assert on default. We cannot take that definition of security interest at face value, however. For example, section 9–339 states that nothing in Article 9 prevents subordination agreements in which a superior creditor subordinates its interest to another. It might be argued that when one creditor of a debtor agrees to subordinate its claim to that of another creditor, the elevated creditor acquires a "security interest," but that would be wrong.

For a second example, suppose a debtor agrees with one of its creditors not to create any security interests in its personal property until the debtor has paid off that creditor. It could be argued that such a "negative pledge" clause creates a security interest in the favored creditor. Perhaps it might seem so under the Code's broad language, but such idiosyncratic and unusual deals fall outside the scope of Article 9. As Professor Gilmore noted early on, the Article was drafted to "regulate certain well-known and institutionalized types of financing transactions."[9] Gilmore argued that interests such as the "negative pledge" may still be valid security interests, but that they are not within Article 9:

> It is fair enough to say that a transaction which sets out to be one of those types should conform to the Article 9 rules or fall by the wayside. But beyond the area of institutionalized transaction, there stretches a no-man's land, in which strange creatures do strange things. For these strange things there are no rules; it makes no sense to measure them against the rules which professionals have developed for professional transactions. The best that can be done is to let the courts pick their way from case to case, working out their solutions ad hoc and ad hominem.[10]

As it happens, section 9–109 and its predecessors have generated relatively little litigation. Even the most deviant of secured transactions generally have fallen under the umbrella of Article 9. The successive rounds of amendments have brought nearly all of them into the fold. To the extent there had been confusion, such things as accounts, chattel paper, payment intangibles, and promissory notes are now clearly included, while securitization of loans and sale of loan participations—both of which generally were excluded from the original Article 9 as "sales" of general intangibles—are now included. Deposit accounts, also originally excluded, now serve as original collateral under Article 9.

---

[9] G. Gilmore, Security Interests in Personal Property § 11.1 at 337 (1965).

[10] *Id.*

Some sellers, by analogy to older law, have tried to retain or reserve title to goods that have been delivered to a buyer (section 2–401), but under Article 9 such provisions are limited to effect the reservation of a security interest. The special property interest of a buyer of goods on identification of those goods to a contract for sale under 2–401 is not a security interest, but a buyer may also acquire a security interest by complying with Article 9. Consignments, which involve goods sent to merchants to hold for sale on thee consignor's behalf, are covered, and consignors now hold security interest in the consigned goods.

1–3   SECURITY INTEREST OR LEASE?

A fecund source of disputes over the years has been whether a particular transaction is a sale with a reserved security interest or a "true lease." Leases are not within the scope of Article 9, but are instead governed by their own Article 2A. While some transactions are easy to categorize, others are not.

The basic difference between a lease and a sale is relatively uncontroversial. A lease involves payment for the temporary possession, use and enjoyment of goods, with the expectation that the goods will be returned to the owner with some expected residual interest of value remaining at the end of the lease term. In contrast, a sale involves an unconditional transfer of absolute title to goods, while a sale with a security interest is also a transfer of title, with only an inchoate interest contingent on default and limited to the remaining secured debt.[11]

But while the distinction is simple in theory, it can be very troublesome in practice. The relevant provision for answering that question is the formidable section 1–203, which is the primary focus of this chapter.

PROBLEM

> Assume that a client comes into your office with a document that has the title "lease" at the top. The "lease" provides that the lessee will make payments of $1,000 per month for 60 months and at the end of that time the lessee has a right to purchase the truck for $100. Your client, the lessor, never filed a financing statement and is now being challenged by the lessee's trustee in bankruptcy. The trustee claims that your client holds only an unperfected security interest in the truck. The trustee points to the hundred-dollar option to buy and says that the practical effect of the

---

[11]   See, Cooper, Identifying a Personal Property Lease Under the UCC, 49 Ohio St. L.J. 195, 197–208 (1988); Gelb & Cubita, Recent Developments in the Recharacterization of Personal Property Leases, 41 Consumer Fin.L.Q. 42 (1987); Naples, A Review and Analysis of the New Article 2A, 93 Com. L.J. 342, 348–351 (1988).

transaction is not a lease of the goods, but is in fact a disguised sale with the retention of security interest.

The trustee is right and your client's interest will be avoided by the trustee who, under Bankruptcy Code section 544, holds a lien that is superior to your client's unperfected security interest. As you see above, the substance of the transaction (sale plus security interest) prevails over the form (lease). This case is relatively easy, but as you will see below, there are some close cases where it will take real skill to distinguish between a lease and a security agreement.

a. The Problem

The rights of a true lessor in personal property do not qualify as an Article 9 security interest. The leased goods are not property of the debtor (although the lease rights themselves may be such) and thus cannot be used to satisfy the lessee's debts. If a levying creditor of the lessee or the lessee's trustee in bankruptcy claims leased goods as against the lessor, Article 9 does not determine the outcome, and the lessor generally prevails under Article 2A. That is so even though no filing or other public record shows the lessor's interest. The drafters of Article 2A and of the revised Article 9 could have required lessors to file financing statements so third parties dealing with the lessee could better learn of the lessor's interests, but they did not. Under 9–505, a lessor nervous about how the transaction will be characterized is permitted, but not required, to file.[12] This will often be desirable.

If, on the other hand, the transaction is not a true lease but rather a disguised installment sale, Article 9 applies and the putative lessor effectively has only a security interest to secure the obligation to buy and pay for the goods. Such a "lessor" who does not comply with section 9–203 will not be entitled to enforce its interest even as against the debtor. If it does not file a required financing statement, it loses to all parties who, under Article 9 and other law, take priority over an unperfected security interest. These include certain purchasers from the "lessee,"[13] certain lien creditors of the "lessee,"[14]

---

[12]   Comment 2 to 9–505 provides:

Doubts may arise whether a transaction creates a relationship to which this Article or its filing provisions apply. For example, questions may arise over whether a "lease" of equipment in fact creates a security interest or whether the "sale" of payment intangibles in fact secures an obligation, thereby requiring action to perfect the security interest. This section, which derives from former section 9–408, affords the option of filing a financing statement with appropriate changes of terminology, but without affecting the substantive question of classification of the transaction.

[13]   §§ 9–102; 9–317; 9–320; 9–323.

[14]   § 9–317.

the "lessee's" trustee in bankruptcy,[15] and others. The "lease vs. security interest" issue continues to be one of the most frequently litigated issues under the Uniform Commercial Code.

You might ask why secured creditors persist in claiming to be lessors. There are many reasons. A lessor, for example, has different rights than a secured creditor on default or on the lessee's bankruptcy.[16] But Article 9 is not the only legal regime out there, and it may not be the most important consideration in how the parties structure their transaction. Under many other bodies of law, a lease may be preferable. There are, for example, important tax considerations. Since a lessee does not own the leased goods, it may escape state or local taxes on personal property, which would be paid by the lessor. Under various versions of Internal Revenue Code (which change frequently) lessees may get larger deductions from income than they would enjoy if they were treated as the owners of the leased goods. Accounting rules also make treatment as a lease preferable—debts owed for purchases always appear on balance sheets as liabilities, but future lease payments in some circumstances may not.[17] Moreover, a true lessor (unlike a seller on credit) is not making a "loan" to the lessee and therefore may not violate state usury laws even when the effective interest rate on a similar sale would.[18]

Sometimes lessees wish to characterize their transactions with financing attributes as leases and not as debt liabilities to keep from breaking promises that they have made to other creditors. Assume, for example, a debtor has signed a covenant with a lender that it will not borrow more money except with that lender's approval. If a "lease" is not a "borrowing" and so falls outside that covenant, the debtor may enter it without the lender's approval.

The distinction between lessor and secured creditor takes on added importance when the debtor is in bankruptcy. If a true lessee goes into bankruptcy, the lessee or trustee ordinarily must affirm the

---

[15]   § 9–317; 11 U.S.C.A. § 544.

[16]   Sections 361–63 of the Bankruptcy Code provide that the debtor in bankruptcy may continue to use the collateral, with or without the consent of the secured party, as long as the secured party is given adequate protection of the value of the collateral. In contrast, a true lease is covered by 11 U.S.C.A. § 365, which provides that a lessee in bankruptcy, or its bankruptcy trustee, must either assume a true lease and give adequate assurances that prior defaults will be cured and future obligations will be performed, or else reject the lease and return the goods to the lessor.

[17]   Accounting rules allow certain lease obligations to be omitted from the lessee's liabilities, whereas secured credit obligations appear on the balance sheet as debt. See, e.g., In re P.W.L. Investments, 92 B.R. 680, 8 UCC2d 163 (Bankr.W.D.Tex.1987) (lease executed so as to not increase balance sheet liabilities).

[18]   True leases are generally exempt from state usury laws. Huddleson, Old Wine in New Bottles: UCC Article 2A Leases, 39 Ala. L. Rev. 615, 623 n. 20 (1988).

lease and keep making full payments, or reject the lease and return the leased goods.[19] The true lessor's rights to these payments or to the return of the goods do not depend upon the filing of a financing statement or the taking of any action to "perfect" the lessor's interest. One claiming to be a lessor, but who is found to be a secured seller, who has filed no financing statement loses to the trustee in bankruptcy as an unsecured creditor. Even a perfected secured creditor may fare worse than a lessor under Chapter 11 of the bankruptcy laws because the debtor may be able to keep the collateral in a "cramdown" (paying its fair market value) instead of the contracted liability. The distinction is important in other contexts as well.

These and other rules like them may lead the lessor (or secured party) to characterize the transaction one way for one purpose (e.g., Article 9 law) and another way for another purpose (e.g., tax law).[20] The lessor's lawyer may also try to draft something that will be accepted as a lease for accounting purposes, yet confer the economic rights of a security agreement.

For these reasons, distinguishing between true leases and disguised secured sales agreements has been troublesome. The trouble has not abated over the years. As noted above, the road sign that directs traffic either to Article 9 (secured transactions) or to Article 2A (leases) is section 1–203.

Consider the purest form of lease and contrast it with the purest form of security agreement. A classic lease would be the lease of a truck for one year. If the truck has a useful life of ten years, the lessor, not the lessee would stand to gain from appreciation in the truck's value or to lose from its depreciation. The lessor has what we might call an "entrepreneurial stake" in the truck, and a valuable "reversionary" interest. Compare that to the position of a bank which lends money to a trucker so he can purchase the truck. If the bank takes security in the truck, the bank, of course, has an interest that the truck not decline below the amount of the debt outstanding, but beyond that the bank has no interest in the truck itself. If the truck proves to be worth twice what was expected, this is a windfall to the debtor, and if the truck is destroyed or declines radically in value, that loss falls on the debtor (provided it is solvent) and not on the bank. The trucker, not the bank, has the entrepreneurial stake.

When the term of a lease gets longer, and inches toward the full economic life of a commodity, when an option to purchase is granted

---

[19]   11 U.S.C.A. § 365 (West 1999).

[20]   See, e.g., Kimco Leasing, Inc. v. State Bd. of Tax Comm'rs, 622 N.E.2d 590 (Ind.Tax 1993) (lessor cannot avoid personal property tax by claiming lease was a security agreement).

to the lessee, and when the lessee assumes many of the risks of ownership (secures for itself most of the benefits or detriments of ownership), a lease begins to look more and more like a secured loan in which the attributes of ownership are held not by the lessor/creditor but by the lessee/debtor. In a 1988 article, Edwin Huddleson suggested that the real issue is whether in a given transaction there is truly a reversionary interest in the hands of the lessor after the agreement is signed.[21] He made the point as follows:

> The central feature of a true lease is the reservation of an economically meaningful interest to the lessor at the end of the lease term. Ordinarily this means two things: (1) at the outset of the lease the parties expect the goods to retain some significant residual value at the end of the lease term; and (2) the lessor retains some entrepreneurial stake (either the possibility of gain or the risk of loss) in the value of the goods at the end of the lease term.[22]

That is a relatively straightforward and analytically useful approach, but it is not the one that the Code drafters and subsequent revisers elected to take. With respect to Article 2A, section 2A–103(1)(j) is of very little help:

> "Lease" means a transfer of the right to possession and use of goods for a period in return for consideration, but a sale, including a sale on approval or a sale or return, retention or creation of security interest or license of information is not a lease. Unless the context clearly indicates otherwise, the term includes a sublease.

The official comment to this section simply directs one to section 1–203 for answers to the hard questions. Article 9 similarly leads readers to the same statute.

Section 1–203 did not attempt to state a bold and explicit definition based on the reversionary interest. Instead, it offered a list of factors that should or should not support an inference of lease. Under 1–203(a), whether a particular transaction is considered a lease or a sale "is determined by the facts of each case."

b. Section 1–203 Sign Posts

Broadly speaking, section 1–203 has two lists of factors, those that militate against or in favor of considering the ostensible lease to be a true lease. Assuming that the transaction is in "the form of a lease," subsection (c) lists the factors that would suggest that the

---

[21] Huddleson, Old Wine in New Bottles: UCC Article 2A Leases, 39 Ala. L. Rev. 615, 625 (1988).

[22] *Id.*

transaction is, in fact, a true lease. If these are met, it is likely (though not certain) that the agreement creates a lease. Subsection (b), however, points in the opposite direction. If its factors are met, the "lease" is probably a secured transaction. Subsections (d) and (e) add definitions and additional wrinkles. We will take these in their statutory order.

1.   *Security Interest, Not a Lease*

Under 1–203(b) the following create "security interests," not leaseholds:

> A transaction in the form of a lease creates a security interest if the consideration that the lessee is to pay the lessor for the right to possession and use of the goods is an obligation for the term of the lease and is *not subject to termination by the lessee*, and:
>
> (1) the original term of the lease is equal to or greater than the remaining economic life of the goods;
>
> (2) the lessee is bound to renew the lease for the remaining economic life of the goods or is bound to become the owner of the goods;
>
> (3) the lessee has an option to renew the lease for the remaining economic life of the goods for no additional consideration or nominal additional consideration upon compliance with the lease agreement; or
>
> (4) the lessee has an option to become the owner of the goods for no additional consideration or nominal additional consideration upon compliance with the lease agreement.

(Emphasis added.) Note the "not subject to termination" language. If the lessee is free to stop paying and return the goods, we would ordinarily see the transaction as a simple at-will lease and Article 9 will not apply. But if the lessee has obligations that run for the entire term of the lease, and the lease is *not* terminable by the lessee, we have to turn to one of the four factors.

Under factors (1) and (2), the lease or the renewal which the lessee is bound to make will absorb the entire economic life of the goods. Assume a lease of truck tires for three years during which time the truck is expected to be driven more than 200,000 miles. The lessor does not expect any significant reversion; while the truck will presumably still have some value, the tires will be worn hulks. The transaction is a secured sale, and the "lease" is a security agreement.

Conditions (3) and (4) deal with the situation in which the lessee has an option to extend the lease or to become the owner of the goods for no money or for only nominal additional consideration. Assume the lessor is leasing a new and expensive luxury automobile for three years under a contract that grants the lessee the right to become the owner at the end of three years by exercising an option and paying $1.00. Unless the present value of those payments over the three years equals the value of the new car, the lessor has made a foolish bargain, because the expected value of such a car after three years is in the thousands or tens of thousands of dollars, and surely the $1.00 option will be exercised. The parties have really signed a three-year secured sale agreement, not a lease.

2.   *Lease, Not a Security Interest*

Turn now to 1–203(c) that provides a general rule for identifying transactions not "for security," i.e., true leases. This rule states six conditions that are not enough alone to make the transaction one for security:

A transaction in the form of a lease does not create a security interest merely because:

(1) the present value of the consideration the lessee is obligated to pay the lessor for the right to possession and use of the goods is substantially equal to or is greater than the fair market value of the goods at the time the lease is entered into;

(2) the lessee assumes risk of loss of the goods;

(3) the lessee agrees to pay, with respect to the goods, taxes, insurance, filing, recording, or registration fees, or service or maintenance costs;

(4) the lessee has an option to renew the lease or to become the owner of the goods;

(5) the lessee has an option to renew the lease for a fixed rent that is equal to or greater than the reasonably predictable fair market rent for the use of the goods for the term of the renewal at the time the option is to be performed; or

(6) the lessee has an option to become the owner of the goods for a fixed price that is equal to or greater than the reasonably predictable fair market value of the goods at the time the option is to be performed.

By these six clauses the drafters sought to overrule a series of decisions under a prior version of section 1–201(37).[23] The results are not always felicitous.

Subpart (1), to begin with, is puzzling. It tells us that something is not a security agreement *merely* because the present value of the projected payments is substantially equal to, or greater than, the fair market value of the goods. Normally one would assume that when that test is met the parties have a secured sale, not a lease. In a line of cases, apparently overruled by 1–203, courts assumed just that.

Could tax and other benefits to the lessee change the equation? To see how that might be so, consider Rushton v. Shea,[24] cited in Comment 2 to section 1–203 in which one party leased railroad tank cars. Over the 15-year lease, the lessor would have received payments with a present value equal to the fair market value of the tank cars plus approximately 1% per month interest. This would seem to indicate that the transaction was a secured sale. But because the tank cars were expected to retain significant residual value which would revert to the lessor at the end of the 15-year lease, the court found the transaction to be a true lease.

You may wonder why a lessee enter into a transaction under which it would pay more and wind up not owning the property. There are several possibilities. First, the lessor and lessee might be controlled by the same party, and the lease might be a device for shifting income from one to the other. Second, there may be unique tax benefits to be gained by the lessee (such as deductions against a high marginal rate representing gain that could be split between the parties). Third, the lessee might be making payments to the lessor to enjoy certain other benefits of the lease such as the avoidance of debt limitations in other loan documents or the avoidance of state and local personal property taxes. Put in economists' words, constructing the transaction as a lease as opposed to a sale may create an externality, i.e., may cause third parties to bear part of the cost of the transaction in the form of reduced claims or smaller tax revenues. The end result is that the lessee realizes a valuable benefit which, when offset against the payments to the lessor, means the net

---

[23] Under section 1–201(37) of the pre-1987 Code, courts often used a "laundry list" approach to distinguish a lease from a security agreement. There were two problems with the laundry list approach. First, some factors were equally consistent with a security agreement or lease. Second, the factors used by courts proved to be so vague it was difficult to predict whether a judge would characterize an agreement as a lease or a security agreement disguised as a lease. Such lists have been characterized as an "enumeration of an arbitrary set of factors, ostensibly based upon the indicia of ownership, identified by the courts on an ad hoc basis." See, Cooper, Identifying a Personal Property Lease under the UCC, 49 Ohio St. L.J. 195 (1988) at 201.

[24] 419 F.Supp. 1349, 22 UCC 273 (D.Del.1976), motion denied, 423 F.Supp. 468, 22 UCC 274 (1976).

amount the lessee is paying to the lessor is not equal to or greater than the fair market value of the goods. Thus, while lease payments that equal the fair market value of the goods *suggest* that a "lease" might in reality be a sale, they do not compel that conclusion.

Subsections (2) and (3) of section 1–203 cover obvious cases. The drafters are telling us in effect that lessees as well as buyer-debtors routinely bear risks of loss, pay taxes, insurance, and registration fees. They are saying that the well-known "triple net" leases (those where the lessee is responsible for taxes, insurance, and maintenance) are still leases even though the lessee bears most of the burden. These seem to be sensible conclusions.

Subsections (4) (5) and (6) of 1–203(c) state a lessee's option to buy at a cost equal to or greater than "the reasonably predictable fair market value" or to re-lease at "the reasonably predictable fair market rent" does not convert a lease into a secured sale. Here the option is with the lessee and, even though the lessee later has to pay (either to rent or buy) the estimated fair market value, the lessor still bears the risk that the lessee will not exercise that option. If, for example, the leased goods are worth substantially less than the parties originally predicted, that loss will be borne by the lessor because, by hypothesis, the lessee will not exercise its option. If, on the other hand, the goods are later worth much more than the parties had predicted, the lessee will probably exercise the option and will thus enjoy the gain. In that transaction the parties have split the entrepreneurial stake. The drafters have concluded that one may yet be a lessor even if he has dealt away one-half of his entrepreneurial stake.

As an example, the Comment to section 1–203 cites the case of Arnold Machinery Co. v. Balls.[25] In that case, the defendant leased a backhoe from the plaintiff for a minimum of six months and thereafter until either party terminated the lease relationship. In conjunction with the lease, the parties made a purchase option agreement whereby the lessee could purchase the backhoe for the full purchase price, plus a 1.25% monthly purchase option charge, plus the cost of any repairs during the lease period, plus any taxes paid during the lease period, less a 100% credit for all rentals paid. The court ruled that this transaction constituted a true lease. If reasonable depreciation is assumed, the purchase option price might be greater than or equal to the reasonably predictable fair market value of the backhoe at the time the option was exercised. It is not a foregone conclusion that the lessee will be economically compelled to exercise the option; the parties have simply split the entrepreneurial

---

[25]   624 P.2d 678, 34 UCC 236 (Utah 1981).

stake. If the backhoe depreciates more rapidly than expected, the lessee will *not exercise* the option and the lessor will receive less than his expected residual value. If, on the other hand, the backhoe depreciates less rapidly than expected, or even appreciates, the lessee is *likely to exercise* the option.

It is useful to compare another case, In re J.A. Thompson & Son, Inc.[26] with *Arnold Machinery*. The lessee in *J.A. Thompson* leased heavy equipment with a purchase option agreement whereby the equipment could be purchased for a specified price plus a 5 1/2% per annum "add-on charge" less a 100% credit for rents paid. The court held this arrangement to be a secured sale because "little additional consideration" was required to exercise the purchase option. In our view, the *J.A. Thompson* court erred in failing to compare the expected value with the option price. Section 1–203 rejects its analysis and endorses *Arnold Machinery*.[27]

The preamble to subsection 1–203(c) says that "a transaction in the form of a lease does not create a security interest *merely* because it provides that . . . ." Are the drafters telling us, for example, that if a lessee assumes the risk of loss or agrees to pay taxes, this is irrelevant in determining whether a transaction is a lease? Or are they saying that none of these is enough alone? We suspect the drafters included (c)(1) through (6) not just because they believed those factors do not carry the day alone, but because they believed those factors not relevant—singly or together. Except perhaps for (1), we regard the factors not only as "not enough," but as generally not relevant in determining whether a document is a lease or a security agreement.[28]

3.   More Section 1–203 Guidelines

Subsections (d)–(e) set out some additional definitions and interpretative rules:

(d) Additional consideration is nominal if it is less than the lessee's reasonably predictable cost of performing under the lease agreement if the option is not exercised. Additional consideration is not nominal if:

(1) when the option to renew the lease is granted to the lessee, the rent is stated to be the fair market rent for the

---

[26]   665 F.2d 941, 33 UCC 356 (9th Cir.1982).

[27]   624 P.2d 678, 34 UCC 236 (Utah 1981).

[28]   Some courts have so held. See, e.g., In re Cole, 100 B.R. 561, 9 UCC2d 234 (Bankr.N.D.Okla.1989), aff'd, 114 B.R. 278, 12 UCC 2d 212 (N.D.Okla.1990); In re Thummel, 109 B.R. 447, 11 UCC2d 948 (Bankr.N.D.Okla.1989); In re Wallace, 122 B.R. 222 (Bankr.D.N.J.1990).

use of the goods for the term of the renewal determined at the time the option is to be performed; or

(2) when the option to become the owner of the goods is granted to the lessee, the price is stated to be the fair market value of the goods determined at the time the option is to be performed.

(e) The "remaining economic life of the goods" and "reasonably predictable" fair market rent, fair market value, or cost of performing under the lease agreement must be determined with reference to the facts and circumstances at the time the transaction is entered into.

First, subsection (e) says that "remaining economic life of the goods" and "reasonably predictable" are to be determined at the time the agreement is made. If the parties enter into a lease of computers expected to have a five-year useful life and the lease term is only two years with no options, the agreement they have signed is a lease, not a security agreement. This is so even if the leased goods, as it turned out, became obsolete after only two years. This is a sensible rule. When the parties sign the contract and become bound, they have either made a lease or a security agreement. That agreement is based upon their present judgments about values, useful life, inflation, risk of non-payment, and other matters. The agreement may prove to be much more beneficial to one than the other, but that does not change its character once the agreement has been signed. Foresight, not hindsight, controls.

c.   Reversionary Interest

Once a court concludes that a lease is not terminable and that none of the conditions in 1–203(b) has been met, its work is not done. Failure to meet one of these conditions signifies only that the document is not *conclusively* a security agreement. Evasion of those four barriers does not make the document a lease. Finding economic life beyond the lease term and seeing no nominal consideration option, what should a court do? The court must then answer whether the lessor retained a reversionary interest. If there is a meaningful reversionary interest—either an upside benefit or a downside risk— the parties have signed a lease, not a security agreement. If not, it is a security interest.

d.   Nominal Consideration

Whether consideration for an option is considered "nominal" may be of substantial importance. Under 1–203(b)(3) a lease with an option to purchase or to renew for the remaining economic life of the goods for a "nominal additional consideration" is a security agreement. But what is "nominal"? An amount considerably less than fair market value might still be more than nominal value.[29]

First, "nominality" is to be tested at the time the agreement is signed. As we have indicated, that is explicit in subsection 1–203(d); something is a security agreement or lease when it is signed. Nominality, therefore, must be determined by considering the parties' *prediction* of concluding value at signing, not by considering the actual value at the conclusion of the term.

But none of this defines nominality in the common case. Assume, for the sake of argument that the parties anticipate that a leased combine will be worth $20,000 at the end of a five-year lease. Clearly, an option price of $1.00 is nominal and an option price of $20,000 is not nominal. Both of those statements are true whether the *actual* value at option time is $40,000 or zero. But where between the two does nominality begin and end? One possibility is to consult the dictionary, under which only "trifling" amounts are nominal. Under that interpretation conceivably $1,000 for a combine expected to be worth $20,000 would not be nominal because $1,000 would not be a trifling amount. We have our doubts.

In our view the proper price against which to measure the option price is the value that the goods are expected to have at the time the option is to be exercised (e.g., $20,000 for the combine). We would allow a substantial deviation from that value and yet conclude the amount is not "nominal." We believe any option price less than 50% of the predicted fair market value (predicted at signing as the value at the option date) should presumptively be nominal, while anything above 50% may still be suspect.

We believe that nominality is, in reality, merely a proxy for the fundamental question: "Is the option price so low that the lessee will certainly exercise it and will, in all plausible circumstances, leave neither risk nor benefit as a reversion for the lessor?" The cases on nominality are in disagreement and many, in our view, are mistaken. We generally endorse the cases that find a payment of less than 50% of the predicted fair market value to be nominal. But we doubt a bright line can be drawn here.[30]

---

[29]   See Official Comment to § 1–201(37) (West 1990).

[30]   See, e.g., In re Hispanic American Television Co., 113 B.R. 453, 11 UCC2d 1226 (Bankr.N.D.Ill.1990); Orix Credit Alliance, Inc. v. Pappas, 946 F.2d 1258, 16 UCC2d 502 (7th Cir.1991); Sine Enterprises, Inc. v. Jaguar Credit Corp., 139 F.3d 912, 35 UCC2d 161 (10th Cir.1998) (an option price representing over 30% of the original purchase price is not nominal).

PROBLEM

> Assume the lease of an aircraft for 10 years. Assume that the aircraft has a useful life of 40 years and that the lessee has an option to renew his lease for an additional 15 years at the end of the first 10. This is a lease, not a security agreement. Because the aircraft has a useful life of 40 years and the maximum time that has been given to the lessee is 25 years, there is a reversionary interest and the lessor has an economic interest in the asset.
>
> Assume the lease of a piece of industrial equipment for five years with a five-year option. The equipment has a 10-year useful life. During the initial term it is not clear whether the lessee will exercise its option. Once the lessee has exercised the option, clearly the transaction has become a security transaction. It is no longer a lease. Assume that the lessor is your client and that the lessee has gone into bankruptcy during the first five-year term. The lessor who has not filed a financing statement asks you whether he will defeat the trustee. The answer is that he will defeat the trustee because there is still a reversionary interest arising from the possibility or even probability that the goods would come back to the lessor at the end of the five-year term. If, on the other hand, the lessee had already exercised its option before the bankruptcy, the outcome is different. Such leases are sometimes called chameleon leases for they change their status upon the exercise of the option. *Marhoefer Packing*[31] is a leading case dealing with such a lease.

1–4 CONSIGNMENTS AS SECURITY INTERESTS

In a typical consignment, an owner puts goods in the possession of a consignee with instructions to sell those goods to third parties. Normally, the consignor agrees to take the goods back if they are not sold. If the goods are sold, the consignee takes a percentage (say 20%) of the sales price and remits the proceeds. Consignments are common in the marketing of certain goods, such as diamonds and books. A typical consignment has some of the economic characteristics of a loan against inventory for the consignor's capital enables the consignee to display inventory on its sales floor and to make sales the consignee could not otherwise make. However, a consignment is not exactly the same as a secured loan, for it leaves the risk of no sale on the consignor/seller not on the consignee/buyer.

Prior to the 1999 revision, most of the Code law on the rights of consignees and their creditors was found in section 2–326 of Article 2. In general, that section subordinated the consignor's interest to rights of the creditors of the consignee in any case in which the consignee did business under a different name than the consignor, unless the consignor could prove that the consignee was "generally

---

[31] Matter of Marhoefer Packing Co., 674 F.2d 1139, 33 UCC 370 (7th Cir.1982).

known to be dealing in goods of another,"[32] or the consignor complied with a relevant sign law showing its interest[33] or filed a financing statement under Article 9.

In addition, former Article 9 contemplated transactions where the parties used consignment language, but the deals were truly "secured transactions," not conventional consignments. If, for example, a debtor borrowed money from a creditor, granted a security interest in inventory and promised to repay the sum *whether or not the goods were sold*, that transaction would be treated in all respects like a secured transaction even if the parties labeled it a "consignment." The foregoing type of transaction differs from the usual consignment in which the consignee has no obligation to pay if it returns the goods. If a court concluded the transaction was in fact intended as security, then knowledge by the consignee's creditors would not save it from the claim of a trustee or a judicial lien creditor, for it would be treated in all respects like a security interest. This division left some "consignments" entirely within Article 9 but some only partly there, and left the courts in doubt about what parts of Article 9 applied to which transactions.

The 1999 revision and the conforming amendments of 2–326 are substantial improvements. First, section 9–102(a)(20) defines consignment as follows:

"Consignment" means a transaction, regardless of its form, in which a person delivers goods to a merchant for the purpose of sale and:

(A) the merchant:

(i) deals in goods of that kind under a name other than the name of the person making delivery;

(ii) is not an auctioneer; and

(iii) is not generally known by its creditors to be substantially engaged in selling the goods of others;

(B) with respect to each delivery, the aggregate value of the goods is $1,000 or more at the time of delivery;

(C) the goods are not consumer goods immediately before delivery; and

---

[32] See, e.g., In re Arthur A. Everts Co., 35 B.R. 706, 37 UCC 1537 (Bankr.N.D.Tex.1984) (consignor must prove "generally known" by the number of creditors, not by the amount of indebtedness).

[33] See, e.g., BFC Chemicals, Inc. v. Smith-Douglass, Inc., 46 B.R. 1009, 40 UCC 1674 (E.D.N.C.1985) (for compliance with § 2–326(3)(a), a consignor must show evidence of a sign in fact and that the sign was conspicuously placed at the consignee's place of business).

(D) the transaction does not create a security interest that secures an obligation.

The definition incorporates most of the conditions of former 2–326. In a second important definitional change, section 1–201(b)(35) states that any consignment (as that term is defined in 9–102(a)), is a "security interest." This means all consignors who are not explicitly excluded by the definition in 9–102(a)(20) hold security interests that are subject to subordination by lien creditors and others under 9–317 if their interests are unperfected. To protect their interests, consignors will have to perfect them like any other security interest. The combination of 9–102(a)(20) and 1–201(b)(35) has moved almost all commercial consignments into Article 9—at least for most purposes.

Certain transactions a layperson would describe as consignments are not consignments, as that term is used by Article 9. Thus, a consignment of used clothing or used furniture, which were "consumer goods" before consignment to a consignment store is not a "consignment" under 9–102(a)(20)(C).

What of the other cases excluded from 9–102(a)(20) by 9–102(a)(20)(D), not because they are not sufficiently secured transactions but because they secure "an obligation"? The drafters here have preserved a distinction between a conventional commercial consignment, defined in 9–102(a)(20), which in almost all cases, is a "security interest," and the unusual commercial consignment which creates a security interest "that secures an obligation." But if all consignments under 9–102(a)(20) must be perfected and enjoy more or less the same priority as any other security interest, who cares whether a transaction is merely a consignment subject to Article 9 or whether it is a security interest "that secures an obligation"? If it secures an obligation, wouldn't Article 9 apply, anyway?

The distinction comes not with respect to whether Article 9 applies, but to the remedies available under foreclosure. The consignor in either case must protect its interest by filing a financing statement and is, for the purposes of perfection and priority, treated like a secured creditor A consignor whose interest also "secures an obligation" under 9–102(a)(20)(D) must follow the same restrictive rules on repossession, resale and the like that apply to other secured creditors. But in the ordinary case where the consignment does not "secure an obligation"—e.g., if it is a standard consignment of diamonds (say) with a duty of sale or return but no duty to pay for unsold goods—it is not so treated for the purpose of foreclosure. The consignor may get its goods back by whatever method is permitted under the state law outside of Article 9. One way to think of the two transactions is to say that a classic consignment creates an interest that behaves like a security interest for the first five parts of Article 9 but not for the sixth, whereas a consignment "that secures an obligation" is a security interest for all parts of Article 9.

That leaves a third type of consignment. These transactions— consignments of consumer goods to a consignment store, consignments of items of less than $1,000, and consignments to a person generally known by its creditors to be substantially engaged in selling the goods or to a consignee who acts in the name of consignor—are not within Article 9. They are governed by 2–326(1), which reads as follows:

> Unless otherwise agreed, if delivered goods may be returned by the buyer even though they conform to the contract, the transaction is:
>
>   (a) a "sale on approval" if the goods are delivered primarily for use, and
>
>   (b) a "sale or return" if the goods are delivered primarily for resale.

The rights of the creditors of the consignee of this third type will have to be determined by looking at the common law of the particular states.

To summarize, if goods are consigned to a merchant in a conventional commercial transaction—where the merchant operates in its own name and not that of the consignor, is not an auctioneer, and is not "generally known by such creditors to be substantially engaged in selling the goods of others"—the transaction is a consignment, and the consignor's interest is a security interest. The consignor must perfect a security interest under Article 9 to protect itself from the consignee's trustee in bankruptcy and from other and later perfected secured creditors. If the transaction falls out of the definition in 9–102(a)(20) because the transaction creates a security interest "that secures an obligation," the rules are practically the same. The consignor is still the holder of a security interest who must perfect it under Article 9. The only difference—probably, in our view, an insignificant one—is that on default this latter consignor must comply with Part 6 of Article 9. We suspect there will be little need under the new law to distinguish between garden-variety commercial consignments under Article 9 and those that are in every respect security agreements because they secure "an obligation."

1–5 QUASI CONSIGNMENT

Consignment has two close neighbors. On the one side it slips off into the land of security interest; on the other it borders on bailments. In "quasi consignment" cases the owner of goods puts them into the hands of another person for manufacturing, processing, or for incorporation in other goods. The parties' plans for goods in these cases are varied and sometimes uncertain. In some cases the owner has the right to get the goods back;[34] in others the processors are to ship the manufactured or processed goods to third parties at the owner's directions;[35] in still others the possibility exists that the processors will sell the goods and remit the proceeds.[36] None are pure consignments or pure bailments; all have some qualities of each.

If the transaction were merely a bailment, it would present no significant issue of law; the law would be clear—the bailed goods are returned to the owner upon promised payment. Without more, the bailee's creditors would have no rights to the goods. But because these transactions also bear some of the earmarks of a sale, the processor's trustee in bankruptcy or its secured creditors will argue that the owner is nothing more than an unsecured creditor or, at best, an unperfected secured creditor.

The possible vice of these transactions is demonstrated by the factual scenarios in cases like In re Bristol Industries Corp.,[37] which arose before the 1999 revisions. There the processor, Bristol, owned metal that it commingled with metal shipped to it and owned by General Motors. Out of this commingled mass of metal, Bristol manufactured finished products that were then sold to General Motors. Creditors of Bristol could plausibly argue that General Motors had enabled Bristol to mislead those creditors about the status of its inventory, since there was no way for them to know that Bristol did not own all of the metal it was holding. There was no public filing, nor was there any outward sign that would put a third party on notice of General Motors' ownership interest in the commingled mass of metal.

Article 9 states the critical question to be whether the goods "have been delivered to a merchant for the purpose of sale." If, despite their processing and commingling, the goods are to be returned to the owner rather than sold to a third person, the transaction is not a consignment under Article 9, and the owner (e.g., General Motors in

---

[34] See, e.g., First Nat'l Bank of Birmingham v. Young, 530 So.2d 834, 7 UCC2d 762 (Ala.Civ.App.1988); B.A. Ballou and Co. v. Citytrust, 218 Conn. 749, 591 A.2d 126 (1991).

[35] See, e.g., In re Medomak Canning Co., 1977 WL 25603, 25 UCC 437 (Bankr.D.Me.1977); Simmons First Nat'l Bank v. Wells, 279 Ark. 204, 650 S.W.2d 236, 36 UCC 126 (1983).

[36] Compare In re Sitkin Smelting & Refining, Inc., 639 F.2d 1213, 30 UCC 1566 (5th Cir.1981) with In re Sitkin Smelting & Refining, Inc., 648 F.2d 252, 31 UCC 887 (5th Cir.1981).

[37] 1981 WL 138044, 38 UCC 989 (Bankr.D.Conn.1981), rev'd on other grounds, 690 F.2d 26, 38 UCC 1001 (2d Cir.1982).

the above case) need not file a financing statement to protect its interest. If, on the other hand, the goods are to be processed and then sold by the processor to persons *to be selected by him*, the transaction is a consignment and filing is required even though the processor is both processing and selling. Comment 14 to 9–102 makes the point as follows:

> The definition of "consignment" requires that the goods be delivered "to a merchant for the purpose of sale." If the goods are delivered for another purpose as well, such as milling or processing, the transaction is a consignment nonetheless because a purpose of the delivery is "sale." On the other hand, if a merchant-processor-bailee will not be selling the goods itself but will be delivering to buyers to which the owner-bailor agreed to sell the goods, the transaction would not be a consignment.

This gives us two clear cases. Where the processor is to return the goods to the owner, there is no consignment; where it free to sell the processed goods to a third party it chooses, there is. But what about situations that fall between the two poles? What if, for example, the processor is to sell to third parties selected by *the owner*? The quoted comment distinguishes between the case in which the contract with the third party purchaser is with the owner/bailor, on the one hand, and the case where the contract is with the processor/bailee, on the other. The comment suggests that in the former case there would be a bailment but in the latter a consignment.

We suspect the person with whom the contract is to be made is not the only factor the courts will consider. For example, if the processor's fee is a function of the price at which the goods are sold, that makes the processor look more like a consignee and less like a bailee. As its fee rises with increasing sales, the bailee looks like someone with a property interest in the goods, not merely a person selling services for a fee. We suspect too that the courts will look at the trade practice, the normal expectations in the industry and whether the goods appear to be inventory or something else. Each of these will give some clue about the reasonableness of a third party's assertion that he was fooled by the bailee's possession.

1–6 SALES OF ACCOUNTS, CHATTEL PAPER, PAYMENT INTANGIBLES, PROMISSORY NOTES

Section 9–102(1)(b) of the 1972 Code covered not only transactions intended to create conventional security interests but also "any sale of accounts or chattel paper." This provision recognized "factoring," a historical form of financing that had long been practiced in many industries. The factor was a person who "bought" accounts; the factor would pay the owner of the account 85, 90 or even 95 cents on the dollar in return for an assignment of 100% of the account. The factor would make its money by collecting 100 cents on the account. The spread (100–90) was the payment for the loan, the equivalent of an interest charge. The classic factor's bargain was "non-recourse"; that is, the factor could look only to the account for repayment, and not "have recourse" to the seller of the account for a deficiency. The buyer of the account agreed to take the full credit risk that the account debtor would not or could not. Thus the factor got both the full upside (100 cents) and the full downside (nothing). In practice there are many variations between full recourse (the debtor promises to pay the full amount if account debtor defaults) and sales completely without recourse (no claim against the seller/debtor even if all account debtors default).

PROBLEM

Your client, Bank, is buying some loans from Small Company. Some were generated by a credit card issued by Small Company, while others were secured loans against automobiles sold to small businesses. Note first that there is a definitional problem here, for in each transaction there are two debtors, (1) the holder of the credit card or the small business, and (2) Small Company; so we need a name to distinguish them. The credit cardholders and the small businesses are called "account debtors"; Small Company is called "the debtor."

A quick look at section 9–309 tells us that sales of certain intangibles such as promissory notes or payment intangibles and certain assignments of accounts are automatically perfected. Which of the two transactions are covered by 9–309?

A quick look at 9–102 tells us that the credit card receivables are "accounts" and so entitled to automatic perfection, but that the loans against the automobiles are "chattel paper" and so require either a filing or possession by your client for perfection. But wait a minute, that's not right; the accounts qualify for automatic perfection only if they are not a "significant part" of Small Company's accounts. So we will need to file as to the accounts too.

Modern practice has grandly expanded the factor's business. The new practice is called "securitization." In a securitization transaction, the creditor sells its accounts to a trustee who in turn sells "shares" or "participations" in the trust to investors. Since former 9–102(1)(b) covered only sales of "accounts or chattel paper," the status of many securitizations was uncertain. Before 1999, Article 9 rights to payment that arose from a *loan* by a creditor to a debtor were "general intangibles" not "accounts"; "accounts" arose only on the sale of goods or services. Thus, for example, a securitization of $100 million of commercial loans or $200 million of credit card receivables would not have been covered by Article 9 because they would have amounted to the "sale of general intangibles" not the "sale of accounts or chattel paper." The change in the definition of accounts (to include credit card receivables, 9–102(a)(2)(vii)) and the expansion of Article 9's coverage (to include sales of payment intangibles and promissory notes, 9–109(a)(3)), brings almost all securitization within Article 9. The new definition of payment intangibles and their inclusion in 9–109(a)(3) brings sale of loan participations into Article 9. As with other parts of Article 9, it is critical in reading older cases to determine whether they are applying the post-1999 rules.

To understand how Article 9 might apply to the sale of various intangibles, consider four cases. (1) General Motors Acceptance Corp. makes 1,000 car loans (complete with perfected security interests) to 1,000 consumer car buyers, then sells those loans (constituting in this case "chattel paper": a security agreement and a note) to a trust that issues shares to investors. (2) Mortgage Company takes notes secured by real estate mortgages from 1,000 account debtor homeowners and transfers its notes and mortgages to a trustee. (3) Credit Card Company sells its receivables. (4) Chase Manhattan lends $100 million to a debtor and then sells off $90 million of "participations" in its $100 million loan to nine other banks so each of the ten banks then owns only $10 million of the loan.

All of these cases are covered by Article 9: The collateral transferred in GMAC's case was "chattel paper"; that transferred by the real estate lender was "instruments" or "payment intangibles"; the credit card company sold "accounts"; and Chase Manhattan transferred "payment intangibles." Although all of these transactions are covered under Article 9, they do not get identical treatment. Under 9–309, the banks who bought loan participations and the purchaser of the notes from the mortgage company are automatically perfected without filing or possession.[38] The buyer from GMAC, however, will either have to file in GMAC's name or take possession of the chattel paper. The buyer of accounts from the credit card company will have to file in the name of the credit card company to perfect its interest.

We note in passing that subsections 9–109(d)(4) through (7) exclude certain transfers of accounts or other intangibles from Article 9. These subsections are, by and large, an attempt to remove from Article 9 a series of transactions that are not really financing

---

[38]   Because there is automatic perfection both for buyers of notes and payment intangibles, it will not be necessary to determine whether the transfers of loan participations are purchases of payment intangibles or transfers of interests in negotiable notes.

transactions. For example, subsection (4) deals with the transfer of accounts in connection with the sale of a business out of which they arose. Here the transfer of accounts or chattel paper is not principally a financing transaction but merely part of the sale of a business. Subsection (5) deals with a case in which a creditor sells its accounts or other intangibles to a collection agency, not for the purpose of financing but for the purpose of collection.

1–7 ARTICLE 9 AND CLAIMS TO INTERESTS IN, AND ARISING FROM, REAL ESTATE

Even though the parties create what looks like a "security interest" within 1–201(b)(35), Article 9 will not apply if the collateral is not "personal property or fixtures." Article 9 generally does not apply to the "creation or transfer of an interest in or lien on real property, including a lease or rents thereunder."[39] This language excludes real estate mortgages and land sale contracts, as well as other forms of security in realty.[40]

But there are several exceptions to the general principle that Article 9 does not apply to realty interests. First, section 9–334 provides that an Article 9 security interest may be created in goods that are fixtures or may continue in goods which become fixtures. According to sections 2–107 and 9–102(a)(44), crops are goods, not realty. To create a security interest in crops one must comply with Article 9. Article 9 does not apply to oil, gas, or minerals before their extraction,[41] but once extraction occurs, real estate security interests in the properties generally terminate and Article 9 takes over.

The challenge in drawing a distinction between real and personal property interests arises when a mortgagee, a seller of land, or a lessor, grants a security interest to a third party in a stream of payments that come from the mortgage note, from the land-sale contract buyer, or from the lessee. Underlying these transactions is a real estate transaction, but our secured creditor has a security interest not in the real estate, but in the stream of payments. Compare section 9–109(d)(11):

> This Article does not apply to . . . (11) the creation or transfer of an interest in or lien on real property, including a lease or rents thereunder, except to the extent that provision is made for:
>
> > (A) liens on real property in sections 9–203 and 9–308;

---

[39] § 9–109(d)(11).

[40] Likewise, if realty is received as "proceeds" of the collateral, the secured creditor cannot rely on § 9–315 for continued perfection.

[41] § 9–102(a)(44).

(B) fixtures in section 9–334;

(C) fixture filings in sections 9–501, 9–502, 9–512, 9–516, and 9–519; and

(D) security agreements covering personal and real property in 9–604.

with 9–109(b):

The application of this Article to a security interest in a secured obligation is not affected by the fact that the obligation is itself secured by a transaction or interest to which this Article does not apply.

The quoted sections and the comments make it quite clear that one can take an Article 9 security interest in a mortgagee's rights to payment, and furthermore, that the secured creditor gets a perfected security interest not only in the note (rights to payment) but also in the "supporting obligations" including the mortgage itself. The secured creditor accomplishes this by perfection under Article 9 and without filing anything in the real estate records. All of this is made clear by 9–203(g) (with respect to attachment):

The attachment of a security interest in a right to payment or performance secured by a security interest or other lien on personal or real property is also attachment of a security interest in the security interest, mortgage, or other lien.

And 9–308(d) (with respect to perfection):

Perfection of a security interest in collateral also perfects a security interest in a supporting obligation for the collateral.

Comment 7 to 9–109 explicitly rejects the older cases that require a real estate recording of the assignment of the mortgage:

It also follows from subsection (b) that an attempt to obtain or perfect a security interest in a secured obligation by complying with non-Article 9 law, as by an assignment of record of a real-property mortgage, would be ineffective. Finally, it is implicit from subsection (b) that one cannot obtain a security interest in a lien, such a mortgage on real property, that is not also coupled with an equally effective security interest in the secured obligation. This Article rejects cases such as In re Maryville Savings & Loan Corp., 743 F.2d 413 (6th Cir.1984), clarified on reconsideration, 760 F.2d 119 (1985).

These rules make an almost clean division between the real estate universe, on the one hand, and the personal property ("stream of payment") universe, on the other. With the former, one must perfect by recording in the real estate records; with the latter, one complies with Article 9. The sole exception to this rule has to do with real estate leases and their rents. Section 9–109(d)(11) excludes a real estate "lease or rents thereunder" from Article 9; those are left to other law—presumably to real estate law. Had the drafters not been burdened by history, they surely would have included lease rents in the personal property universe and allowed for perfection under Article 9. Failure to do so is probably a bow to existing practices and recognition that the practices were blessed by a similar provision in former Article 9. In any case, real estate lease rents are not subject to Article 9 perfection rules.

This conclusion on rent does nothing to resolve the persistent question in bankruptcy court whether the rights to hotel and motel daily rentals are to be regarded as "accounts" or "proceeds of accounts"—subject to Article 9, or as real estate "rents"—outside of Article 9. The 1994 amendments to the Bankruptcy Code have improved the prospects for the real estate mortgagee's claims to these fees, but neither Article 9 nor the Bankruptcy Code[42] resolves the issue.

In conclusion, Article 9 applies only to security interests in personal property or fixtures. But now more clearly than was formerly true, rights to payments that are themselves secured by real estate mortgages are covered by Article 9; perfecting a security interest in those rights to payment also perfects an interest in the mortgage or other supporting document (against the mortgagee's creditors) without any recording in the real estate files. Note, too, that many of the transactions that have their start in real estate will not only be covered by Article 9 but will also enjoy automatic perfection under 9–309(3) and (4). One lending against rights to payments secured by mortgages in "mortgage warehousing" transactions will not only be covered by Article 9 but will typically have a perfected security interest merely by attachment.

PROBLEM

> Usually buyers or lenders against notes and real estate mortgages take an interest in substantial pools of notes and mortgages and there are many different account debtors. Your client plans to lend $1 million to a mortgagee who holds only three mortgages, each for $400,000. Having read the material above you assure your client that personal property filing against the mortgagee will adequately protect him in case of the mortgagee's bankruptcy.

---

[42]   See 11 U.S.C.A. § 541(d) (West 1999).

In response to that assurance, he asks whether this is an evasion of the real estate filing rules. He suggests, for example, a case in which a third party purchases the underlying real estate from the account debtor. How would your filing in the personal property records protect you against that person? Momentarily dumbstruck, you realize that your filing would not protect you. What protects you against that person is the recording (which you hope has been done by the mortgagee) of the mortgage in the real estate records. If the debtor/mortgagee has not recorded his mortgage, he leaves you open to challenge by later purchasers of and lenders against the real estate.

So what should we do? In all cases we should certainly get a warranty from the mortgagee that he has properly recorded his mortgages, and since there are only three of them it might make sense to do our own search of the real estate records. If we were buying 100 or 1,000 notes and mortgages, we might feel comfortable in relying upon the debtor's warranty about his own recording of the mortgages but where there are only three mortgages our eggs are all in one basket and checking the real estate records would be comparatively inexpensive.

1–8   AGRICULTURAL AND OTHER STATUTORY LIENS, SECTION 9–109(a)(2)

Article 9 generally excludes coverage of statutory liens ("a lien, other than an agricultural lien, given by statute or other rule of law for services or materials," 9–109(d)(2)). There are two broad categories of liens. First, there are "judicial" liens, which arise from lawsuits and from writs issued to the sheriff in attempts to collect money owed in those lawsuits. Second, and more important for our purposes, are "statutory" liens. These are specific rights granted to certain types of creditors by state statute. For example, most states grant "mechanics" liens to laborers and construction companies against properties on which they have expended labor or materials. Many states also give liens to commercial laundries against their patrons' clothing. There are many others. Some depend upon the creditor's continued possession of the collateral (e.g., the patron's clothing), while others require the lien holder to make a public records filing (e.g., those against real estate). The state statutes that create these liens commonly state rules for their priority.

One form of statutory lien, the "agricultural lien," has been brought within Article 9 for the purpose of perfection and priority. An agricultural lien is not a "security interest" under Article 9, because it is not consensual—it arises by operation of law.[43] Generally, agricultural liens are statutory liens given to certain creditors who

---

[43]   The underlying transactions leading to the agricultural liens are, of course, generally consensual, but the farmer/buyer did not specifically consent to the creation of a security interest.

supply things like seed, fertilizer, feed, and veterinary services to farm operations. Given their importance in farm operations, state statutes sometimes provide a kind of super-priority for agricultural liens.

For Article 9 purposes, agricultural liens are defined a follows in 9–102(a)(5):

"Agricultural lien" means an interest, other than a security interest, in farm products:

(A) which secures payment or performance of an obligation for:

(i) goods or services furnished in connection with a debtor's farming operation; or

(ii) rent on real property leased by a debtor in connection with its farming operation;

(B) which is created by statute in favor of a person that:

(i) in the ordinary course of its business furnished goods or services to a debtor in connection with a debtor's farming operation; or

(ii) leased real property to a debtor in connection with the debtor's farming operation; and

(C) whose effectiveness does not depend on the person's possession of the personal property.

Excluded from this definition is the farm lender who acquires a "security interest" through a "security agreement" that is secured by "farm products." Such lenders have ordinary security interests created by agreement, not agricultural liens created by statute. To qualify as an agricultural lien, it must (1) be "created by statute"; (2) run in favor of those who furnish goods and services (or rental property) in the ordinary course of business in connection with farming operations, and (3) be non-possessory—i.e., must not depend upon the possession by the creditor. Almost all agricultural liens run in favor of landlords (for rent), or trade creditors who sell goods (feed, seed and the like) or provide services (custom cutting, veterinary services and the like). Any of these creditors could, if they chose, also obtain a security agreement with the farmer, but they are not obliged to.

A comparison of 9–322(a) (covering priorities in agricultural liens) with 9–322(g) (allowing super priority to the agricultural lien if the statute creating the lien so provides), shows that the agricultural lien has one foot in Article 9 and one foot outside of it. Moreover, Comment 12 to 9–322 suggests that the Article does not grant a "security interest" in proceeds of agricultural liens; thus no Article 9 security interest can arise in those. Agricultural liens also get somewhat different treatment in Part 6 of Article 9 than security interests do. For example, under section 9–601(e)(3) an agricultural lien would relate back to "any date specified in a statute under which it was created." So too, section 9–606 specifies that "default" occurs when the lien holder "becomes entitled to enforce the lien in accordance with the statute under which it was created." With respect to perfection, section 9–310 makes no concessions to the agricultural lien. With the exceptions provided in 9–310(b) (none of which applies to agricultural liens), "a financing statement must be filed to perfect all . . . agricultural liens."

Section 9–322(g) grants potential super priority only to a "perfected agricultural lien." Presumably the drafters contemplated that other statutes could grant greater priority but could not provide for a mode of perfection other than the filing of a financing statement that is specified in 9–310(a). Assume that a statute which created an agricultural lien on behalf of veterinarians provided that the lien should be prior to all other liens and all security interests whether perfected and whether prior in time. Assume further that the veterinarian did not file a financing statement. In that case, the veterinarian would have an unperfected agricultural lien and would therefore not enjoy the super priority granted by 9–322(g). If, on the other hand, the veterinarian filed a financing statement, it would presumably defeat not only a prior perfected security interest, 9–322(g), but also a prior lien creditor by virtue of 9–317(a)(1) (which subordinates the lien creditor in the same circumstances that section 9–322 subordinates a perfected secured creditor). Of course, the veterinarian lien statute could be construed to override contrary provisions of Article 9 and, if that is what the legislature (which can give priority to whomever it chooses) intended.

1–9   EXCLUSIONS, SECTION 9–109(c) AND (d)

Subsections 9–109(c) and (d) read as follows:

(c) [Extent to which article does not apply.] This article does not apply to the extent that:

(1) a statute, regulation, or treaty of the United States preempts this article;

(2) another statute of this State expressly governs the creation, perfection, priority, or enforcement of a security interest created by this State or a governmental unit of this State;

(3) a statute of another State, a foreign country, or a governmental unit of another State or a foreign country, other than a statute generally applicable to security interests, expressly governs creation, perfection, priority, or enforcement of a security interest created by the State, country, or governmental unit; or

(4) the rights of a transferee beneficiary or nominated person under a letter of credit are independent and superior under section 5–114.

(d) [Inapplicability of article.] This article does not apply to:

(1) a landlord's lien, other than an agricultural lien;

(2) a lien, other than an agricultural lien, given by statute or other rule of law for services or materials, but section 9–333 applies with respect to priority of the lien;

(3) an assignment of a claim for wages, salary, or other compensation of an employee;

(4) a sale of accounts, chattel paper, payment intangibles, or promissory notes as part of a sale of the business out of which they arose;

(5) an assignment of accounts, chattel paper, payment intangibles, or promissory notes which is for the purpose of collection only;

(6) an assignment of a right to payment under a contract to an assignee that is also obligated to perform under the contract;

(7) an assignment of a single account, payment intangible, or promissory note to an assignee in full or partial satisfaction of a preexisting indebtedness;

(8) a transfer of an interest in or an assignment of a claim under a policy of insurance, other than an assignment by or to a health-care provider of a health-care-insurance receivable and any subsequent assignment of the right to payment, but sections 9–315 and 9–322 apply with respect to proceeds and priorities in proceeds;

(9) an assignment of a right represented by a judgment, other than a judgment taken on a right to payment that was collateral;

(10) a right of recoupment or set-off, but:

(A) Section 9–340 applies with respect to the effectiveness of rights of recoupment or set-off against deposit accounts; and

(B) Section 9–404 applies with respect to defenses or claims of an account debtor;

(11) the creation or transfer of an interest in or lien on real property, including a lease or rents thereunder, except to the extent that provision is made for:

(A) liens on real property in sections 9–203 and 9–308;

(B) fixtures in section 9–334;

(C) fixture filings in sections 9–501, 9–502, 9–512, 9–516, and 9–519; and

(D) security agreements covering personal and real property in section 9–604;

(12) an assignment of a claim arising in tort, other than a commercial tort claim, but sections 9–315 and 9–322 apply with respect to proceeds and priorities in proceeds; or

(13) an assignment of a deposit account in a consumer transaction, but sections 9–315 and 9–322 apply with respect to proceeds and priorities in proceeds.

Even though an interest is a "security interest" under 1–201(b)(35) and even though it is an interest in "personal property or fixtures," Article 9 may not apply because either subsection 9–109(c) or (d) excludes it. Exclusions in subsection (c)(1) apply most importantly to the laws and regulations of the United States. We discuss those in chapter 1–11 infra. Subsections (c)(2) and (3) deal with special laws concerning governmental debtors. Example 1 in Comment 8 illustrates the operation of this section by posing a New Jersey state commission's claim in a New York court. If the New Jersey law grants special rights to the New Jersey state commission as a debtor, the New York court (under its own version of 9–109(c)) applies New Jersey law. Of course one would need to look at New Jersey law to be sure it had special rules.

Most of the exclusions in subsection (d) can be justified on the ground that the transactions described do not involve conventional secured loans. Some of them, such as the rules on landlord's liens and on other statutory liens in (d)(1), represent well developed bodies of state law that vary from state to state.

Section 9–109 narrows the exclusions as compared to prior law in several ways. First, it brings within Article 9 some assignments of "health care insurance receivables . . . ." This section recognizes that rights to payments asserted against the health care insurers are more like conventional receivables than they are like one-shot payments from the conventional liability insurers.

To permit the taking of a direct security interest in deposit accounts (formerly excluded by 9–104), the old exclusion was removed. But subsection 9–109(d)(13) does exclude deposit accounts that secure liability arising out of a "consumer transaction." Note that a security interest in a consumer deposit account may be granted under Article 9 as long as the debt is a non-consumer debt (and vice versa), but if the security is granted in a transaction under which a person "incurs an obligation primarily for personal family or household purposes" *and* the deposit account is held primarily for personal family purposes (all defined in 9–102(a)(26)), then a security interest in the deposit account is not possible under Article 9. Advocates for consumer debtors feared that consumers unknowingly would grant security to their banks.

Finally, 9–109(d)(12) permits Article 9 security interests in "commercial tort claim[s]."

1–10 APPLICABILITY OF ARTICLE 9 TO "SECURITY INTERESTS" THAT ARISE UNDER ARTICLE 2 ON SALES, SECTIONS 9–109(a)(5), 9–110

There are some situations in which sellers and buyers are entering into sales or lease transactions that involve security interests in goods, but the buyer does not yet have possession of the goods. Article 2 provides that sellers or buyers have security interests in many of these cases that arise by operation of law, such as in 2–401(seller who retains title to the goods), 2–505 (seller who ships "under reservation") and 2–711(3) (buyer in possession of rejected goods). Article 9 covers these sorts of interests, along with analogous interests created under 2A–508(5). The relevant provision is section 9–110, which gives recognition and priority to those claiming Article 2 and 2A security interests, but only "until the debtor obtains possession of the goods." Section 9–110 reads in full as follows:

> A security interest arising under section 2–401, 2–505, 2–711(3), or 2A–508(5) is subject to this Article. However, until the debtor obtains possession of the goods:
>
>   (1) the security interest is enforceable, even if section 9–203(b)(3) has not been satisfied;
>
>   (2) filing is not required to perfect the security interest;

(3) the rights of the secured party after default by the debtor are governed by Article 2 or 2A; and

(4) the security interest has priority over a conflicting security interest created by the debtor.

Since the Article 2 and 2A interests are (in Article 9 terms) non-consensual, it makes sense to dispense with the security agreement. Since they are dependent upon the debtor's not having possession of conforming goods, it also makes sense to dispense with filing and to grant priority over other security interests created by the debtor. By hypothesis, the debtors never have possession of the collateral in these cases, or if they did, have already transferred the assets in an ordinary course transaction to a buyer. So it is unlikely that these Article 2 liens will prejudice third parties despite the fact there is no security agreement and no financing statement.

Once the debtor obtains possession, the protection of 9–110 is gone and the explicit incorporation of these rights into Article 9 by 9–109(a)(5) means that any Article 2 creditor's claim is then no different from the claim of any other consensual creditor under Article 9. It is dependent upon the conventional rules of attachment and perfection. Thus the seller who sells goods and purports to retain a "security interest," but does not file a financing statement, will be an unperfected secured creditor—and perhaps less—once buyer gets possession. The rule seems sensible and the section on priorities has cleared up most of the uncertainty in the former law.

There are still other rights in Articles 2 and 2A that have some of the attributes of security interests yet are not explicitly recognized as such by Article 2 or by Article 9. Comment 5 to 9–110 addresses these as follows:

> This Article does not specifically address the conflict between (i) a security interest created by a buyer or lessee and (ii) the seller's or lessor's right to withhold delivery under section 2–702(1), 2–703(a), or 2A–525, the seller's or lessor's right to stop delivery under section 2–705 or 2A–526, or the seller's right to reclaim under section 2–507(2) or 2–702(2). These conflicts are governed by the first sentence of section 2–403(1), under which the buyer's secured party obtains no greater rights in the goods than the buyer had or had power to convey, or section 2A–307(1), under which creditors of the lessee take subject to the lease contract.

The last sentence of the comment seems to suggest that anytime a seller can stop goods on their way to the buyer, or can reclaim them from the buyer, any transferee from the buyer (such as a secured creditor) would likewise be subject to the seller's stoppage or reclamation rights. That is plainly wrong with respect to a seller's rights to reclaim under 2–702(3). which makes the seller's right to reclaim "subject to the rights of a buyer in ordinary course or other good faith purchaser." The last sentence of the comment is accurate with respect to 2–705 for, by hypothesis, there the buyer would never have had possession of the goods, and the same is probably true of 2–507. This competition between a seller who has certain stoppage or reclamation rights under Article 2 and a buyer or transferee from the buyer is not governed by Article 9, but by the explicit rules in Article 2–702(3) or by inference from the relevant Article 2 rule or, where there is no rule, by the common law.

Assume, for example, Seller ships goods to an insolvent buyer who has granted a perfected security interest to a bank. Assume further that the bank's security interest has a conventional after-acquired property clause that causes the security interest to attach to the goods delivered by Seller. Seller's right to reclaim under 2–702 will lose to bank's security interest because of 2–702(3)—the bank is a purchaser in good faith. Thus, the bank wins, not because of Article 9 priority rules, but because of Article 2 priority rules.

Sections 9–109 and 9–110 clarify the rights of the holders of Article 2 security interests. The comments make clear that one must look elsewhere for rules to govern the competition between Article 2 claimants (with interests that are not security interests).

1–11   FEDERAL LAW THAT OVERRIDES ARTICLE 9

Even though Article 9 applies to a transaction, other federal or state law may displace the Article in whole or in part. For the most part, in this section we ignore state law that overrides Article 9 security interests. That law, found in consumer protection statutes and sometimes in the law on state tax liens or other statutory liens, is far from uniform. We do not have the space to deal with it here, but the lawyer should beware and should examine closely the consumer law in the states where clients do business. Federal law which can preempt Article 9 and 9–109(c)(1) reminds us of this:

This article does not apply to the extent that:

(1) a statute, regulation, or treaty of the United States preempts this article[.]

Federal conflicts fall into three large categories. First are federal statutes that appear to establish federal filing systems for perfection of transfers or assignments—possibly including security interests. Most of these acts are fragmentary and typically do not deal coherently with perfection of security interests. One exception is the federal income tax lien law, which includes a comprehensive set of perfection and priority rules for federal income tax liens.[44] Filing systems for aircraft and ship mortgages are also comprehensive. Systems for patents, trademarks, and copyrights are neither comprehensive nor coherent.[45]

The second type of conflict arises when the federal government or a federal agency is the lender. For example, the Department of Defense and the Farmers' Home Administration are frequent lenders. When they find themselves in trouble, they often resort to federal "common law" to make up for their failure to have perfected their security interests.

Finally, there are federal forfeiture laws and federal laws that otherwise subordinate secured creditors in the pursuit of various federal policies. Among these are laws having to do with drug enforcement, environmental law, and federal labor law.

To return to the first category, consider the variety of federal acts that deal with security.[46] Even when these acts clearly cover filing (as does the federal law dealing with aircraft), they typically leave open matters like creation of the interest, priorities, and foreclosure. When that happens, many courts have accepted the invitation of the drafters in former section 9–104(a) and its comment, to flesh out the statutory skeleton by analogy to Article 9 law.[47]

---

[44]   Int. Rev. Code of 1954 §§ 6321 et seq.

[45]   See, e.g., 35 U.S.C.A. § 261 (West 1984); 17 U.S.C.A. §§ 101–603 (1977 & West Supp.1993); 15 U.S.C.A. §§ 1051–1128 (1976 & West Supp.1993).

[46]   Some of these are:

(1) Truth in Lending Act of 1968, Pub.L.No. 90–321, §§ 123, 128, 129, 130, 82 Stat. 152, 153, 15, 156, as amended, Act of 1974, Pub.L.No. 93–495, Title II–IV, 88 Stat. 1511–1521, 15 U.S.C.A. §§ 1635, 1638, 1639, 1640 (1974);

(2) Act of 1958, Pub.L.No. 85–726, Title V, §§ 503, 504, 72 Stat. 772, as amended, Act of 1959, Pub.L.No 86–81, §§ 1–4, 73 Stat. 180, 49 U.S.C.A. §§ 1403, 1404 (1976) (recording of aircraft ownership);

(3) Ship Mortgage Act of 1920, ch. 250, §§ 30 Subsections A–W, 41 Stat. 1000, as amended 46 U.S.C.A. §§ 911–984 (1976);

(4) Revised Interstate Commerce Act of 1978, Pub.L.No. 95–473, 92 Stat. 1431, 49 U.S.C.A. § 11304 (1979) (recording of security interests in certain motor vehicles);

(5) Revised Interstate Commerce Act of 1978, Pub.L.No. 95–473, 92 Stat. 430, 49 U.S.C.A. §§ 11303 (1979) (recording of railroad equipment trust agreements).

[47]   For ships, see, e.g., Chemical Bank v. Miller Yacht Sales, 173 N.J.Super. 90, 413 A.2d 619, 28 UCC 1160 (App.Div. 1980); Brown v. Baker, 688 P.2d 943, 39 UCC 1105 (Alaska 1984); In re McLean Industries, 132 B.R. 271, 15 UCC2d 1062 (Bankr.S.D.N.Y.1991).

For aircraft, see, e.g., Cessna Finance Corp. v. Skyways Enterprises, Inc., 580 S.W.2d 491, 26 UCC 212 (Ky.1979); Bitzer-Croft Motors, Inc. v. Pioneer Bank & Trust Co., 82 Ill.App.3d 1, 401 N.E.2d 1340, 37 Ill.Dec. 247, 30 UCC 317 (1980).

Though it has been more than half a century since the Code was widely adopted, the law on perfection of security interests in intellectual property is still confused. The leading cases dealing respectively with patents, copyrights, and trademarks are *Otto Fabric, Peregrine Entertainment,* and In re Roman Cleanser.[48] Under *Otto Fabric,* a UCC filing is sufficient to perfect a security interest in patents vis à vis a lien creditor (and bankruptcy trustee). However, a federal filing may be necessary to perfect vis à vis a subsequent purchaser or mortgagee.[49] Under *Peregrine Entertainment,* however, a UCC filing is ineffective to perfect a security interest in a copyright (and perhaps in related accounts receivable) even as against lien creditors. Therefore, a federal filing is necessary. Under the reasoning of the In re Roman Cleanser court, a UCC filing is sufficient and necessary to perfect a security interest in a federally registered trademark. A bankruptcy court in In re 199Z, Inc.[50] held a federal recordation ineffective.[51]

The law is still confused. The holding in *Peregrine Entertainment,* written by Circuit Judge Alex Kozinski when sitting by designation, has been criticized as "novel and questionable" by one court,[52] but was subsequently adopted (though not extended) by the Ninth Circuit.[53] Some subsequent cases have held that state filings are effective with respect to copyrights that were not filed with the federal copyright office,[54] while others have applied *Peregrine Entertainment* even to unregistered copyrights.[55] The complexities are illustrated by the 2015 decision in Prodigy Distribution, Inc. v.

---

[48]   City Bank and Trust Co. v. Otto Fabric, Inc., 83 B.R. 780, 5 UCC2d 1459 (D.Kan.1988); In re Peregrine Entertainment, Ltd., 116 B.R. 194, 11 UCC2d 1025 (C.D.Cal.1990); In re Roman Cleanser, Co., 43 B.R. 940, 39 UCC 1770 (Bankr.E.D.Mich.1984), aff'd, 802 F.2d 207, 2 UCC2d 269 (6th Cir.1986).

[49]   The Official Comment to former section 9–104 states that a filing under the federal patent statute is "recognized as the equivalent" of an Article 9 filing. However, the *Otto Fabric* court reasoned that a recordation of a security interest at the federal level would take the form of an absolute assignment and thus offer significant protection but at the cost of flexibility. For example, a debtor could not unilaterally grant a license or sue for infringement after the secured creditor's recordation.

[50]   137 B.R. 778, 17 UCC2d 598 (Bankr.C.D.Cal.1992).

[51]   A creditor and debtor may agree to make an absolute assignment of the collateral which would require a federal filing. The lender who chooses this route should exercise caution due to the possibility of lender liability. See Torres v. Goodyear Tire & Rubber Co., 901 F.2d 750 (9th Cir.1990) (trademark licensor is subject to the "enterprise theory" of strict products liability under Arizona law if it was significantly (but indirectly) involved in the manufacturing and distribution process).

[52]   MCEG Sterling, Inc. v. Phillips Nizer Benjamin Krim & Ballon, 169 Misc.2d 625, 646 N.Y.S.2d 778, 33 UCC Rep.Serv.2d 305 (Sup. Ct. N.Y. Cty. 1996).

[53]   In re World Auxiliary Power Co., 303 F.3d 1120, 1125 (9th Cir. 2002).

[54]   See, e.g., *id.* at 1129–30.

[55]   Zenith Productions, Ltd. v. AEG Acquisition Corp., 161 B.R. 50 (9th Cir. BAP 1993), aff'g 127 B.R. 34 (Bankr.C.D.Cal.1991); In re Avalon Software Inc., 209 B.R. 517 (D.Ariz.1997).

Seven Arts Entertainment, Inc.[56] In that case, the creator of a film gave a security interest in the unregistered copyrights to a lender, who perfected under Article 9. The creator/debtor subsequently registered the copyright and claimed the earlier security interest was improperly perfected. The court disagreed, holding that a security interest perfected before registration was valid, even though it would not have been valid if the copyright had been registered first.

It is safe to say that no one can be confident that a state law filing will give adequate protection to secured creditors in intellectual property. The language in the federal statutes appears to distinguish between security interests and outright assignments, and among lien creditors, mortgagees, bona fide purchasers and others. This archaic language leaves all kinds of troublesome inferences for the secured creditor.[57]

As we have suggested above, any federal agency that lends money will argue that it is protected by federal common law when it gets backed into a corner because of its failure to perfect its security interests under Article 9. In United States v. Kimbell Foods,[58] the Supreme Court greatly restricted the power of federal lenders to invoke federal common law. In that case, the Court concluded first that federal lenders are normally governed by federal law. That was the good news for the government. The bad news was that federal common law should, at least in this context, be found by looking to Article 9 of the Uniform Commercial Code. In that case the Small Business Administration—which had not filed under state law—claimed it had priority over a secured creditor who had perfected its secured interest under state law. The Supreme Court rejected the SBA's argument. Although the Court recognized that there might be cases where courts ought not to adopt state law (e.g., where Congress plainly intended a uniform federal law to govern), the Court concluded that state commercial Codes are sensible and in no way inconsistent with adequate protection of federal interests. Thus, state law should normally be the source of federal common law.[59] Not

---

[56]   2015 WL 12672739 (C.D. Cal. May 21, 2015).

[57]   The ABA Task Force on Security Interests in Intellectual Property reported to the Permanent Editorial Board for the Uniform Commercial Code in favor of a "mixed" system, apparently with the support of the Patents and Trademarks Office and the Register of Copyrights. Preliminary Report of the ABA Task Force on Security Interests in Intellectual Property (Working Document No. M6–52), May 13, 1992, as reported in Appendices to Report, PEB Study Group, Uniform Commercial Code, Article 9 (1992). As adopted by the Permanent Editorial Board Study Committee, this proposal called for a revision of both Article 9 and federal law to allow for state filings, federal "tract filings" (according to the particular property) and a federal notice-filing system. Although Article 9 was revised in 1999, federal law regarding filing has remained the same.

[58]   440 U.S. 715, 99 S.Ct. 1448, 59 L.Ed.2d 711, 26 UCC 1 (1979).

[59]   Id. at 729, 26 UCC at 10.

every court has been true to the *Kimbell Foods* instruction, but the case has been an enormous boon for Article 9 and it has greatly restricted the power of federal lenders to thumb their noses at state law.

We do not have space here to shine a light on every dark corner of federal law that poses a threat to the secured creditor; there are many such. We cite but one case as an example and refer the reader to our practitioner's edition. In Citicorp Industrial Credit, Inc. v. Brock,[60] the Court held that a perfected secured creditor, who had lawfully foreclosed under its security agreement, could not transport the collateral in interstate commerce because the collateral had been manufactured in violation of the federal minimum wage requirements. That had happened because the debtor had failed to pay its employees' wages upon its financial failure. Although the Court denied it was "granting a lien" to the wage earners, the practical effect was the same. Since the FLSA (Federal Labor Standards Act)[61] explicitly prohibits shipment or sale of goods until the wage requirements are fulfilled and since a willful violation of the act is a crime, the rights of the employees are even better than a lien. The woods are full of statutes like this. Walk with care.[62]

We have been hoping for several years—ever since the 1999 amendments to Article 9—that federal laws on security interests in intellectual property will be modified by Congress. Congress could create a comprehensive and coherent set of rules, but we are not sanguine about the will or interest to deal with the issue. We expect that forfeiture issues will come and go as particular interests are accommodated by Congress, in one way or another, without any comprehensive thought of their integration into Article 9 or any other system. To work out these problems is one of the joys of being a lawyer in a federal system.

---

[60] 483 U.S. 27, 107 S.Ct. 2694, 97 L.Ed.2d 23 (1987).

[61] 29 U.S.C.A. §§ 201–219 (West 1978).

[62] D. Taube, Civil Forfeiture, 30 Am. Crim. L. Rev. 1025 (1993). Some of the more prominent federal forfeiture statutes include:

> (1) Organized Crime Act of 1970 ("Racketeer Influenced and Corrupt Practices Act," or "RICO"), Pub.L.No. 91–452, 84 Stat. 922, as amended by the Comprehensive Crime Control Act, Pub.L.No. 98–473, 98 Stat. 1937, 18 U.S.C.A. § 1963 (criminal forfeiture).

> (2) Comprehensive Drug Abuse Prevention and Control Act of 1970, ("Controlled Substances Act"), Pub.L.No. 91–513, 84 Stat. 1236, as amended by the Comprehensive Crime Control Act, Pub.L. No. 98–473, 98 Stat. 1937, 21 U.S.C.A. § 881 (civil forfeiture) and 21 U.S.C.A. § 853 (criminal forfeiture).

> (3) Money Laundering Control Act of 1986, Pub.L.No. 99–570, §§ 1351–1367, 100 Stat. 3207–35, as amended by Pub.L.No 102–393, 106 Stat. 1729; Pub.L.No. 101–647, §§ 103, 2508, 2524, 2525, 3531, 104 Stat. 4791, 4862, 4873, 4874, 4924; Pub.L.No. 100–690, §§ 6463, 6469–71, 102 Stat. 4374, 4377, 4378, 18 U.S.C.A. § 981 (civil forfeiture).

Chapter 2

CREATION AND PERFECTION OF ENFORCEABLE ARTICLE 9 INTERESTS

Analysis

2–1 INTRODUCTION

Article 9 applies to two kinds of property interests: ordinary security interests in personal property and fixtures,[1] and the interests of *buyers* of accounts and certain other intangibles (which the Code also calls "security interests").[2] Section 9–203 lays out the steps a party must take to create an Article 9 enforceable security interest. Once these steps are taken the security interest comes into existence. When a security interest becomes enforceable against the debtor (with respect to the collateral), section 9–203(a) states that the interest "attaches" to the collateral.

Attachment has two general consequences. First, if the debtor defaults, the secured creditor can foreclose or otherwise realize on the collateral to satisfy the claim. Second, the security interest becomes "enforceable against . . . third parties."[3] In other words, the secured party can, in general, take the collateral from, or to the exclusion of, third parties with priority inferior to the secured creditor's security interest. There are important exceptions. Many third parties will defeat an attached but "unperfected" security interest. And if a party with an attached security interest fails to comply with Part 6 of Article 9 on default procedures, the party may lose its rights even as against the debtor. Additionally, an unconscionable clause in a security agreement may be unenforceable.

---

[1]   § 9–109.

[2]   § 9–109.

[3]   § 9–203(b).

The mere attachment of a security interest to collateral, in most cases,[4] Article 9 distinguishes attachment of a security interest from its "perfection." It is perfection (filing of a financing statement, taking possession or control of the collateral, as appropriate, etc.) that affords maximum secured creditor protection against third parties, including the trustee in bankruptcy. But even the perfected secured creditor does not defeat all third parties.

2–2 CREATION OF ENFORCEABLE ARTICLE 9 SECURITY INTERESTS—BASIC REQUIREMENTS

How does a secured party create an enforceable Article 9 security interest? Section 9–203 requires only a few steps. In general:

a. *Value:* the creditor must give value,

b. *Debtor rights in collateral:* the debtor must have rights in the collateral,

c. *Security agreement:* there must be a security agreement,

d. *Description of collateral:* the security agreement must describe the collateral, and

e. *Authentication:* either the security agreement must be in a writing signed by the debtor or there must be some other "authenticating" event, as described in 9–203(b)(3), to provide grounds for concluding that the parties have entered into a security agreement. There might, for example, be an authenticated security agreement that was not in writing,[5] the creditor's taking possession under 9–313, the creditor's taking "delivery" of certificated securities under 8–301, or by the creditor's achieving "control" over certain kinds of collateral.

Nine times out of ten, an enforceable security interest will arise from a loan or extension of credit by the creditor to the debtor (value),

---

[4]   Exceptions to this general rule arise, for example, under § 9–110, which deals with security interests created under UCC Articles 2 or 2A. In these cases, where the security interest arises under §§ 2–401, 2–505, 2–711(3), or 2A–508(5), the security interest is enforceable, no filing is required to perfect the security interest, the rights of the secured party are determined under Articles 2 or 2A, and the security interest has priority over conflicting security interests created by the debtor.

[5]   Under § 9–102(a)(7)(B), authentication means either signing a record or attaching or logically associating with a record an electronic sound, symbol, or process with the present intent to adopt or accept the record. Thus, recording a security agreement on a smartphone voice memo app with the debtor's name at the end would constitute an authenticated security agreement that would satisfy § 9–203(b)(3), at least if the debtor put its name on it with the intention of identifying itself and becoming bound by the terms of the security agreement.

the debtor's ownership of the collateral (rights in the collateral), and a written agreement that describes the collateral and is signed by the debtor (9–203(b)(3)(A)). The remaining 10% of the cases, or perhaps only 1%, involve no signed writing but only possession by the creditor, an electronic record or control. Consider how little can suffice to bind the debtor. For example, it is enough for the debtor to write on the back of an envelope, "I hereby grant bank a security interest in my cattle, John Jones." If the bank makes a loan and the debtor owns the cattle, the parties created a valid security interest despite the informality.

2–3 CREATION OF ENFORCEABLE ARTICLE 9 SECURITY INTERESTS—"ATTACHMENT" AND "ENFORCEABILITY"

Section 9–203 reads in part as follows:

(a) [Attachment.] A security interest attaches to collateral when it becomes enforceable against the debtor with respect to the collateral, unless an agreement expressly postpones the time of attachment.

(b) [Enforceability.] Except as otherwise provided in subsections (c) through (i), a security interest is enforceable against the debtor and third parties with respect to the collateral only if :

(1) value has been given;

(2) the debtor has rights in the collateral or the power to transfer rights in the collateral to a secured party; and

(3) one of the following conditions is met:

(A) the debtor has authenticated a security agreement that provides a description of the collateral and, if the security interest covers timber to be cut, a description of the land concerned;

(B) the collateral is not a certificated security and is in the possession of the secured party under section 9–313 pursuant to the debtor's security agreement;

(C) the collateral is a certificated security in registered form and the security certificate has been delivered to the secured party under section 8–301 pursuant to the debtor's security agreement; or

(D) the collateral is deposit accounts, electronic chattel paper, investment property, or letter-of-credit rights, and the secured party has control under section 9–104, 9–105,

9–106, or 9–107 pursuant to the debtor's security agreement.

. . .

(f) [Proceeds and supporting obligations.] The attachment of a security interest in collateral gives the secured party the rights to proceeds provided by section 9–315 and is also attachment of a security interest in a supporting obligation for the collateral.

(g) [Lien securing right to payment.] The attachment of a security interest in a right to payment or performance secured by a security interest or other lien on personal or real property is also attachment of a security interest in the security interest, mortgage, or other lien.

a. Security Agreement

Although security agreements are seldom oral, they can be. For example, one might make an oral pledge of jewelry to a pawnbroker; section 9–203 would recognize such an agreement provided one of the other requirements in 9–203(b)(3) was met.

The typical security agreement is labeled "security agreement" but unorthodox documents labeled "collateral pledge," "security assignment" or "title retention agreement" are also likely to be recognized as adequate security agreements. Indeed, agreements without a trace of security agreement terminology (e.g., many "leases"[6]) qualify as security agreements regardless of the parties' subjective intent to create or avoid creating such an agreement. It is also true that certain transfers "absolute in form," such as the sale of accounts or payment intangibles now create "security interests" and specific "words of grant" are not required.

What then are the essential features of a "security agreement"? First, the document must show, to an objective observer, that debtor intended to transfer an interest in personal property *as security*[7] to a creditor. This could be done by a security agreement masquerading as a lease[8] as well as by a conventional security agreement containing words of grant.

Second, the collateral must be identified, either by description in the security agreement or through some alternative means. Strictly speaking, a description of the collateral is not always required. The parties may define the collateral by description or by

---

[6]   See § 1–203(b).

[7]   That is, for the purpose of securing payment or performance of an obligation. UCC § 1–201(35) ("security interest").

[8]   UCC § 1–203.

other methods such as the creditor's possession of particular collateral or the creditor's "control" of particular collateral. But where a creditor without possession or control of the collateral seeks to satisfy 9–203 by an authenticated security agreement, that agreement must contain a description of the collateral, for there is no other way of identifying the collateral subject to the agreement.

Third, although the agreement need not follow any particular form and even though unorthodox agreements may constitute security agreements, there are some limits. When trouble comes, secured creditors who have filed a financing statement are sometimes unable to locate a written security agreement. They may then argue that the financing statement itself suffices as the security agreement when supported by other documents, such as a resolution by the debtor's board of directors, or "security" notations on a note. Since the debtor does not sign a post 1999 financing statement, that document does not alone have the necessary "authentication" to be a security agreement. Still, a clever secured creditor might tack the signature on a note to a financing statement or to a document referring to the grant of a security interest and so cobble together an "authenticated security agreement."

We are generally sympathetic to the argument that an authenticated security agreement can be proven by the use of multiple documents, as in the leading case of In re Numeric Corp.[9] In that case the person claiming to be a secured creditor was unable to produce a written, signed security agreement. Although he maintained there was such an agreement, all he could produce was a financing statement that listed the collateral and the minutes of the board of directors of the debtor that approved the granting of a security interest. The court concluded that the financing statement

---

[9]   485 F.2d 1328, 13 UCC 416 (1st Cir.1973). See also In re ProvideRx of Grapevine, LLC, 507 B.R. 132, 154 (N.D. Tx. Bankr. Ct. 2014) ("a security agreement need not be evidenced by a single document; two or more writings, considered together, may constitute a security agreement.") (quoting Looney v. Nuss (In re Looney), 545 F.2d 916, 918 (5th Cir. 1977)); In re Weir-Penn, 344 B.R. 791, 793 (W.V. N. Bankr. Ct. 2006) ("No requirement exists that there be a separate written document labeled 'security agreement' that has express language granting a security interest: once a debtor signs the financing statement the writing requirement is met, and the determination of whether the parties intended to create a security interest is an issue of fact that is garnered by reviewing 'a collection of documents, no one of which contains granting language, but which in the aggregate disclose an intent to grant a security interest in specific collateral.'") (quoting Terry M. Anderson, Marianne B. Culhane, and Catherine Lee Wilson, *Attachment and Perfection of Security Interests Under Revised Article 9: A "Nuts and Bolts" Primer*, 9 Am. Bankr. Inst. L. Rev. 179, 188 (2001) and citing In re Numeric Corp., 485 F.2d 1328, 1331 (1st Cir. 1973)), Weinandt v. Peckman, 84 UCC Rep. serv. 2d 118 (Minn. Ct. App. 2014) (unpublished) (recognizing majority rule that a financing statement by itself is insufficient to create a security agreement and citing favorably the "composite document rule" adopted by In re Numeric Corp.).

satisfied the Statute of Frauds requirement in 9–203 and that the directors' resolution established that an agreement in fact existed to give security. Noting that the UCC should be "liberally construed," the court found that the secured creditor had proved an enforceable security agreement. Even when there is no fully formed security agreement, in most cases, the loan will be manifest. Notes, payments, and other performance will show it. There will also be considerable evidence of intention to grant security (written inventories of collateral, identification of collateral in one way or another, and filed financing statements).

b. Description

Section 9–203(b)(3)(A) requires that an authenticated security agreement "provide a description of the collateral." Possession under (3)(B) and delivery to the secured party under (3)(C) obviate the need to describe the collateral. To a lesser extent the same is true under subsection (3)(D) with respect to deposit accounts and investment property over which a secured party has "control". Even though (3)(D) does not require a description as such, the secured creditor will somehow have to identify the deposit accounts or investment property in which it has control.[10] So even in that case there may be a description problem.

Article 9 treats the sufficiency of the description in the security agreement separately from the sufficiency of the description ("indication of collateral") in the financing statement. The description in the security agreement is covered by 9–108 while 9–504 covers the description on the financing statement. Lawyers beware: certain descriptions, such as "super generic" descriptions, e.g., "all the debtor's assets," are explicitly rejected for the purposes of security agreements, yet are explicitly permitted for financing statements.[11] Thus, anything that is an adequate description under 9–108 for the security agreement is adequate under 9–504 for the financing statement, but there may be descriptions (in addition to super generic descriptions) that are adequate for the financing statement but inadequate for the security agreement.

---

[10]   See UCC § 9–203(b)(3)(D) cmt. 4 ("[U]nder subsection (b)(3)(D), control of investment property, a deposit account, electronic chattel paper, or a letter-of-credit right, or electronic documents satisfies the evidentiary test if control is pursuant to the debtor's security agreement.").

[11]   Compare UCC § 9–108(c) ("A description of collateral as 'all the debtor's assets' or 'all the debtor's personal property' or using words of similar import does not reasonably describe the collateral.") with UCC § 9–504 (financing statement sufficiently indicates the collateral if it provides a description conforming with § 9–108 or provides "an indication that the financing statement covers all assets or all personal property.").

Subsections 9–108(a) and (b) read:

(a) [Sufficiency of description.] Except as otherwise provided in subsections (c), (d), and (e), a description of personal or real property is sufficient, whether or not it is specific, if it reasonably identifies what is described.

(b) [Examples of reasonable identification.] Except as otherwise provided in subsection (d), a description of collateral reasonably identifies the collateral if it identifies the collateral by:

(1) specific listing;

(2) category;

(3) except as otherwise provided in subsection (e), a type of collateral defined in [the Uniform Commercial Code];

(4) quantity;

(5) computational or allocational formula or procedure; or

(6) except as otherwise provided in subsection (c), any other method, if the identity of the collateral is objectively determinable.

A description can be insufficient either because it is too narrow, and so excludes collateral intended by the parties to be covered, or because it is too broad and may include property not intended. Section 9–108(c) states that super generic descriptions are not effective. If the description is too narrow, the secured creditor lives with the description and, unless it can persuade the court to hear testimony, receives a security interest only in the collateral duly described.

Presumably subsection (b) with its six examples of adequate descriptions is intended to encourage the courts to be generous here. Common descriptions that are blessed in subsection (b) include descriptions in Article 9, such as "inventory" or "farm products." The blessing of "category" in subsection (2) presumably would allow a description such as "all livestock," and the computational or allocational formula described in (5) authorizes a security interest in "50% of debtor's grain stored in the Harlan elevator."

Subsection (b)(6) permits any other method of identification provided "the identity of the collateral is objectively determinable." Presumably this means that a court should sometimes hear testimony to show how the description "objectively determines" the identity of the collateral. For example, if a debtor granted a security interest in all of its inventory located at its plant at 625 S. State St., a court would need testimony about what was located at that plant at the relevant time in order to determine the nature of the collateral.

Likewise a description of a truck that described it as a "2018 Mack Anthem Truck with serial number AB7777" would be an adequate description even though the serial number was in fact AB7888. Comment 2 rejects "any requirement that a description is insufficient unless it is exact and detailed (the so-called serial number test)." If the debtor owned only one Mack Anthem Truck, it would be objectively determinable that the parties intended to create a security interest in that truck. Thus, there will be many cases where the court may require testimony or other proof to determine the nature of the collateral. That is not to say a court must always hear testimony about the particular intention of the debtor or creditor in using particular words but only that the words, as objectively understood, may refer to items of collateral that must be identified by further investigation, as by viewing the inventory at 625 S. State St., or examining the debtor's statement of account from Merrill Lynch.

Since 9–203 is intended only as a Statute of Frauds (and is entitled to no more respect than any other Statute of Frauds), a court should be ready to allow testimony that will enable it to objectively determine the collateral under 9–108(b)(6), if necessary. Thus, where the security agreement is fragmented and is not an integration of the agreement, a court should allow testimony about what the parties did or did not intend to cover by potentially ambiguous language in the security agreement. There will almost always be some performance or extrinsic evidence that will show that the parties intended to secure a particular loan by particular collateral. Consequently, a court should be receptive to proof—particularly evidence that describes performance under the loan such as inventories taken and lists submitted—to broaden the description. It is worth noting that in many cases involving allegedly ambiguous descriptions of collateral, the debtor is not the party challenging the adequacy of the description. Rather, such challenges may originate with third parties, such as the trustee in bankruptcy or another creditor. It is disingenuous in such cases for the third party challenger to say the debtor and creditor ought to have been clearer about the collateral in their private security agreement simply because there is an apparent ambiguity in the writing.

A final point that is easy to overlook in drafting a security agreement is the identification of the loan to be secured. Sometimes the parties have in mind merely a single loan, e.g., "securing a note of even date." Once a new advance is made, or a "note of even date" is rewritten, there may be a question whether the security agreement covers the new obligation. Sophisticated secured creditors cover this problem by using an expansive definition of liabilities to be covered that refers not only to future advances or to commercial loans, but to liabilities of all sorts. Absent such a broad description of the loan covered, a court should apply conventional, sensible rules of interpretation that would normally include rewritings of the original loan as a covered loan.

c.   Authenticate

The "signed writing" required in former 9–203, reappears within the broader concept of "an authenticated . . . security agreement" in the 1999 Code[12] (9–203(b)(3)(A)). Digital security agreements are developing rapidly[13] (particularly for high volume consumer lenders), but for now by far the most common form of authenticated security agreement will continue to be a signed writing. Signing after all is the traditional method of authentication of paper documents and, at least for security agreements, we expect that physical paper (or at least an electronic copy of paper documents) will remain important. "Signed" is defined in 1–201(b)(37) and includes "any symbol executed or adopted with present intention to adopt or accept a writing." Courts have interpreted this provision liberally; a typed name may satisfy it, so may a photocopy of a signed signature, as well as many other symbols.[14]

But what does "authenticate" mean? What else does it allow? According to 9–102(a)(7) it means:

(A) to sign; or

(B) with the present intent to adopt or accept a record, to attach to or logically associate with the record an electronic sound, symbol, or process.

The language in (B) permits security agreements in electronic and other non-written media. For this purpose one can only authenticate "a record"; 9–102(a)(70) defines a record as:

(70) . . . information that is inscribed on a tangible medium or which is stored in an electronic or other medium and is retrievable in perceivable form.

While Comment 9(a) states:

A "record" need not be permanent or indestructible, but the term does not include any oral or other communication

---

[12] The 2010 amendments to Article 9 made no changes to § 9–203 beyond updating the cross reference to § 1–203 (2001).

[13] The rapid development of blockchain-based smart contracts and similar technologies, for example, suggest that in many contexts electronic agreements based entirely or partly in self-executing code will likely become a dominant mechanism for making, monitoring, and possibly even recording secured transactions.

[14] It is enough in most cases if parol evidence establishes an intention to authenticate with use of the symbol.

that is not stored or preserved by any means.... Information that has not been retained other than through human memory does not qualify as a record.

If, for example, the parties negotiated a security agreement and stored it in a computer file located in a cloud storage form such as the Google Cloud Platform or Box.com (or perhaps even just preserved as an attachment to an email chain), the adoption of a symbol (or apparently the encryption of the document without adoption of a symbol) with the present intention of "identifying" themselves and "adopting or accepting" the record, would make the data computer file an enforceable security agreement. Although encryption is a sufficient method of authentication, it is not a necessary one.

Comment 9(b) states:

> The terms "authenticate" and "authenticated" generally replace "sign" and "signed." "Authenticated" replaces and broadens the definition of "signed," in section 1–201, to encompass authentication of all records, not just writings.

Nor is it necessary that the "symbol" have the characteristics of a signature or secret code; the symbol adopted with the intention of identifying a person need not be unique like a manual signature or a fingerprint. Typing the name "John Jones" or "First Day Ditching Company by John Jones" (with Jones' approval) into the document which is recorded on a floppy disk would itself be adequate to authenticate even though the typed name would give no assurance that the person whose name appears at the end of the document authorized the use of his name.[15]

Authentication requires both "present intent" to identify the person authenticating and to "adopt, accept" or "establish the authenticity" of a "record or term." There can be no authentication as that term is used in 9–102(a)(7) of something that does not qualify as a record under 9–102(a)(70). To be a record something must be "retrievable in perceivable form." (9–102(a)(70)). So the security agreement recorded on the cloud storage platform would be adequate. Presumably the same is true of the security agreement recorded on the secured creditor's hard drive. But the "retrievable in perceivable form" requirement is not so clear with voice mail where there is a limited capacity to retrieve the record. Comment 9 to 9–102 explicitly blesses e-mail as well as certain other technology: "examples of

---

[15] It is important here to emphasize that "authentication" under 9–102(a)(7) requires a "present intent to adopt or accept a record." A mere forgery or unauthorized typing of John Jones's name at the end of a record would not have been attached with the present intent to adopt or record that record.

current technology commercially used to communicate or store information include, but are not limited to, magnetic media, optical disk, digital voice messaging systems, electronic mail, audio tapes and photographic media as well as paper." Remember, a record must be on a "tangible medium" or, "stored" and "retrievable in perceivable form." The question remains, for how long? At least under the Comment, one could argue that a security agreement sent by the debtor to the creditor by e-mail or phone mail and later destroyed would nevertheless constitute a record that could be proven by oral testimony in the same way one could prove the existence of a writing that had been destroyed.

We suspect the questions inherent in the word "authenticate" and the definition of a "record" will be slow in rising to the surface in secured transactions. Secured creditors are nothing if not careful and conservative. We suspect they will be slow to abandon signed, written documents. On the other hand, many lenders will soon store most of their agreements and other documents in electronic form, and it is easy to imagine a case in which the secured creditor loses or, by mistake, destroys the original written document and will have to rely upon the electronic copy in case of litigation.

d. Value

Section 1–204 defines "value":

[e]xcept as otherwise provided in Articles 3, 4 [and] 5, [and 6], a person gives value for rights if the person acquires them:

(1) in return for a binding commitment to extend credit or for the extension of immediately available credit, whether or not drawn upon and whether or not a charge-back is provided for in the event of difficulties in collection;

(2) as security for, or in total or partial satisfaction of, a preexisting claim;

(3) by accepting delivery under a preexisting contract for purchase; or

(4) in return for any consideration sufficient to support a simple contract.

Lending money is giving value. Likewise, a binding obligation to make a loan is value sufficient to support a security interest. Consideration in the form of a promise is value. There are few cases on what is value and fewer yet are noteworthy. Of course, it is possible for the debtor and creditor to sign an agreement that does not oblige the creditor to lend money. In those circumstances the creditor will not have given value until the loan is made, but also in those cases there will almost never be an issue whether value has been given because there will be no Article 9 dispute unless a loan is made.

e.   Rights in the Collateral

Occasionally courts illegitimately invoke the requirement that the debtor have "rights in the collateral" to solve priority disputes. They do this by concluding the debtor had no "rights in the collateral," and therefore could convey nothing to the secured creditor who in turn received nothing. This version of the rule *nemo dat quod non habet*[16] probably should be attributed to section 2–403 or to other law, but not to 9–203. If the debtor's title is defective and if the competitor is not otherwise subordinated by 9–322 or other provisions of Article 9, then in truth there is no conveyance to the secured creditor and the secured creditor takes nothing. We doubt the "rights in the collateral" language of 9–203 embodies that rule.

In general, debtor's rights in the collateral are not determined by Article 9, but by Articles 2 and 2A, by the common law and by other rules. Thus, for example, a debtor's "title" might depend on a local certificate of title law, 2–401 and 2–403 of Article 2, or on common law rules dealing with bailment and the like. Viewed that way, "rights in the collateral" merely states a truism, namely that the debtor can normally only convey something once it has something and that the debtor's interest might be less than the full bundle of rights that one with absolute title would own.

Under section 9–203 "rights in the collateral" goes beyond title to the collateral to include any case where the debtor has "the power to transfer rights in the collateral to a secured party." According to the second paragraph of Comment 6, this phrase recognizes that a debtor may have the power to transfer greater rights than the debtor has. These would include cases where, for example, the debtor had made a transfer of a security interest to a creditor who had not perfected and the debtor had later made a second transfer of the same collateral to another creditor who first perfected. Under the rules of priority in Part 3, the creditor whose transfer was second but who first perfected would have priority, and that would be so despite the fact the debtor was transferring greater rights to the second creditor than the debtor still held.

The debtor's rights to which the security interest attaches can, of course, be far less than full ownership. A lessee can convey a security interest in its interest; a joint owner of an asset can convey a security interest in its share, etc. Nothing in Article 9—some courts

---

[16]   One cannot give what one does not have.

to the contrary notwithstanding—shows any intention to limit the power of a debtor to convey a security interest in any rights held by the debtor, however slight.

2–4 PERFECTION IN GENERAL

Perfection is a term of art in Article 9. Sections 9–308 through 9–316 specify how one perfects in each of the various transactions under Article 9. We devote the remainder of this Chapter to mapping perfection's boundaries.

A secured creditor gains significant benefits by perfecting its security interest. The perfected secured creditor is nearly as far above the unperfected secured creditor in the priorities pecking order as the unperfected secured creditor is above the general creditor. Perfection also earns the secured party priority over a subsequent lien creditor. The lien creditor *par excellence* is the trustee in bankruptcy wielding rights under section 544(a) of the Bankruptcy Code. Thus, a secured party who perfects before bankruptcy usually enjoys a solitary feast, but an unperfected secured party will invariably have to eat from the general creditors' trough in bankruptcy. Likewise, the date of the perfecting act is commonly the date from which priority is measured vis à vis other perfected secured creditors. Usually, though not invariably, a creditor who perfects takes priority over secured creditors who perfect later, yet is subordinate to those who perfected previously.

Security interests can be perfected in four ways. These methods of perfection include: (1) filing a financing statement, (2) possession of the collateral by the creditor, (3) control of certain types of collateral by the creditor, and (4) automatic perfection with respect to certain types of collateral.

Filing a financing statement. First, the most common and important method of perfection is the filing of a financing statement.[17] This document is usually filed with the secretary of state at the state capital. The financing statement is a relatively simple document that merely purposes to provide public notice to readers that the named creditor may claim an interest in described collateral of the debtor. Only rarely is the financing statement also the operative document which creates the security interest between the parties.

Possession of the collateral by the creditor. A second method for perfection of security interests occurs where the secured creditor

---

[17]   UCC § 9–310.

possesses the collateral. This method *may* be used with respect to certain kinds of collateral[18] and *must* be used with respect to cash.[19]

Control of the collateral by the creditor. A third method, useable with some kinds of intangible collateral, is "control."[20] A direct security interest in a deposit account or letter of credit may be perfected *only* by taking control; it is a permissible but not the exclusive mode of perfection for investment property and electronic chattel paper. "Control" is to intangibles as "possession" is to goods. Where a bank might "possess" a tractor and so perfect its security interest in the tractor, the bank might achieve "control" over its customer's account at Merrill Lynch (by putting the bank's name on the account, for example) and so perfect a security interest in the debtor's stock and bonds.

Automatic perfection. Finally, some security interests are automatically perfected at the time of their creation (attachment) without any additional act of the secured creditor.[21] The most important of this group of automatically perfected interests are purchase money interests in consumer goods.[22]

Why do we insist on perfection? What is to be gained by a public filing or by the creditor taking possession or control of the debtor's assets? The public filing will give notice to any third party smart enough to search, and taking possession will give notice to anyone who does an inventory of the debtor's assets. In theory, these public acts minimize the capacity of the debtor to borrow twice against the same collateral or otherwise to mislead subsequent potential creditors. Again, however, the public filing is merely a "notice." The drafters of Article 9 consciously rejected the typical real estate "recording" system under which the operative document, e.g., the mortgage, is put in a public recording system. The examination of a financing statement tells little about any existing loan or security interest. The principle functions of the financing statement are to inform the searcher that other creditors may have a claim against the collateral and direct the searcher toward finding more information. As we will see, in some cases, the drafters concluded that the benefits of public disclosure were outweighed by the costs of making that disclosure.

Article 9 does not state rules for perfection with respect to all security interests in all types of personality. For example, security

---

[18]   UCC § 9–313.
[19]   UCC §§ 9–312(b)(3), 9–313.
[20]   UCC §§ 9–312(b), 9–314.
[21]   UCC § 9 309.
[22]   UCC § 9–309(1).

interests in aircraft are perfected according to a federal law by filing in Oklahoma City. Federal filings may also be required in certain cases for interests in patents, copyright and trademarks. As to collateral or transactions that are excluded from Article 9 under 9–109, taking and perfecting a secured interest may nevertheless be possible under the common law or under some other statute of a particular state.

2–5 AUTOMATIC PERFECTION, IN GENERAL

For most secured transactions, to maximize rights against third parties a secured creditor must enter an enforceable security agreement that attaches to the collateral *and* take additional steps to perfect that security interest. These steps usually consist of either filing or possession, which perfect the creditor's interest against third parties. But in certain specialized cases, the Code in section 9–309, grants "automatic" perfection to some security interests merely upon their attachment under 9–203, that is, without any filing nor shift of possession or control of the collateral to the creditor. Most common is the purchase money security interest in consumer goods—the pre-Code "conditional sale" dressed in Code attire.

The remaining security interests that are automatically perfected under section 9–309 are a motley lot of transactions, each one of which is automatically perfected for good reason but for reasons that themselves are quite different from one transaction to another. For example the transactions in 9–309(3), (4) and (5)—sales of payment intangibles, promissory notes, or assignment of health care insurance receivables to health care providers—are clearly important commercial financing transactions. Here someone convinced the drafters that filing was unnecessary and inappropriate. The sale of payment intangibles covers, among other things, the granting of loan participations by large banks to smaller banks. We suspect the banks thought it would be unseemly to have another bank file a financing statement in their name and argued that these transactions were so tightly controlled within a limited number of creditors and debtors that filing was unnecessary.

A similar claim was made about sales of promissory notes in "mortgage warehousing." In mortgage warehousing, a creditor lends to a mortgage lender and takes a security interest in the pool of notes and mortgages pending the securitization and sale of those notes and mortgages to third parties.

Some of the other automatic perfection provisions are tolerable because they are not traditional financing transactions, lie quite far removed from Article 9, and have persisted for a long time without the necessity for filing. Among these are the security interest identified in 9–309(6) (Articles 2 and 2A, security interests), (7) (Article 4, collecting bank security), and (8) (Article 5, issuer or nominated party under a letter of credit).

As we will explain more fully below, sections 9–309(9) and 9–309(10) grants automatic perfection, respectively, to a broker or securities intermediary who gets "delivery" of a financial asset[23] and to a broker who takes a security interest in its customer's brokerage account. Section 9–309 reads as follows:

The following security interests are perfected when they attach:

(1) a purchase-money security interest in consumer goods, except as otherwise provided in section 9–311(b) with respect to consumer goods that are subject to a statute or treaty described in section 9–311(a);

(2) an assignment of accounts or payment intangibles which does not by itself or in conjunction with other assignments to the same assignee transfer a significant part of the assignor's outstanding accounts or payment intangibles;

(3) a sale of a payment intangible;

(4) a sale of a promissory note;

(5) a security interest created by the assignment of a health-care-insurance receivable to the provider of the health-care goods or services;

(6) a security interest arising under section 2–401, 2–505, 2–711(3), or 2A–508(5), until the debtor obtains possession of the collateral;

(7) a security interest of a collecting bank arising under section 4–210;

(8) a security interest of an issuer or nominated person arising under section 5–118;

(9) a security interest arising in the delivery of a financial asset under section 9–206I;

(10) a security interest in investment property created by a broker or securities intermediary;

(11) a security interest in a commodity contract or a commodity account created by a commodity intermediary;

---

[23]   Presumably delivery could have been defined as another mode of perfection instead of a condition for automatic perfection under 9–309.

(12) an assignment for the benefit of all creditors of the transferor and subsequent transfers by the assignee thereunder; and

(13) a security interest created by an assignment of a beneficial interest in a decedent's estate.

2–6 AUTOMATIC PERFECTION—PURCHASE MONEY SECURITY INTERESTS IN CONSUMER GOODS, SECTION 9–103

Should merchants or banks with security interests in consumers' chairs, stoves, or washing machines be required to file like most other secured creditors? Pre-Code law granted perfected status without filing to sellers of consumer goods and to those who lent the purchase price of consumer. The Code's "automatic" perfection on creation of such interests replicates this pre-Code doctrine. In this case, automatic perfection reduces what would otherwise be heavy transaction costs with slight benefits. If creditors had to file with respect to every consumer credit transaction, the filing offices would be bulging at the seams. Further, the benefits to be gained from filing these security interests are marginal. Since potential creditors have long been aware of automatic perfection of such "conditional sales," they are on guard when a consumer attempts to borrow against consumer goods. Finally, most consumer goods cost little and depreciate quickly; creditors, other than purchase money lenders, seldom rely on such goods in making loans, so it is unlikely that any subsequent creditor will be fooled by the absence of a public filing.

The case law has revealed only two significant lawyer problems. First, what is a purchase money security interest? Second, what are "consumer goods"?

a. Purchase Money Status

In most circumstances identification of a purchase money security interest is easy. If the seller has retained an interest in goods sold to secure payment of some or all of the price, the seller has a purchase money security interest. The words the parties use to describe their contractual relationship is irrelevant. Whether the agreement with the buyer is called a "conditional sales contract," a "bailment lease," or something else, what matters is the substance of the transaction, specifically whether the transaction satisfies the requirements of 9–103(b). Moreover, the creditor in such situations may be the seller of the goods or software to the debtor or a third party (for example, a bank or finance company) that lends money to a prospective buyer to enable the buyer to purchase.[24] Under § 9–103(a)(2), that person must make advances or incur an obligation "to enable the debtor to acquire rights in or the use of the collateral," and, the money lent must be "in fact so used." Elsewhere we will consider the importance of the limitations of (a)(2). For now, it suffices to understand that the third party has a purchase money security interest only if that party can show that the money the third party lent was "in fact" used to acquire an interest in the collateral in question.

To be automatically perfected, a security interest must retain its status as a "purchase money" security interest. Thus it is often in the interest of a trustee in bankruptcy or some other competitor to claim that a security interest which was originally "purchase money" has lost that status or, in some cases, never attained that status. The challenge to the purchase money status comes in two forms. First, the challenger might argue that the mixture of a purchase money and non-purchase money security interest in the same security agreement renders the entire security agreement non-purchase money. Second, the challenger might acknowledge the existence of two security interests, one purchase money and one non-purchase money, but argue that the debtor's payments should be allocated first to the purchase money security interest and so reduce that one to the benefit of the trustee (who, by hypothesis, can defeat the non-purchase money unperfected interest but who cannot defeat the purchase money perfected interest). Revised Article 9 explicitly provides that a single document can create two security interests in business transactions: one purchase money and one non-purchase money. But section 9–103 declines to take a position on that issue in consumer cases. So, unless a court chooses to apply the business rule by analogy to consumer cases too, we are left with uncertainty.[25]

There are two common circumstances in which purchase money status is uncertain. First is the case where the debtor makes several consecutive purchases from the same seller. Assume the debtor buys a refrigerator in month one, a television in month two, and a stereo in month three. Assume further that each of the purchases is financed by the seller who takes a security interest in each of the

---

[24]   UCC § 9–103(a)(2).

[25]   For a discussion of the positions courts have taken on the status of purchase money security interests where the consumer purchase involves both a purchase money security interest and a non-purchase money security interest, see In re Mancini, 390 B.R. 796, 806–808 (Bankr. M.D. Penn. 2008). There, the court noted that courts have adopted two separate rules for addressing this problem. The " 'transformation rule' converts the entire claim into a non-purchase money claim, eliminating any purchase money portion of the claim." In contrast, the " 'dual status rule' allows the portion of the claim which is a purchase money security interest to remain so, even if part of the claim is non-purchase money." Id.

assets purchased. Since each would be financed by the seller, each would be a purchase money security interest and so be automatically perfected. But life is not so simple. In all likelihood, our seller will combine the three items into one security agreement and that security agreement will provide that each asset is collateral, not only for its own purchase price but also for the purchase price of the other two items.[26] Now there is a problem. Because the purchase price for the refrigerator was "purchase money" only as to the refrigerator and not as to the television or stereo, to the extent that the television and stereo stand as collateral for the price of the refrigerator, the security is "non-purchase money."

The second circumstance arises when a loan is re-financed or when a debtor makes payments against a loan that is secured by two security interests, one purchase money and one non-purchase money. Assume, for example, the debtor borrows $2,000 from the bank in a purchase money loan to buy a stereo system. Six months later the bank "refinances" the loan. At that time, the debtor borrows an additional $1,000. Has the refinancing caused the security interest to lose its purchase money status? For consumer cases, 9–103 declines to give an answer; however, for business cases, 9–103 rules that the purchase money status is retained.[27] So section 9–103 leaves a court free to follow its own rule (if it has one), to apply the business rule by analogy, or to reason from other cases. In these cases we believe the courts should apply the business rule by analogy.

Even if it is conceded that the original security interest retains its purchase money status, the new loan ($1,000) will not be a purchase money loan and will not be automatically perfected. Now, assume the debtor pays $1,000 against its consolidated debt. Does this $1,000 reduce the loan that is secured by the purchase money security interest, does it extinguish the $1,000 loan that is secured by non-purchase money security interest, or is it allocated pro rata? This will be important if the secured creditor is depending on the automatic perfection provisions associated with purchase money loans. If the $1,000 payment is allocated on a FIFO (first in, first out) basis to the earliest loan, $1,000 of the loan is now secured by a

---

[26] This financing and security interest structure is highly similar to the "add-on" installment security clause analyzed under UCC § 2–302 in the famous case of Williams v. Walker-Thomas Furniture Co., 350 F.2d 445 (D.C. Cir. 1965). Notably, there are many variations on this type of security arrangement, and such clauses are not necessarily unconscionable in particular transactions.

[27] UCC § 9–103(f) ("In a transaction other than a consumer-goods transaction, a purchase-money security interest does not lose its status as such. . . ."). Comment 8 further clarifies that this exclusion of consumer-goods transactions was deliberate: "Under subsection (h), the limitation of subsections (e), (f), and (g) to transactions other than consumer-goods transactions leaves to the court the determination of the proper rules in consumer-goods transactions."

perfected security interest (purchase money) and $1,000 is secured by an unperfected security interest. If, alternatively, the payments are allocated on a LIFO basis to the last loan, the secured creditor retains a perfected security interest as to its entire remaining loan because the payment would have been treated as a payment against the second loan secured by a non-purchase money security interest.

Where there are multiple purchases and later payments, one faces the same allocation problem. If I have paid the price of the item first purchased, do I at least own that? If a court recognizes a "dual status" security agreement, it needs to find an allocation method to determine how a single payment per month by the debtor should be allocated among the various purchase money interests and the non-purchase money interests. Should it be FIFO, LIFO or some other method? Some courts were offended (see, e.g., Williams v. Walker-Thomas Furniture Co.)[28] by allocation schemes that held every piece of collateral subject to the security interest until the last penny was paid. Other courts found a solution to that problem in state law providing an allocation scheme.[29] In any case the creditor needs to provide an allocation scheme by its agreement or to find one in the law. Finally, there are cases where the loan was rewritten or "consolidated." In those too, the courts have been in confusion and disagreement, some finding that the rewriting or consolidation deprived the new loan entirely of the purchase money status; others concluding the opposite.

The drafters of the 1999 Code lost heart when they got to consumer purchase money loans. By setting out explicit rules that generally favored purchase money status in business transactions, the drafters showed that they understood the proper rules and had the capacity to state them clearly. It is regrettable they did not apply the same rules to consumer transactions, but, at least, they left the courts free to apply the business rules by analogy to consumer cases. In section 4 of Chapter 4 we deal with purchase money security interests in the business context. In that context, purchase money status does not earn perfection; rather it raises the priority this secured creditor would otherwise enjoy.

Other pitfalls await creditors relying on automatic perfection. For example, if the goods are to become fixtures, the filing exemption will not protect the retailer (see sections 9–334 and 9–604). Observe

---

[28]   Williams v. Walker-Thomas Furniture Co., 350 F.2d 445, 2 UCC 955 (D.C.Cir.1965) (though identical to the standard retail installment pro-rata allocation scheme, the court suggested that a contract providing each payment by debtor would be pro-rated to various items of collateral in proportion to the price of each was unconscionable).

[29]   See, e.g., Michigan Retail Installment Sales Act, M.C.L.A. 445.861 (West 1999); Pristas v. Landaus of Plymouth, Inc., 742 F.2d 797, 39 UCC 1 (3d Cir.1984).

that purchase money status is important not merely for perfection; it is also necessary to preserve a security interest in consumer goods from extinction in bankruptcy under 522(f).

Under the pre-1999 law, the cases dealing with consumer purchase money security interest were in disarray. Some, such as In re Manuel,[30] declined to recognize the dual status where there were cross collateral clauses and found (or implied) that the secured creditor was unperfected if the creditor had not filed and that none of its security interest was purchase money. Others recognized dual security interests in business cases—with no suggestion that a different rule would apply in consumer cases.[31]

b. Consumer Goods

The second question presented by 9–103 involves classification of the collateral: consumer goods or not? Is a stove designed for home use necessarily a consumer good? Is a $50,000 house trailer a consumer good? According to subsection 9–102(a)(23): "[g]oods are 'consumer goods' if they are used or bought for use primarily for personal, family or household purposes . . . ." Note that section 9–102 does not classify goods according to design or intrinsic nature but according to the use to which their owner puts them. It follows that as use changes, either because the owner finds some new task for the goods, or because an owner sells the goods to another who uses them for a different purpose, the classification of the goods will also change. Of course, borderline cases, such as a physician's car or a farmer's jeep, will arise. When they do, the factfinder must determine whether the debtor used the goods "primarily" for personal, family, or household purposes.

One troublesome problem in defining consumer goods has arisen in cases involving house trailers. In the case of In re Sprague,[32] a secured creditor claimed an automatically perfected security interest in a house trailer. The trustee argued that the trailer was not a consumer good because it was large and expensive and it would not be "consumed" (i.e., depreciate) as quickly or as fully as most items that qualify as consumer goods. The trustee's argument seems to disregard the clear command of 9–102. Design, size, weight, shape and cost are irrelevant; use or intended use determines proper categorization. The policy underlying 9–309, however, supports the trustee's argument. One important justification for tolerating

---

[30]   507 F.2d 990, 16 UCC 493 (5th Cir.1975).

[31]   See, e.g., In re Express Air, Inc., 136 B.R. 328, 17 UCC2d 936 (Bankr.D.Mass.1992); In re Ionosphere Clubs, Inc., 123 B.R. 166, 13 UCC2d 1276 (S.D.N.Y.1991); In re Hemingson, 84 B.R. 604, 7 UCC2d 187 (Bankr.D.Minn.1988).

[32]   1966 WL 8932, 4 UCC 702 (Bankr.N.D.N.Y.1966).

unfiled, and therefore, secret liens under 9–309, is that most consumer goods are relatively inexpensive and decline rapidly in value after they are taken from the merchant's premises. Subsequent creditors are thus not likely to lend in reliance upon such goods and so not likely to be misled to their injury by the absence of a public filing. Quite clearly this policy does not fit house trailers. As Referee Ryan pointed out, the drafters of the Code recognized the substantial residual value in a motor vehicle, and excluded it from the automatic perfection provision.[33] This principle applies *a fortiori* to even more permanent, more expensive mobile homes. Referee Ryan decided the Sprague case against the secured creditor on two grounds: (1) the house trailer was not consumer goods, and (2) it was a motor vehicle and so excluded from the automatic perfection provisions of former 9–302(1)(d). On the appeal of a companion case, Judge Foley accepted Referee Ryan's holding that the secured creditor was not perfected but he relied exclusively upon a finding that the house trailer was a motor vehicle under New York law. At least by implication, he rejected Referee Ryan's interpretation of the words "consumer goods."[34]

Under the definition, the house trailer should be regarded as a consumer good. One could explicitly require filing of security interests in mobile homes and other reasonably expensive collateral but the Code's Editorial Board rejected this approach.[35] Or one could limit the value for which the exemption applies.[36] Durable, valuable "consumer goods" which a creditor is likely to rely upon for collateral, include not only mobile homes, but also jewelry, paintings and other works of art, pleasure boats, or even above ground swimming pools. The legislature and not the courts, however, should solve this problem. The unfocused balancing test implicit in Referee Ryan's opinion would produce a long series of ad hoc judgments having to do with the useful life, size, and value of various goods. In sum, until legislators say otherwise, mobile homes, yachts, diamond wedding rings, and dining room chandeliers remain "consumer goods" along with kitchen salt and Rolling Stones' CDs and in all of these (except

---

[33]   The uniform automatic perfection provision, former 9–302(1)(d), excluded motor vehicles.

[34]   In re Vinarsky, 287 F.Supp. 446, 5 UCC 1042 (N.D.N.Y.1968), aff'g,1966 WL 8933, 4 UCC 707 (Bankr.N.D.N.Y.1966). See also In re Brown, 45 B.R. 766, 768, 40 UCC 684 (Bankr.N.D.N.Y.1985) (mobile home is consumer goods but is also "motor vehicle required to be licensed or registered"; therefore excepted from automatic perfection).

[35]   "Public policy as to mobile homes ought not to be frozen in a Uniform Code." Perm.Ed.Bd. UCC Rev.Comm. Art. 9, Final Report 237 (1971).

[36]   At least two states do not permit automatic perfection when the consumer goods' price, or the amount financed, exceed a certain price: Kansas (purchase price over $3,000) and Maine (amount financed over $2,000). See 3A U.L.A. 16 (1999 Supp.).

where a certificate of title law applies), a purchase money security interest is automatically perfected under 9–309.

PROBLEM

Assume that Bank takes a security interest in the inventory of a series of hardware stores. That inventory is composed of hand tools, lawn mowers, garden tractors and the like; almost all of it is intended for sale to consumers. For some reason Bank fails to file a financing statement. On hardware stores' bankruptcy, Bank claims that it is a perfected secured creditor, because it has a purchase money loan against consumer goods.

Bank is wrong. The shovels, lawn mowers and the like in the hands of the hardware store are inventory under 9–102(a)(48). Once a lawn mower that is inventory in the hands of the hardware store is sold to a consumer, that very same lawn mower becomes a consumer good under 9–102 (a)(23). Had the lawn mower been sold to a landscape business, it would have become equipment under 9–102(a)(33).

Since inventory does not fit within the automatic perfection rules of section 9–309, the bank is unperfected, and its security interest will be avoided by the trustee in bankruptcy.

c. Conclusion

While claiming not to modify the rules concerning purchase money security interest in consumer goods, section 9–103 of the 1999 Revision in fact provides a template which courts can follow and which in our opinion they should follow, namely 9–103(e) and (f). Whether a security interest in consumer goods is a purchase money security interest is important for at least three reasons: First, it is important for the purposes of 9–309. If the security interest is a purchase money security interest in consumer goods, it is automatically perfected without filing or any other act. If the security interest is not a purchase money security interest, the creditor will normally have to file a financing statement in order to perfect and achieve priority over a trustee in bankruptcy and many other claimants. Second, in bankruptcy a consumer debtor may be able to avoid certain non-purchase money security interests in household goods and the like under Bankruptcy Code § 522(f)(1)(B)—even if they are perfected. Finally, the taking of a non-purchase money security interest in certain household goods may be an unfair trade practice under the FTC regulation, 16 C.F.R. § 444.2(a)(4).[37] So, the

---

[37]   "In connection with the extension of credit to consumers . . . it is an unfair act or practice . . . for a lender or retail installment seller directly or indirectly to take or receive from a consumer an obligation that . . . (4) Constitutes or contains a nonpossessory security interest in household goods other than a purchase money security interest." 16 C.F.R. § 444.2(a)(4).

purchase money status of a security interest in consumer goods has potential significance beyond automatic perfection.

Some of the rules discussed above also apply to purchase money status in business transactions. In these cases, the rules in 9–103 are quite clear. These rules become relevant when a creditor who is second in time claims first priority because of its purchase money status. We discuss those cases in Chapter 4.

2–7 AUTOMATIC PERFECTION—CERTAIN INTANGIBLES, SECTION 9–109

From the very first, Article 9 distinguished among various transfers of intangible rights. Some were excluded from Article 9, others were accorded automatic perfection, and yet others were treated like transfers of conventional collateral under which the secured creditor was required to file a financing statement in order to perfect its interest. Revised Article 9 introduces a nuanced and complex treatment of security transfers of various intangible rights. First, certain transfers are entirely excluded from Article 9 (9–109(d)(3)–(9)). For example, 9–109(d)(5) excludes assignments of accounts to collection agencies for obvious reasons and section 9–109(d)(6) excludes the assignment of a right to payment to an assignee who also assumes the obligation to perform the contract—presumably because the assignee is not a financing party but a person in the assignor's business.

An addition to Article 9 following the 1999 Revision, is automatic perfection under 9–309(3) and (4) for the "sale" of "a payment intangible" and "a promissory note." Comment 4 to 9–309 explains these automatic perfection rules as follows: "[t]hey reflect the practice under former Article 9. Under that Article, filing a financing statement does not affect the rights of a buyer of payment intangibles or promissory notes, inasmuch as the Article [does] not cover those sales." Before 1999, the Code covered only sales of accounts, not sales of intangibles or instruments. Thus, the statement in the Comment, while accurate, falls short of a reasoned explanation why, once included, these transactions should enjoy automatic perfection.

We suspect this exclusion of the foregoing sales from Article 9's filing rules is attributable to the influence of banks and other parties who do not wish to file in loan participation or "mortgage warehousing" cases. In the former case, a bank with a large loan might sell off parts of that loan to third parties. If that transaction were within Article 9 and subject to conventional perfection rules, the buyer would have to file a financing statement (or if there were a note, take possession of the note). In a case of "mortgage warehousing" in which a bank might be extending a line of credit to a commercial mortgagee, the "warehousing" lender would either have to take possession of the notes (under the old Code) or either file or take possession of the notes (under 1999 Article 9). The statute would have been easier to understand, less complicated, and more logical if the drafters had not excluded these cases from the conventional perfection rules, but as the Comment suggests, these transactions have caused little problem in the past, so it may be that little is lost in granting automatic perfection.

Automatic perfection applies only if there is a "sale" of the intangible or note. If a transaction is not a "sale," such as the grant of a security interest or a mere assignment for security, the transaction is within Article 9, and the automatic perfection provisions of 9–309 do not apply. How does one distinguish a sale versus a grant of a security interest or a non sale assignment? The distinction lies mostly in the amount of recourse the transferee has against the transferor. In a classic factoring "sale" of accounts the factor purchases the accounts from the obligee and frees the obligee (the seller of the accounts) from any recourse in case the account debtor fails to pay. In effect, the entire risk of nonpayment by the account debtor (and the entire benefit of full payment) is transferred to the factor or buyer. If, on the other hand, one chose to "lend" against a debtor's accounts, the debtor might be asked to sign a note and grant a security interest in the accounts as security for the note. The debtor in this case would have an obligation to make up the difference out of other assets when the accounts proved to be inadequate for payment. In effect, the debtor would retain the credit risk associated with the accounts and, if the account debtors failed, would have to make up that difference in order to pay the note in full.[38]

It is common for assignors and assignees of intangibles to write contracts that leave them somewhere between a pure sale and a pure secured loan. For example, a bank who is purchasing "automobile paper" from an automobile dealer may require the automobile dealer to buy back any loan that fails within 6 months of the sale. Such a transaction is a "sale," but to the extent there is recourse against the

---

[38] See, e.g., In re De-Pen Line, Inc., 215 B.R. 947, 34 UCC2d 502 (Bankr.E.D.Pa.1997) (where debtor transfers accounts receivable to a factor but retains risk of nonpayment on the accounts, the transfer is not a true sale of accounts receivable and does not enjoy automatic perfection); In re Qualia Clinical Service, Inc., 411 B.R. 325 (2011) ("Where the 'seller' retains 'virtually all of the risks of noncollection,' the transaction cannot properly be considered a true sale."); Pascack Community Bank v. Universal Funding, LLP, 16 A.2d 1097 (N.J. Super. 2011) (despite document indicating "sale" of invoices to factor, factor's agreement to advance monies equal to 85% of invoices and also to charge back to debtor amount of invoices that were not paid made it unclear that risk of nonpayment was transferred to factor or retained by debtor).

dealer in the first 6 months, the transaction has some of the characteristics of a loan. We cannot examine every possible variation here. But the lawyer should be aware that adding too many elements of recourse (or leaving too many other elements of ownership with the seller), the lawyer runs the risk that the transaction is no longer a sale and that the buyer's interest is no longer automatically perfected. We suspect that at least outside the loan participation and mortgage warehousing arenas, most lenders will perfect by filing a financing statement anyway, and so need not depend on the automatic perfection of 9–309(3) and (4).

Section 9–309(2) grants automatic perfection to assignments of accounts or payment intangibles if those assigned do not constitute a "significant part" of the assignor's outstanding accounts or payment intangibles. What assignments do not amount to a "significant part" of the outstanding accounts of the assignor? Courts have used at least two tests: the "casual and isolated" test and the "percentage" test.[39] The "casual and isolated" test found support in Comment 5 to former 9–302 which identifies such assignments as targets of eligibility for automatic perfection. The Comment provided further backhanded support for this theory in advising that "[a]ny person who regularly takes assignments of any debtor's accounts should file."

Under the "percentage" test, the factfinder disregards the professional status of the assignee and asks only what percentage of the total accounts of the assignor were assigned and whether that percentage constitutes a "significant" part of the whole. While he does not articulate the alternate theory, Judge Nims in the case of In re Boughner[40] appears to reject the "casual and isolated" analysis. *Boughner* holds that the transfer by an insurance agent of all the agent's commissions to a third party, not in the business of lending, was the assignment of a significant part and was therefore not automatically perfected under former 9–302(1)(e). Neither *Boughner* nor any other case clearly indicates what percentage is "significant" under the percentage test. One district court case in Arkansas found that 16 percent of the outstanding accounts was not a significant

---

   39   For an example of the "casual and isolated" test, see In re Barrington, 34 B.R. 55, 37 UCC 540 (Bankr.M.D.Fla.1983). For examples of courts employing the percentage test, see, e.g., In re Arctic Air Conditioning, Inc., 35 B.R. 107, 37 UCC 1353 (Bankr.E.D.Tenn.1983) (67% was "significant"); In re Hostetler, 49 B.R. 737, 41 UCC 643 (Bankr.W.D.Pa.1985) (5% and 13.6% not "significant"). Some courts require a passing grade on both tests to avoid filing. See St. Paul Mercury Ins. Co. v. Merchants & Marine Bank, 882 So.2d 766, 54 UCC Rep.Serv.2d 671 (Miss. 2004) (more than 25% was significant under "casual and isolated" test).
   40   1970 WL 12620, 8 UCC 144 (Bankr.W.D.Mich.1970).

part.[41] A district court in New York, however, found "just under 20 percent" significant.[42]

It might appear that a percentage test would be certain, but the cases reveal that this certainty is illusory. No distinct percentage demarcating the border between significant and insignificant amounts readily suggests itself; nor have the courts identified one.[43] There are further questions: on what calculation of "total accounts" should the percent assigned be figured, and at what time? Should "uncollectible" accounts be included? Excluded? Included but discounted?[44] Should the total be figured at the time of assignment? At the time of the bankruptcy proceeding? On some sort of "average" of the totals between assignment and bankruptcy? As several courts have found, the resolution of these questions may significantly affect the exempt-nonexempt determination.[45]

Of course, the "casual and isolated" test is also mushy. But whatever degree of certainty either of these alternate approaches affords, certainty in planning should have little relevance in construing this provision. The exception seeks to cover only transactions so isolated or so insubstantial that "no one would think of filing."[46] Most actors in the commercial world, especially those dealing in accounts, will realize that Article 9 applies to these transfers. Special exceptions cover several situations in which assignees will not think to file.[47] The desirability of providing public notice of interests in such ephemeral property, and the ease with which assignees can file, suggests that courts should generally construe the exception narrowly. Close cases should be resolved in

---

[41]   Standard Lumber Co. v. Chamber Frames, Inc., 317 F.Supp. 837, 8 UCC 139 (E.D.Ark.1970). See also In re Sun Air Int'l, Inc., 24 B.R. 135, 34 UCC 1369 (Bankr.S.D.Fla.1982) (approx. 14% of accounts assigned to debtor's attorneys "not significant").

[42]   Miller v. Wells Fargo Bank Int'l Corp., 406 F.Supp. 452, 18 UCC 489 (S.D.N.Y.1975), aff'd, 540 F.2d 548 (2d Cir.1976).

[43]   See In re Vigil Bros. Const., Inc., 193 B.R. 513, 29 UCC Rep.Serv.2d 15 (9th Cir. Bankr. App. 1996) (noting, after surveying both percentage test and casual and isolated test and appearing to adopt percentage test, "Courts have attempted to define what percentage constitutes a significant part of the assignor's account receivables."), aff'd In re Vigil Bros. Const., Inc., 1997 WL 377160 (9th Cir. 1997).

[44]   Particularly in the sale of accounts, this issue can have real consequences. Consider a hypothetical distressed debtor that determines that 50% of its accounts receivable are uncollectible and sells those accounts to a factor for only 5% of nominal value. Which percentage should be applied to determine whether the sale is "significant"? Business realities seem to strongly favor discounting (and therefore automatic perfection), while the relative size (and possibly number) of the accounts lean toward a determination of significance.

[45]   See In re Arctic Air Conditioning, Inc., 35 B.R. 107, 37 UCC 1353 (Bankr.E.D.Tenn.1983).

[46]   § 9–309, Comment 4.

[47]   § 9–109(d)(3)–(7).

favor of filing, and the creditor should bear the burden of demonstrating the exemption's applicability.[48] Noting that all the creditors involved were "in the business of agricultural financing" and familiar with the filing procedures, the court, in the case of In re Bindl,[49] pointed out that although the percentages of the debtor's total accounts taken by each assignee-creditor ranged from about 2.5% to 13%, none of the actual dollar amounts was so small as to be "de minimis," (referring to the $500 limit on automatic perfection of consumer goods). Given the likelihood of subsequent additional assignments to other creditors, notice of the pre-existing assignments would be a matter of significant interest to these subsequent assignees. Therefore, the court found none of the assignee-creditors was exempt from filing under former 9–302(1)(e).

2–8 PERFECTION BY POSSESSION, SECTION 9–313

As we have indicated, automatic perfection aside, perfection generally requires some action such as filing or possession which would put a diligent searcher on notice of the secured party's claim. Section 9–313(a) authorizes perfection by possession of "negotiable documents, goods, instruments, money, or tangible chattel paper and by 'delivery' of a certificated security."[50] Section 9–203(b)(3)(B) also renders the security agreement of a possessing creditor enforceable even though there is no signed writing or other authenticated record. So possession can fulfill two functions: enforceability (9–203) *and* perfection (9–313).

a. Pledgeable Property

One who reflects on the nature of the collateral covered by Article 9 will appreciate that the pledge[51] is uniquely suited to certain kinds of collateral, and quite unsuited to others. Since the creditor's possession (and the debtor's lack of it) puts third parties on notice, the collateral must be something that one can see, touch, and move. The collateral must have a physical embodiment that is recognizable as the exclusive representation of the right. It follows that accounts and general intangibles cannot be perfected by possession. Even if one collects ledger cards, journals, computer print-outs, sales slips and any other items believed to represent receivables, the creditor

---

[48]   In re Vigil Bros. Const., Inc., 193 B.R. 513, 29 UCC Rep.Serv.2d 15 (9th Cir. Bankr. App. 1996) ("The assignee has the burden of proving 'insignificance.' ").

[49]   13 B.R. 148, 32 UCC 337 (Bankr.W.D.Wis.1981).

[50]   Where the debtor has a certificate registered to him, giving possession to the creditor is "delivery," § 8–301.

[51]   The term "pledge" is usually used in modern commercial vernacular to describe security interests that are perfected by possession.

will not, by those acts, perfect a security interest in accounts or general intangibles. Article 9's treatment of these items as non-possessable comports with the pre-Code common law and with the abstract nature of that property. For example, since no exclusive embodiment of accounts is recognized, one creditor might seize ledger cards, another creditor could possess a computer print-out, and a third creditor might hold sales slips or a second print-out. When no "res" represents the property interest to the exclusion of all other indices of ownership, possession cannot be a reliable method of perfection.

Accounts and general intangibles must therefore be distinguished from instruments, and that is not as simple as it sounds.[52] In many cases courts have struggled with the fuzzy distinction between "accounts" and "general intangibles," which are *not* perfectible by possession, and "instruments," which under the former Code were perfectible *only* by possession. Because investment property can be completely intangible (stock for which no certificate has ever been issued), or the converse (a stock certificate bearing the owner's name and held in its paw), rules for stocks and bonds are especially complex.[53]

---

[52]   See § 9–102(a)(2). "Account," except as used in "account for," means a right to payment of a monetary obligation, whether or not earned by performance, (i) for property that has been or is to be sold, leased, licensed, assigned, or otherwise disposed of, (ii) for services rendered or to be rendered, (iii) for a policy of insurance issued or to be issued, (iv) for a secondary obligation incurred or to be incurred, (v) for energy provided or to be provided, (vi) for the use or hire of a vessel under a charter or other contract, (vii) arising out of the use of a credit or charge card or information contained on or for use with the card, or (viii) as winnings in a lottery or other game of chance operated or sponsored by a State, governmental unit of a State, or person licensed or authorized to operate the game by a State or governmental unit of a State. The term includes health-care-insurance receivables. The term does not include (i) rights to payment evidenced by chattel paper or an instrument, (ii) commercial tort claims, (iii) deposit accounts, (iv) investment property, (v) letter-of-credit rights or letters of credit, or (vi) rights to payment for money or funds advanced or sold, other than rights arising out of the use of a credit or charge card or information contained on or for use with the card.

Section 9–102(a)(42) "General intangible" means any personal property, including things in action, other than accounts, chattel paper, commercial tort claims, deposit accounts, documents, goods, instruments, investment property, letter-of-credit rights, letters of credit, money, and oil, gas, or other minerals before extraction. The term includes payment intangibles and software.

Section 9–102(a)(47) "Instrument" means a negotiable instrument or any other writing that evidences a right to the payment of a monetary obligation, is not itself a security agreement or lease, and is of a type that in ordinary course of business is transferred by delivery with any necessary indorsement or assignment. The term does not include (i) investment property, (ii) letters of credit, or (iii) writings that evidence a right to payment arising out of the use of a credit or charge card or information contained on or for use with the card.

[53]   See § 9–102(a)(49): "Investment property" means a security, whether certificated or uncertificated, security entitlement, securities account, commodity contract, or commodity account.

Even as to collateral that is "possessable," and so subject to perfection by possession, possession plays a minor role by comparison with filing. Few debtors can afford to give up possession in order to enable their creditors to perfect security interests. A debtor needs its equipment and inventory to stay in business; it could hardly give possession of its motor vehicles to a creditor in order to perfect that interest. Only unusual collateral, collateral not "used" by the debtor, is likely to be perfected by possession. A debtor might be in a position to give up possession of a negotiable instrument not yet due, or of chattel paper, or of stock certificates. A familiar pledge used by consumers of modest means is the pawnshop. Even counting all of these types of cases, the pledge is still little used in commercial transactions and is probably declining in importance; it is ill-suited to modern commercial practice.

b. Possession

Apart from the question what assets can be duly possessed, and so be "pledgeable," section 9–313 poses only two questions of any significance. The first involves the meaning of the word "possession." The second concerns the identity of the person who must "possess."

Possession is a notoriously plastic idea. Historically it has taken many different shapes depending on the circumstances. Property law recognizes and distinguishes among constructive possession, physical possession, actual possession, mere custody, and other similar notions. Criminal courts deal with possession in determining whether a defendant has committed larceny. In some property cases the courts must decide whether a deed has been delivered into the possession of the transferee, whether a party has commenced adverse possession, or whether possession was sufficient to put some other party on notice of an interest. In the course of the many decisions which have dealt with its meaning, the word "possession" has taken varied form and has accommodated itself to the needs of real property law, the law of consignment, insurance, and criminal law.

The drafters of the UCC were aware of this history, and they have declined the futile task of defining possession in the Code. Traditionally, possession of personal property in the law of security interests has been important because of the notice it gives to prospective creditors, a fundamental policy of this branch of law. In societies with no method of perfection other than possession— societies in which possession was more likely to equal ownership than it does in our society—the courts were understandably insistent that creditors unquestionably take possession in order that the debtor not mislead other creditors. We are left, therefore, with several hundred years of cases and with the policy of Article 9 to help us define the word possession. Fortunately, the pledge is now restricted largely to circumstances in which the creditor's possession will be unmistakable (for example, the bank puts debtor's valuables in its vault).

c. Possession by Whom

What if someone other than the creditor purports to hold possession for the creditor? Comment 3 directs us to the law of agency to determine whether the person in possession is the agent of the secured creditor and so satisfies the requirement that the "creditor" have possession.[54] Where an agent may represent both parties, such as an escrow agent, the question is difficult. Comment 3 to 9–313 deals with that question as follows:

> This section does not define "possession." . . .[I]n determining whether a particular person has possession, the principles of agency apply. For example, if the collateral clearly is in possession of an agent of the secured party for the purposes of possessing on behalf of the secured party, and if the agent is not also an agent of the debtor, the secured party has taken actual possession without the need to rely on a third-party acknowledgment. See subsection (c) and Comments 4 and 8. However, if the agent is an agent of both the secured party and the debtor, prudence might suggest that the secured party obtain the agent's acknowledgment in order to ensure perfection by possession. The debtor cannot qualify as an agent for the secured party for purposes of the secured party's taking possession. And, under appropriate circumstances, a court may determine that a third person in possession is so closely connected to or controlled by the debtor that the debtor has retained effective possession, even though the third person may have agreed to take possession on behalf of the secured party. If so, the third person's taking possession would not constitute the secured party's taking possession and would not be sufficient for perfection. See also section 9–205(b). In a typical escrow arrangement, where the escrowee holds possession of collateral as agent for both the secured party and the debtor, the debtor's relationship to the escrowee is not such as to constitute retention of possession by the debtor.

---

[54]   See, e.g., Haft v. Haft, 671 A.2d 413, 30 UCC2d 323 (Del.Ch.1995) (transfer of possession of stock certificates into hands of secured party's lawyer was sufficient to perfect security interest).

Of course, the debtor cannot qualify as an agent for the secured party. Similarly, some third persons in possession might be so closely connected to the debtor that the debtor in reality retains effective possession, even though the third person may have agreed to take possession on behalf of the secured party. If so, possession by such a closely connected third person could not constitute possession by a secured party, and would not be sufficient for perfection.[55]

A more difficult question arises if the collateral is in the hands of a bailee. Bailees might be professional warehousemen or persons possessing under less formal terms, such as those boarding horses. If a bailee has issued a document of title[56] such as a warehouse receipt or a bill of lading, perfection is covered by 9–312(c) and (d), not by 9–313. Those subsections read as follows:

(c) [Goods covered by negotiable document.] While goods are in the possession of a bailee that has issued a negotiable document covering the goods:

(1) a security interest in the goods may be perfected by perfecting a security interest in the document; and

(2) a security interest perfected in the document has priority over any security interest that becomes perfected in the goods by another method during that time.

(d) [Goods covered by non-negotiable document.] While goods are in the possession of a bailee that has issued a non-negotiable document covering the goods, a security interest in the goods may be perfected by:

(1) issuance of a document in the name of the secured party;

(2) the bailee's receipt of notification of the secured party's interest; or

(3) filing as to the goods.

If the bailee has issued a negotiable document, the secured creditor must perfect an interest in the document. That can be done by taking possession of the document or by filing as to the document. Where the goods are covered by non-negotiable documents, the secured creditor may perfect by having the document issued in the name of the secured party, by filing as to the goods, or by notifying

---

[55]   UCC § 9–205(b).

[56]   See §§ 9–102(a)(30) ("Document" means a document of title or a receipt of the type described in § 7–201(b)). Section 7–201(b) provides that "[i]f goods . . . are stored under a statute requiring a bond against withdrawal or a license for the issuance of receipts in the nature of warehouse receipts, a receipt issued for the goods is deemed to be a warehouse receipt even if issued by a person that is the owner of the goods and is not a warehouse."

the bailee. These rules are the natural result of the fact that a negotiable document is thought fully to represent the goods but a nonnegotiable document is merely a contract dealing with the goods. In any case where the goods are covered by documents of title one must look to 9–312 and not to 9–313.

Where the third party possesses on behalf of a secured creditor, but has not issued a document of title, 9–313(c) and (h) govern. Here the bailee must acknowledge that it possesses on behalf of the secured creditor and that acknowledgement must be in a record.[57] Unlike the case where there is a non-negotiable document outstanding, it is not sufficient for the secured creditor to inform the possessor of its interest.

Where the secured party had possession of the collateral, itself or through an agent, it remains perfected under subsection (h) despite delivery to a third person (excluding the debtor or debtor's lessee), if that person is instructed to hold possession of the collateral for the secured party's benefit or to redeliver the collateral to the third party. With admirable candor (or less admirable pique), Comment 9 explains that subsection (h) was put in to satisfy the "mortgage warehouse lenders." The drafters were persuaded that it would be "unduly burdensome and disruptive" to require mortgage warehousers to get authenticated acknowledgements as subsection (c) generally requires in other cases.

But since the language of subsection (h) does not identify mortgage warehousers, there is the potential for conflict between (c) and (h). What if a creditor, not in the mortgage warehousing business, fails to get an authenticated record acknowledging possession? May it claim that it is covered under subsection (h) and thus perfected? The only condition to subsection (h) is that the secured creditor (or the secured creditor's agent acting as the secured creditor) have "possession" and itself deliver the collateral to the third person. If the goods are delivered by the debtor to a third person, one would have to comply with subsection (c). These sections could cause trouble, not necessarily in the mortgage warehousing business, but in cases not now foreseen for persons not intended for subsection (h) who nevertheless claim the protection of that section.

It is plain that certain persons should *not* be recognized as a proper agent of the creditor. Obviously this is true of the debtor and the debtor's agent as is suggested above in the quote from Comment 3. The same is true of a "lessee of the collateral from the debtor in the ordinary course of business" (subsection (c)). Obviously possession by

---

[57]   UCC § 9–102(a)(70) ("Information inscribed on a tangible medium or which is stored in an electronic or other medium and is retrievable in perceivable form.").

a lessee is no evidence of the rights of a third party who has loaned money to the lessor, debtor. Section 9–313(i) absolves a third person possessor, under subsection (h), from any duty to the secured creditor and from any general obligation to acknowledge its possession on behalf of the secured party.

Finally, subsection (b) makes clear that a creditor cannot perfect a security interest in goods covered by a certificate of title, such as an automobile, by taking possession of the goods. That rule is subject to a limited exception in 9–316(d) for goods covered by certificates of title that are moved from one state to another. In summary, section 9–313 sharpens the edges of old 9–305. It works no fundamental changes in the law, and complicates as well as clarifies. We foresee trouble only in the potential conflict between subsection (c) and (h).

2–9 CONTROL, SECTION 9–314

Security interests in investment property (stocks, bonds, brokerage accounts and the like) and electronic chattel paper may be perfected by control; with limited exceptions, a security interest in deposit accounts and letter of credit rights can *only* be perfected by control. The idea of "control" as a means of perfection first came to Article 9 via the 1994 revision to Article 8. That revision of Article 8 recognized control as a mode of perfecting a security interest in investment property, particularly stocks, bonds, and other assets held in brokerage accounts. By a 1994 amendment to Article 9, made concurrently with the adoption of a new Article 8, the idea also found its way into former section 9–115. With the 1999 revision, the concept of control has been expanded beyond investment property to include the other intangible interests listed above.

Control is the intangible's equivalent to possession of tangibles. As we have said above, security interests in intangibles for which there is no indispensable "res" to be possessed (like a negotiable instrument) cannot be perfected by possession. Yet some of these intangible interests can be put under the "control" of a secured creditor to the exclusion of others, and this will put third parties on notice.

What is control? Sections 9–104 (control of deposit accounts), 9–105 (control of electronic chattel paper), and 9–107 (control of letter of credit rights) define it. For investment property, section 9–106 directs one to Article 8, particularly 8–102, 8–106, 8–301 and 8–501.[58] "Control" comes into play mostly in cases where a person's

---

[58] UCC § 9–106(a) provides that "A person has control of a certificated security, uncertificated security, or security entitlement as provided in Section 8–106." Section 9–106(b) defines control over commodity contracts, and § 9–106(c) provides that secured parties having control "of all security entitlements or commodity contracts

rights are represented by something that is usually called an "account" in layman's terms. The two most common applications are with bank accounts (where the account holder might grant a security interest to the bank that holds the account or to a third party and, give control to the creditor), and brokerage accounts (where the owner of the account might do the same thing with respect to the broker who held the account or with respect to a third party). In this discussion we ignore control of letter of credit rights as defined in 9–108, and control of electronic chattel paper as defined in 9–105.

a. Deposit Accounts

A deposit account must be distinguished from other accounts. The definition in subsection 9–102(a)(29) reads as follows:

> (29) "Deposit account" means a demand, time, savings, passbook, or similar account maintained with a bank. The term does not include investment property or accounts evidenced by an instrument.

Subsections 9–104(a) and (b) specify:

> (a) [Requirements for control.] A secured party has control of a deposit account if:
>
> (1) the secured party is the bank with which the deposit account is maintained;
>
> (2) the debtor, secured party, and bank have agreed in an authenticated record that the bank will comply with instructions originated by the secured party directing disposition of the funds in the account without further consent by the debtor; or
>
> (3) the secured party becomes the bank's customer with respect to the deposit account.
>
> (b) [Debtor's right to direct disposition.] A secured party that has satisfied subsection (a) has control, even if the debtor retains the right to direct the disposition of funds from the deposit account.

There are three ways to achieve control over a deposit account. The first—and the most common—is to have the deposit account maintained with the secured party. Every bank that enters into a security agreement with its depositor that covers the debtor's deposit account *ipso facto* has control over that account and becomes a perfected secured creditor on lending to the depositor.[59] This is where the action will be; we predict banks will routinely make security

---

carried in a securities account or commodity account has control over the securities account or commodity account."

[59]   See UCC §§ 9–104 & 9–314.

agreements (as to any future loans) part of their form deposit agreements.

Less common will be security interests that the depositor grants in a deposit account to creditors other than the depositary bank. Such creditors can achieve control over the debtor's deposit account either by: (1) getting the appropriate authenticated agreement from the depositary bank "that the bank will comply with the instructions . . . of the secured party" even in the face of contrary instructions by the debtor, or (2) by becoming the "bank's customer with respect to the deposit account." (See 9–104(a)(2) and (3)). We suspect it will be rare that a third party will gain control over deposit accounts under 9–104(a)(2), because depositary banks will be hesitant to grant control by agreement to third parties. Although it is clear from subsection (b) that a depositary bank or a third party can have control and yet allow the debtor to make deposits and withdrawals, banks will foresee much that is bad and little that is good to come from recognizing a third party's right in a bank account.[60]

A bank might say it already has enough trouble making sure the conventional debits and credits are made to the typical person's account in the right order and in the correct amount, and it is certainly not looking for ways to complicate its obligation to the customer by adding yet another obligation to a third party who is a creditor of the depositor. A moderately neurotic banker could think of many scenarios under which a third party creditor might sue. Assume for example, the third party creditor instructs the bank to close down the account and give it the funds. But, because of a mistake or of uncertainty about the third party's rights, the bank delays. In the meantime the depositor withdraws the funds. Does the depositary bank have liability to the third party lender? Probably yes. What does the depositary bank get for bearing that responsibility? Nothing, unless it bargains for it.

But depositary banks will not be able to keep a third party from getting control of a deposit account under 9–104(a)(3). For example, Ann Arbor Ditching Company clearly could give Finance Company control over its deposit account at National City by transferring the account to the name of Finance Company. If that were done, Ann

---

[60]   On the other hand, the 2010 amendments to § 9–104 added a new example to Comment 3 regarding requirements for control by the depositor's bank that recognized that the depositor's bank could take a security interest in the account and also act as an agent for third parties. "Example: D maintains a deposit account with Bank A. To secure a loan from Banks X, Y, and Z, D creates a security interest in the deposit account in favor of Bank A, as agent for Banks X, Y, and Z. Because Bank A is 'a secured party' as defined in Section 9–102, the security interest is perfected by control under [§ 9–104(a)(1)]." The amended comment also clarifies that "[a]s is the case with possession under Secion 9–313, in determining whether a particular person has control under subsection (a), the principles of agency apply."

Arbor Ditching would no longer have the right to draw on the account and would have lost its use.

What if Ann Arbor Ditching made Finance Company a joint depositor? Would that, in the terms of 9–103(a)(3), make Finance Company "the bank's customer with respect to the deposit account" or would Finance Company have to be the sole customer on the account? The statement in the third paragraph of Comment 3: "as the customer, the secured party would enjoy the right (but not necessarily the exclusive right) to withdraw funds from, or close the deposit account" suggests that a joint account owner is a "customer" and so has control. This also is consistent with 9–104(b)—that a party can have control yet allow the debtor to continue to make withdrawals.

In summary, we anticipate that the combination of 9–314 and 9–104 will routinely transform depositary banks who lend money to their depositors into perfected secured creditors as to the debtor's deposit accounts. We believe 9–104(a)(2) will be little used, but that third party lenders will sometimes become joint owners of accounts and so gain control.

b.   Investment Property

Subsection 9–102(a)(49) gives the following definition of "investment property" which is only moderately helpful:

(49) "Investment property" means a security, whether certificated or uncertificated, security entitlement, securities account, commodity contract, or commodity account.

We do not have the space to visit the long-running dispute in federal securities law on the question what is and what is not a "security." We suspect it will not be obvious to many readers in today's world whether a security is "certificated" or not. And the idea of "a securities entitlement" will itself be mysterious. Let us summarize in a way that may be helpful, if not completely accurate. Most "securities" are stocks and bonds. Typically, "security entitlements" are rights the customer has against his or her broker as represented by the statement the stockbroker provides the customer monthly or quarterly. That statement will often show that the customer owns interests in both certificated and uncertificated securities. To say that a customer's interest in a stock is "certificated" means only that there is a certificate in someone's hands somewhere, representing that customer's interest. In modern practice, the certificate is likely to be in the basement of the Deposit Trust Co. in Manhattan which holds "jumbo certificates" on behalf of a particular broker and the broker in turn holds its interest on behalf of various customers. Thus, even though the customer will never see a certificate, the customer's interest may be in a "certificated security."

Today stocks issued by most American companies are certificated (excluding those that are issued as part of dividend reinvestment programs). On the other hand, the mutual funds in the brokerage account are probably not represented by any certificate anywhere; these are uncertificated securities. It is also possible that a customer will actually have a certificate with the customer's name printed on its face showing that the customer owns a designated number of shares in the company that issued the certificate. For many reasons, fewer and fewer customers today actually have possession of stock or bond certificates.

Secured parties' control for the purpose of certificated securities and security entitlements is defined in section 8–106 of Article 8. For commodity contracts, 9–106(b) has its own rule. Section 8–106 reads in part as follows:

(a) A purchaser has "control" of a certificated security in bearer form if the certificated security is delivered to the purchaser.

(b) A purchaser has "control" of a certificated security in registered form if the certificated security is delivered to the purchaser, and:

(1) the certificate is indorsed to the purchaser or in blank by an effective indorsement; or

(2) the certificate is registered in the name of the purchaser, upon original issue or registration of transfer by the issuer.

(c) A purchaser has "control" of an uncertificated security if:

(1) the uncertificated security is delivered to the purchaser; or

(2) the issuer has agreed that it will comply with instructions originated by the purchaser without further consent by the registered owner.

(d) A purchaser has "control" of a security entitlement if:

(1) the purchaser becomes the entitlement holder;

(2) the securities intermediary has agreed that it will comply with entitlement orders originated by the purchaser without further consent by the entitlement holder. . . .

(e) If an interest in a security entitlement is granted by the entitlement holder to the entitlement holder's own securities intermediary, the securities intermediary has control.

Because of the existence and "remote holding" (by Deposit Trust) of stock certificates, it will be uncommon for secured creditors to get control of such a stock under (b) (certificated security delivered to the secured creditor) or (c) (uncertificated security). Typically, neither a local broker nor the customer will possess the certificate. Also, the certificate itself will be registered in the name of an intermediary such as the Deposit Trust Corporation. Nevertheless, the debtor's interest will be in a "certificated security," not an uncertificated one, so subsection (c) will not apply. Because the "certificate" will neither be in the possession of nor registered in the name of the debtor, subsection (b) will be unavailable. This means the typical lender who seeks an interest in most of the securities in the conventional securities account will have to qualify under (d) or (e).

Subsection (e) makes it easy for a broker when it makes a loan to its own customer. Most brokers are also lenders to their customers. The common term for these loans is "margin" loans. The margin refers to the amount by which the value of the stocks, bonds or other investment property that is given as collateral must exceed the amount of the loan. Under the terms of the typical margin loan, the customer must put up additional collateral. If the value of the stocks and bonds declines, the customer is said to receive a "margin call." When that happens, the broker is free to sell the customer's collateral. If he is not free to do so, the broker will likely need to make a prompt margin call. Doubtless the rules on control by a broker/lender were devised to facilitate this well recognized mode of secured lending.

A third party lender will be faced with the same kind of problem it faces when it seeks to gain control over a bank account. Under subsection (d), that lender can get control by: (1) getting its name on the brokerage account as the "entitlement holder" (here, as there, we believe being a joint entitlement holder is enough), or (2) getting an agreement from the broker that it will "comply with the entitlement orders" of the secured creditor.

Finally, recall that control can also facilitate attachment of the security interest under section 9–203(b)(3)(D). That is, when there is control, the security agreement need not be an authenticated record.

PROBLEM

Debtor borrows $300,000 from Bank. Debtor offers its $500,000 brokerage account at Merrill Lynch as collateral. Bank lends the money and sends a formal letter to Merrill, which states "we have made a loan to your customer, Robert Jones, and have taken a security interest in his brokerage account, number 7777, held with you. We claim control of that account."

> Debtor goes into bankruptcy and trustee claims that Bank is not perfected, because it failed to get control and did not file.
>
> Trustee wins. The stocks and bonds held in the Merrill account are undoubtedly "security entitlements" because brokers these days seldom hold certificated shares for their customers. For a third party to have "control," the "securities intermediary," namely Merrill, must agree that it will comply with orders issued by the secured creditor. Merrill has made no such agreement here.

2–10   PERFECTION BY FILING, IN GENERAL

Perfection by filing is by far the most common method of perfecting a security interest under Article 9. Section 9–310(a) identifies filing as the norm and, except when they are proceeds, there is no other way to perfect a security interest in most accounts (as distinguished from deposit accounts) and general intangibles. Filing is a permissible method, but not the only method of perfection as to goods, chattel paper, documents and investment property. For the first time, in the 1999 Code, filing is a permitted method of perfecting a security interest in instruments, see 9–312(a).[61]

At the other end of the spectrum, filing cannot be used to perfect certain security interests, such as deposit accounts (9–312(b)(1)), letter of credit rights (9–312(b)(2)), and money (9–312(b)(3))—except when those assets are proceeds.[62] Also a UCC filing is not adequate for goods covered by a certificate of title such as automobiles, trailers, boats, and similar goods for which a state has created a separate certification of title scheme that provides for security interests "to be indicated on the certificate of title as a condition or result of perfection."[63] Nor is a UCC filing adequate if federal law calls for a federal filing (9–311(a)(1)).

We suspect that for more than 90% of the universe, perfection occurs by some form of filing of a document which the UCC calls a "financing statement." As we have explained above, the financing statement omits almost all of the important terms of the parties' agreement. Filing of a financing statement as to personal property was revolutionized by the initial adoption of the UCC, and later by the widespread use of electronic data storage. Prior to the Code's filing system, filing was haphazard and nonuniform. Some states maintained state-wide filing systems for some kinds of collateral, while other states provided for recording of chattel mortgages in the

---

[61]   One should not read the clarification in 9–312(a) (specifying that security interests in certain kinds of collateral "may be perfected by filing") to exclude other things such as goods.

[62]   UCC § 9–312(b) provides generally that §§ 9–315(c) and (d) control the treatment of proceeds.

[63]   UCC § 9–311(a)(2). See also UCC § 9–311(a)(3).

local offices where real estate mortgages were recorded. The first revolutionary act of the UCC in this field was to provide for the "filing" of a separate skeletal document in place of the "recording" of the actual document executed by the parties with all of its terms, as in the case of a chattel mortgage. The second major innovation was to move a substantial part of filing out of local registries into a single state-wide registry.

The proposal for state-wide filing conflicted with local practices and traditional policies. It was generally thought that local creditors should be able to walk to the local courthouse and examine the files, and the local recorder of deeds should collect a fee with each filing. Nevertheless, the drafters of the 1962 Code (and the 1972 Code) proposed three alternative filing systems. These were designed to minimize the political objections of local filing officers who might lose fees from a state-wide system and also to meet the concerns of people who still wished to be able to determine a debtor's status from local files. Even at the outset, the drafters recognized the efficiency of a state-wide filing system; creditors could search at one place and filers could file at one place. Both would avoid the mistakes of searching and filing in the wrong place.

In the first alternative (all alternatives appeared in 9–401), one filed locally only with respect to timber to be cut, oil and gas, and "fixture filings." Under this alternative all other filings were in one state-wide office, usually the office of the Secretary of State. The second alternative was the most widely adopted; it added consumer and farm collateral to local filing. The third alternative not only adopted all the local filing requirements of the second alternative, but also in some cases, required a filing both state-wide and locally in cases where the debtor's place of business was in only one county in the state.[64] As more state filing systems became computerized, it became possible to search by computer and ultimately, to file electronically. The convenience of being able to walk across the street to the courthouse therefore disappeared, and the cost associated with local filing could no longer be justified. In the 1999 revision, section 9–501 calls for state-wide filing, with only three exceptions: fixture

---

[64] If, under the third alternative of former 9–401(1), a debtor had a "place of business" in only one county within the state, the secured party needed to file both centrally and locally. However, the Code failed to define "place of business" despite its central importance to filing. Two plausible tests existed to determine the limits of this unfocused phrase. The first involved a measurement of the quantity of business work accomplished at a place: how much revenue is attributable to that place, what is its permanence, how many letters are sent there, how many letters are sent from there, how many employees are there, etc. The alternative test focused on "notoriety": to what extent do creditors and others regard the debtor as doing business at the place in question? Nearly all courts wrestling with this problem relied on the notoriety test.

filings, "as-extracted" collateral (oil, gas and minerals), and timber to be cut.

Of course, both states and the federal government maintain other filing systems beyond the state-law-based financing statement filing system created by Article 9. Section 9–311 must bow to federal filing systems that preempt Article 9. Clearly the federal filing system with respect to aircraft fits this definition. The extent to which the federal filing rules as to patents, copyrights, and trademarks preempt the UCC is unclear. To understand some of the difficulties with these federal intellectual property recording statutes, we consider the federal law on copyright. Under section 205(a) of the Copyright Act "[a]ny transfer of copyright ownership or other document pertaining to a copyright may be recorded in the Copyright office."[65] Filing is effectively made mandatory by section 205(d) which grants priority to a second-in-time recorded transfer over a prior unrecorded transfer,[66] and by Judge Kozinski's decision that federal copyright law preempts the UCC filing system[67] (at least for copyrights that have been filed in the federal registry).

In an article on software financing, Professor Mann has explained the gross defects in the federal filing requirements of the Copyright Act.[68] First, since there must be a filing as to each copyright, filing can be significantly more costly than under a system such as that found in Article 9 where one filing *per debtor* will often suffice for many assets. The cost of perfecting a security interest in a large portfolio of collateral can be prohibitive where there must be a separate filing and a separate fee paid for each copyright. Second, registration requirements pose substantial risks for some secured creditors. Before a creditor can file, the debtor-owner must register with the Copyright Office by depositing two copies of its material in a form "visually perceptible without the aid of a machine or device."[69] Software developers, for example, are reluctant to release printed copies of source codes for fear of educating their competitors. Thus, it

---

[65] 17 U.S.C. § 205(a).

[66] 17 U.S.C. § 205(d).

[67] In re Peregrine Entertainment, Ltd., 116 B.R. 194, 11 UCC2d 1025 (C.D.Cal.1990). Judge Kozinski held a state UCC filing wholly insufficient to perfect a creditor's security interest in a copyright library of films. Compare this with developments in trademark law. In the case of In re Together Development Corp., 227 B.R. 439, 37 UCC2d 227 (Bankr.D.Mass.1998), Judge Queenan held that the only method to perfect a security interest in a trademark is to file a UCC financing statement. Federal filing alone is insufficient. For an excellent survey and analysis of the tensions inherent in perfecting security interests in intellectual property, see Xuan-Thao Nguyen, *Financing Innovation: Legal Development of Intellectual Property as Security in Financing, 1845–2014*, 48 Ind. L. Rev. 509 (2015).

[68] Ronald J. Mann, *Secured Credit and Software Financing*, 85 Cornell L. Rev. 134 (1999).

[69] 37 C.F.R. § 205.20(c)(2)(vii)(A).

is possible that the debtor's collateral would be a copyright, as to which a UCC filing might be inadequate, but not yet subject to a secured creditor's filing under the federal law because the debtor had not yet registered its copyright there.[70]

The certificate of title notation rules take the place of Article 9 filings with respect to goods covered by certificates of title. Thus, because of 9–311, a secured creditor perfects its security interest in an automobile for which a certificate of title has been issued, by complying with the state's certificate of title law (usually notation on the certificate of title). This *state* exception to Article 9 filing is subject to an exception for cases where cars or other goods subject to the certificate of title laws are held in inventory for sale, (9–311(d)). In that case the vehicles are treated like any other inventory and so must be the subject of an Article 9 filing for perfection.

Prior to 1999 Article 9, it was always possible to file both locally and at the state capital when there was any question about the classification of the collateral (as with consumer goods calling for a local filing or equipment calling for a state-wide filing) or when there was a question whether a debtor was engaged in business in only one county in the state. But many secured creditors did not file in both places, and the courts were called upon to determine, for example, whether large broods of laying hens should be classified as "inventory" (calling for a filing in the state capital) or "farm products" (calling for a local filing); or whether a boat used for Coast Guard volunteer work was "equipment" as opposed to "consumer goods"; or whether a computer bought initially for home use became "equipment" when it was devoted to business use. Section 9–501 sweeps all these questions away. Whether the debtor's goods are consumer goods or business equipment, the filing is at the state capital (the filing for a debtor's computer is at the state capital whether the debtor uses it for personal or business purposes). And the searchers search in state-wide databases.

With the combination of a state-wide filing system and the substantial elimination of local filing, and given the advances in electronic filing, data storage and searching, we may be sure that further advances will revolutionize the states' filing systems. As state databases become available on the internet for searches by anyone with a computer connection, and as the software for searching becomes more sophisticated, the filing and search problems will shrink. Likewise, developments in blockchain technology and distributed ledger record keeping systems raise the possibility of

---

[70]   See In re World Auxiliary Power Co. 303 F.3d 1120 (9th Cir. 2002) (interests in registered copyrights must be filed according to federal Copyright Act while security interests in unregistered copyrights are perfected by filing under Article 9.

secure, transparent, real time recording with respect to a variety of interests, including secured transactions. The possibility will decline that a creditor who has made a good faith attempt to perfect by filing will find itself unperfected because it filed in the wrong place or filed the wrong document, and the probability that a searcher will discover a proper filing will increase.

2-11 THE BASICS OF FILING AND THE EFFECTS OF IMPERFECT FILING OR INDEXING

Section 9–502 states the minimum data that must be included on a financing statement for it to be effective. Section 9–516 states additional requirements and has rules on the extent of the effectiveness of imperfect financing statements. Section 9–520 specifies the duties of the filing office with respect to certain defective financing statements and the legal effects of those statements if they are accepted.

Subsections 9–502(a) and (b) state what is necessary (if not in all cases sufficient) for a document to qualify as a financing statement:

(a) [Sufficiency of financing statement.] Subject to subsection (b), a financing statement is sufficient only if it:

(1) provides the name of the debtor;

(2) provides the name of the secured party or a representative of the secured party; and

(3) indicates the collateral covered by the financing statement.

(b) [Real-property-related financing statements.] Except as otherwise provided in section 9–501(b), to be sufficient, a financing statement that covers as-extracted collateral or timber to be cut, or which is filed as a fixture filing and covers goods that are or are to become fixtures, must satisfy subsection (a) and also:

(1) indicate that it covers this type of collateral;

(2) indicate that it is to be filed [for record] in the real property records;

(3) provide a description of the real property to which the collateral is related [sufficient to give constructive notice of a mortgage under the law of this State if the description were contained in a record of the mortgage of the real property]; and

(4) if the debtor does not have an interest of record in the real property, provide the name of a record owner.

Under the predecessor of 9–502 (9–402(1)) a financing statement had to include the addresses of the debtor and secured parties, and had to be signed by the debtor to be effective. The drafters of Revised Article 9 apparently concluded that the debtor's signature was an unnecessary technicality and that the addresses of the parties were useful but not critical, since a searcher could find the address of any earlier secured creditor and presumably the searcher has the address of its debtor. (The requirement for addresses now appears in 9–516(b) where, as we will see, their omission has only limited adverse consequences for the secured creditor.) The section allows the use of a mortgage as a financing statement in certain real estate transactions and, like the former law, requires a financing statement that is to be filed for record in the real property records to contain a description of the real property and to state to the filing officer that it must be filed in those records. The troublesome requirement of a real estate description for a financing statement covering growing crops is gone; security interests in growing crops are now perfected by a plain vanilla financing statement without any mention of real estate.

Section 9–516(b) contains certain additional requirements, for example, a financing statement is to provide a "mailing address for the debtor" (9–516(b)(5)(A)). Section 9–520(a) directs the filing officer to refuse to accept a record that does not meet the additional requirements of 9–516(b). Yet, if the filing officer accepts a financing statement which meets the conditions of 9–502 but not the additional requirements of 9–516(b), there has been a filing that is effective for most purposes. So we now have two classifications of defective financing statements: defective (satisfies 9–502 but fails to satisfy 9–516(b)) and *really* defective (fails to satisfy 9–502). If a filing officer mistakenly accepts two defective financing statements, the first being defective because it omits the name of the secured party (so failing 9–502), and the second because it omits the address of the secured creditor (so failing 9–516(b) but not 9–502); the first creditor is not perfected, but the second one is.

What are these additional requirements of a financing statement stated in 9–516?

(b) [Refusal to accept record; filing does not occur.] Filing does not occur with respect to a record that a filing office refuses to accept because:

(1) the record is not communicated by a method or medium of communication authorized by the filing office;

(2) an amount equal to or greater than the applicable filing fee is not tendered;

(3) the filing office is unable to index the record because:

(A) in the case of an initial financing statement, the record does not provide a name for the debtor;

(B) in the case of an amendment or information statement, the record:

(i) does not identify the initial financing statement as required by section 9–512 or 9–518, as applicable; or

(ii) identifies an initial financing statement whose effectiveness has lapsed under section 9–515;

(C) in the case of an initial financing statement that provides the name of a debtor identified as an individual or an amendment that provides a name of a debtor identified as an individual which was not previously provided in the financing statement to which the record relates, the record does not identify the debtor's surname; or

(D) in the case of a record filed [or recorded] in the filing office described in section 9–501(a)(1), the record does not provide a sufficient description of the real property to which it relates;

(4) in the case of an initial financing statement or an amendment that adds a secured party of record, the record does not provide a name and mailing address for the secured party of record;

(5) in the case of an initial financing statement or an amendment that provides a name of a debtor which was not previously provided in the financing statement to which the amendment relates, the record does not:

(A) provide a mailing address for the debtor; or

(B) indicate whether the name provided as the name of the debtor is the name of an individual or an organization; or

(6) in the case of an assignment reflected in an initial financing statement under section 9–514(a) or an amendment filed under section 9–514(b), the record does not provide a name and mailing address for the assignee; or

(7) in the case of a continuation statement, the record is not filed within the six-month period prescribed by section 9–515(d).

If the filing officer refuses to accept the filing, but does so based upon reasons not identified in 9–516(b), then the attempted filing is effective under 9–516(d) (provided 9–502(a) and (b) are met), "except as against a purchaser of the collateral which gives value in reasonable reliance upon the absence of the record from the files." One has to make several rather far-fetched assumptions to raise the issues that are buried in section 9–516(d). First, one has to assume the secured creditor presents a financing statement which complies with 9–502. Second, one has to assume the filing officer refuses the filing based on reasons *other than* non-compliance with 9–516(b). Third, one must assume the filing officer either failed to tell the secured creditor of its refusal to accept the filing, or the secured creditor and the filing officer got into an angry standoff. Finally, one must assume that a "purchaser" gives value in reasonable reliance on the absence of the filing. Among those who would qualify as "purchasers" would be buyers of the collateral and also other secured creditors who might take a security interest in the collateral in ignorance of the earlier and unrecorded security interest. If each of these improbable events comes to pass, the unindexed financing statement is valid against non-reliance creditors but not against those who acted in reliance upon the absence of the filed financing statement. Presumably the most likely set of events are those in which the filing officer refuses the filing but, by mistake, fails to notify the secured creditor. The debtor then goes bankrupt and the secured creditor of the bankruptcy case has to prove that it attempted to make a filing and that it qualifies for the protection of 9–520(c).

If the filing office does the converse, accepts for filing a record it should refuse (only because of defects of the kind described in 9–516(b)), section 9–520(c) makes that filing effective but opens the possibility that certain subsequent parties would take free of the security interest if they were misled by the inaccuracies on the financing statement, see 9–338. Assume creditor one files a financing statement which indicates debtor is an individual when debtor is a corporation; that financing statement is defective under 9–516(b)(5)(B). Assume further that a second creditor examines the filing and concludes that there is no filing against its debtor of the same name because that debtor is a corporation, not an individual. In that case the combination of 9–520(c) and 9–338(1) would subordinate the earlier secured creditor who had provided inaccurate information—at least if the later secured creditor could show it had given "value in reasonable reliance upon the incorrect information."[71]

---

[71]   Sometimes an uncommonly diligent searcher discovers a filing made in the wrong place. Under the pre-1999 law the creditor who discovered the improperly filed financing statement was bound as though it had been properly filed and, under old 9–401(2), his knowledge subordinated him. The new Code treats a filing at the improper place—and even the discovery of that filing by a subsequent creditor—as irrelevant to the priority conflict between the filer and the subsequent party.

Notwithstanding 9–520(a)'s direction to decline financing statements that fail 9–516(b), filing officers will in practice have some discretion about the financing statements they will accept. If the filing officer refuses a financing statement because it fails one of the requirements in 9–516(b), there has never been a filing.[72] If, on the other hand, the filing officer accepts the financing statement despite the failure, the secured creditor is properly filed (except against subsequent purchasers who are misled by its errors) if its financing statement contains the minimum requirements of 9–502. Conceivably the filing officers in some states will insist upon compliance with every part of 9–516(b); others may not do so. Some of the requirements are merely common sense obligations that must be fulfilled in order to get an understandable financing statement properly indexed. For example, if an electronic record is communicated by a "medium of communication" that is incompatible with the electronic communication system of the filing officer, presumably no filing is possible because the filing officer will be unable to get the communication out of its system in comprehensible form.

Section 9–520 states the limits of the filing officers' discretion:

(a) [Mandatory refusal to accept record.] A filing office shall refuse to accept a record for filing for a reason set forth in section 9–516(b) and may refuse to accept a record for filing only for a reason set forth in section 9–516(b).

(b) [Communication concerning refusal.] If a filing office refuses to accept a record for filing, it shall communicate to the person that presented the record the fact of and reason for the refusal and the date and time the record would have been filed had the filing office accepted it. The communication must be made at the time and in the manner prescribed by filing-office rule but [, in the case of a filing office described in section 9–501(a)(2),] in no event more than two business days after the filing office receives the record.

---

[72]   As Comment 3 observes with respect to a rightfully rejected filing: "A financing statement or other record that is communicated to the filing office but which the filing office refuses to accept provides no public notice, regardless of the reason for the rejection. However, this section distinguishes between records that the filing office rightfully rejects and those that it wrongfully rejects. A filer is able to prevent a rightful rejection by complying with the requirements of subsection (b). No purpose is served by giving effect to records that justifiably never find their way into the system, and subsection (b) so provides." In contrast, with respect to wrongfully rejected records, Comment 3 observes: "Subsection (d) deals with the filing office's unjustified refusal to accept a record. Here, the filer is in no position to prevent the rejection and as a general matter should not be prejudiced [outside of the special rule protecting third-party purchasers who rely on the absence of the record] by it."

(c) [When filed financing statement effective.] A filed (i.e., accepted) financing statement satisfying section 9–502(a) and (b) is effective, even if the filing office is required to refuse to accept it for filing under subsection (a). However, section 9–338 applies to a filed financing statement providing information described in section 9–516(b)(5) which is incorrect at the time the financing statement is filed.

(d) [Separate application to multiple debtors.] If a record communicated to a filing office provides information that relates to more than one debtor, this part applies as to each debtor separately.

We read 9–520(a) as a legislative direction to the filing officer to refuse to accept filings which fail any of the tests in 9–516(b), although the sentence is awkward. More important, Comment 2 gives a stern warning to filing officers; it basically tells them to keep their fingers out of the pot in other respects: "under this section, the filing officer is not expected to make legal judgments and is not permitted to impose additional conditions or requirements." And, according to Comment 3 to 9–516: "neither this section nor section 9–520 requires or authorizes the filing office to determine, or even consider, the accuracy of information provided in a record."

It seems likely that most filing officers will insist upon most of the requirements in subsection 9–516(b) and such insistence will improve the quality of the filings and index. For example, (b)(3)(D) permits the filing officer to require a sufficient description of the real estate, and (b)(4) and (5)(A) authorize the requirement of the mailing address of the secured party and the debtor.

We reiterate: (1) if a financing statement fails to meet the conditions of 9–502, the filing is not effective, even if it is accepted and indexed, (2) if a financing statement satisfies 9–502 but not 9–516(b), and the filing officer refuses to accept it because of its failure, the filing is not effective, (3) if a financing statement satisfies 9–502 but not 9–516(b) and the filing officer accepts it, the filing is effective (for most purposes), and (4) if a financing statement satisfies section 9–502 and the filing officer refuses to accept it for reasons other than those stated in section 9–516(b) (we never take financing statements from red haired people), the filing is effective (for most purposes).

Revised Article 9 went well beyond the former law. Among other things section 9–521 set forth a uniform financing statement form— updated further with the 2010 amendments to Article 9—which has been adopted by most states. The form was worked out in consultation with the filing officers of several states. The combination of the use of identical documents throughout the states and conformity to uniform requirements on numbering and indexing as specified in 9–522, should facilitate uniformity and minimize the cases in which filing is done improperly or where proper searches fail to find filed financing statements.

PROBLEM

> Bank makes loans of $1 million each to the three subsidiaries of Albert's hardware: Albert Indiana, an Indiana corporation, Albert Mississippi, a Mississippi corporation and Albert Arizona, a Delaware corporation doing business only in Arizona.
>
> With respect to Albert Indiana, Bank files a financing statement at the secretary of state's office in Indianapolis. Bank has recently changed its name, and the person who makes up the statement mistakenly enters the old name. The financing statement describes the collateral as "inventory."
>
> With respect to Albert Mississippi, Bank files in Jackson, but its financing statement fails to indicate that Albert is a corporation. That financing statement describes the collateral as "hardware goods."
>
> With respect to Albert Arizona, Bank's financing statement is rejected in Delaware, because the financing statement has the old and not the new name for the bank. Bank also files in Phoenix, the state capital of the state where the debtor conducts all of its business.
>
> All of the subsidiaries go bankrupt, and in each case, a trustee in bankruptcy challenges the filing as deficient.
>
> The Indiana filing arguably flunks 9–516(b)(4) and the trustee will argue that it also flunks 9–502. Bank will respond that the reference in 9–520(c) to subsection (b)(5), and the fact that an earlier name was included on the financing statement, should be good enough. It will also point out that anyone searching the records could easily have determined who the secured creditor was from the former name. We think the trustee loses, but we are not positive.
>
> The Mississippi filing's description of the collateral seems fine. There is no obligation to use the code definitions in one's financing statement and the listing of a hardware store together with a description of "hardware goods" would surely be adequate. The failure to state that the name of the debtor on the financing statement is the name of a corporation violates 9–516(b)(5)(B) but since the office took the filing there is no problem, especially since the trustee cannot use 9–520's invitation to 9–338. Look at 9–338—the trustee is neither a purchaser nor a secured creditor. Also, there is no reliance on the mistake here.
>
> The issues for Arizona are more complicated. First, the filings in Phoenix are worthless; filings need to be at the "location" of the debtor and the location of a corporate debtor is at its place of incorporation, Delaware. If the Delaware refusal is construed to be a justified objection under section 9–516(b), then there is no filing and the trustee wins. If on the other hand, Bank convinces the court that the old name is an adequate indication of the name of the secured party, Bank will be treated as though it had

successfully filed. As above, we think that is the right outcome, but we are not sure. (Of course, this is a highly improbable hypothetical, since the official rejecting the filing is obliged to give notice, and we must assume that Bank ignored the notice.)

2–12 FILING, THE BASICS

Combining the basic requirements of 9–502 with the additional requirements of 9–516(b) produces the following checklist for an acceptable filing:

1.   names of debtor and creditor

2.   description of collateral

3.   mailing address for debtor and creditor

4.   statement whether the debtor is an organization or an individual

5.   identification   of   individual   debtor's   surname (Christian Peter or Peter Christian?)

6.   properly communicated

7.   fee tendered

8.   compliance with 9–502(b) as to real estate related collateral (description of real estate)

We suspect most of these requirements will be easy to satisfy and that the combined effect of 9–502, 9–516 and 9–520 will considerably clarify the duties and rights of the filer, the filing officer, and the searcher.

a.   Name of Debtor

Why is the debtor's name on the financing statement so important? The filing officer uses debtors' names to compose the index, and subsequent parties use the index to search for a filing under the debtor's name. If the debtor's name is wrong, the index will be wrong and subsequent parties misled. The debtor's name can be wrong for a variety of reasons. First, a debtor's trade name might be used instead of the actual name of the individual, partnership or corporation. Second, the debtor's actual name might be misspelled or otherwise improperly reproduced in a variety of ways. For example, Vaughan may be spelled Vaught,[73] "Inc." may be left off a corporate name,[74] or the filing officer may not be able to tell whether "Peter" or "Christian" is the debtor's surname. Similarly, the debtor's name

---

[73]   In re Vaughan, 1967 WL 8935, 4 UCC 61 (Bankr.W.D.Mich.1967).

[74]   General Motors Acceptance Corp. v. Haley, 329 Mass. 559, 109 N.E.2d 143 (1952).

might be represented with characters not possible to reproduce in the filing system database or it may be longer than the permitted field length in that database.

The most significant 2010 amendments to Article 9 arguably were the changes to § 9–503 rules on debtor name. These changes can be roughly divided into (1) mechanisms for dealing with the names of individual debtors and (2) mechanisms for dealing with names of debtors who are entities.

Individual debtors. With respect to individual debtor names, § 9–503 provides states with two alternatives for adoption: Alternative A, known as the "only if" rule, and Alternative B, the "safe harbor" rule. In addressing names of individual debtors, § 9–503 provides:

(a) **[Sufficiency of debtor's name.]** A financing statement sufficiently provides the name of the debtor:

[Alternative A]

(4) subject to subsection (g), if the debtor is an individual to whom this State has issued a [driver's license] that has not expired, only if the financing statement provides the name of the individual which is indicated on the [driver's license];

(5) if the debtor is an individual to whom paragraph (4) does not apply, only if the financing statement provides the individual name of the debtor or the surname and first personal name of the debtor; and

(6) in other cases:

(A) if the debtor has a name, only if the financing statement provides the individual or organizational name of the debtor; and

(B) if the debtor does not have a name, only if it provides the names of the partners, members, associates, or other persons comprising the debtor, in a manner that each name provided would be sufficient if the person named were the debtor.

[Alternative B]

(4) if the debtor is an individual, only if the financing statement:

(A) if the debtor has a name, only if the financing statement provides the individual or organizational name of the debtor; and

(B) provides the surname and first personal name of the debtor; or

(C) subject to subsection (g), provides the name of the individual which is indicated on a [driver's license] that this State has issued to the individual and which has not expired; and

(5) in other cases:

(A) if the debtor has a name, only if the financing statement provides the individual or organizational name of the debtor; and

(B) if the debtor does not have a name, only if the financing statement provides the names of the partners, members, associates, or other persons comprising the debtor, in a manner that each name provided would be sufficient if the person named were the debtor.

_____

[End of Alternatives]

(c) **[Debtor's trade name insufficient.]** A financing statement that provides only the debtor's trade name does not sufficiently provide the name of the debtor.

(d) **[Representative capacity.]** Failure to indicate the representative capacity of a secured party or representative of a secured party does not affect the sufficiency of a financing statement.

(e) **[Multiple debtors and secured parties.]** A financing statement may provide the name of more than one debtor and the name of more than one secured party.

_____

[Alternative A]

(g) **[Multiple driver's licenses.]** If this State has issued to an individual more than one [driver's license] of a kind described in subsection (a)(4), the one that was issued most recently is the one to which subsection (a)(4) refers.

[Alternative B]

(g) **[Multiple driver's licenses.]** If this State has issued to an individual more than one [driver's license] of a kind described in subsection (a)(4)(C), the one that was issued most recently is the one to which subsection (a)(4)(C) refers.

[End of Alternatives]

Individual names raise unique difficulties for a filing system that attempts to provide filers with "a simple and predictable system in which they can have a reasonable degree of confidence that, without undue burden, they can determine a name that will be sufficient so as to permit their financing statements to be effective."[75] Similarly, searchers need the financing statement filing system to provide "a simple and predictable system in which they can have a reasonable degree of confidence that, without undue burden, they will discover all financing statements pertaining to the debtor in question."[76] Individual names create challenges for these goals by virtue of the fact that individuals do not always use the same name for all purposes. A birth certificate might show one name while credit cards, state I.D. cards, drivers' licenses, passports, and other identifying documents might state that name in the diminutive or add or drop a middle name or initial, might lack characters necessary to represent the name correctly, might lack sufficient space in the data field to represent the full name, or may show only a previous name or a business name of a sole proprietor.

All of these problems—and others—create uncertainties for filers and searchers. While such problems in reality are likely rare, the 2010 Amendments to Article 9 attempted to simplify the debtor name requirements of 9–503. With respect to individual names, the Amendments provided states with two alternatives for the information permitted or required to be used to identify individual debtors on the financing statement: the "only if" rule under Alternative A and the "safe harbor" rule under Alternative B.

The "only if" rule prioritizes an individual's driver's license as the source of the correct debtor name to be entered on the filing statement. Specifically, under this alternative, if the individual holds an unexpired driver's license issued by the state in which the financing statement is to be filed, the financing statement sufficiently provides the name of the debtor "only if the financing statement provides the name of the individual which is indicated on the [driver's license]. . . ."[77] If the debtor does not hold an unexpired

---

[75]   UCC § 9–503, cmt. d.

[76]   *Id.*

[77]   UCC § 9–503(a)(4) [Alternative A].

driver's license issued by the correct jurisdiction, the financing statement must provide "the individual name of the debtor or the surname and first personal name of the debtor. . . ."[78]

The "safe harbor" rule does not prioritize any particular source of the debtor's individual name. For jurisdictions adopting Alternative B, the financing statement sufficiently provides the name of the debtor if it provides the individual name of the debtor, provides the surname and first personal name of the debtor, *or* the name of the individual which is indicated on an unexpired driver's license issued by the state of filing.[79]

Debtor name for registered organizations, collateral being administered by a personal representative of a decedent, and collateral held in trust that is not a registered organization. The 2010 Amendments to § 9–503 clarified the debtor name requirements for financing statements regarding collateral held by registered organizations, personal representatives of a decedent debtor's estate, and trusts that are not registered organizations.

Registered organizations. The 2010 Amendments clarified the definition of a "registered organization" to identify the "public organic record" of such an organization as the source of the debtor name for the financing statement. Section 9–102(a)(71) (2010) states that a registered organization is an organization "formed or organized solely under the law of a single State or the United States *by the filing of a public organic record with, the issuance of a public organic record by, or the enactment of legislation by the State or the United States.*" (emphasis added). The new term "public organic record" is a change from the prior definition that focused on "public record" and which left open ambiguity regarding whether that term meant, in the example of a corporation the articles of incorporation, certificate of incorporation, state business name database, tax filings, securities filings, and similar public records that might contain the organization's name. Instead, § 9–102(68) (2010) defines "public organic record" as:

> (68) . . . a record that is available to the public for inspection and is:

> (A) a record consisting of the record initially filed with or issued by a State or the United States to form or organize an organization and any record filed with or issued by the State or the United States which amends or restates the initial record;

---

78   UCC § 9–503(a)(5) [Alternative A].
79   UCC § 9–503(a)(4) [Alternative B].

(B) an organic record of a business trust consisting of the record initially filed with a State and any record filed with the State which amends or restates the initial record, if a statute of the State governing business trusts requires that the record be filed with the State; or

(C) a record consisting of legislation enacted by the legislature of a State or the Congress of the United States which forms or organizes an organization . . . .

Amended § 9–503(a)(1) clarifies that debtor registered organizations must be identified on the filing statement by the name contained on the most recently filed public organic record that "purports to state, amend, or restate the registered organization's name. . . ."

Collateral being administered by the personal representative of a decedent. Where collateral is being administered by a personal representative of a decedent, the financing statement must indicate the name of the decedent as the name of the debtor.[80] Pursuant to § 9–503(f), the name of the decedent on the financing statement is the name of the decedent "indicated on the order appointing the personal representative of the decedent issued by the court having jurisdiction over the collateral." The financing statement must also indicate separately that the collateral is being administered by a personal representative.[81]

Collateral held in a trust that is not a registered organization. In the case of collateral held in trusts that are not registered organizations, the financing statement must show as the name of the debtor the name of the trust specified in the organic record of the trust, and separately the financing statement must indicate that the collateral is held in trust.[82] If the organic record of the trust does not specify a name for the trust, then the debtor name is the name of the settlor or testator, and separately the financing statement must provide sufficient information to distinguish the trust from other trusts which also list the same settlor or testator.[83]

Section 9–503(c) purports to outlaw trade names (but section 9–506 saves filings in trade names if a search in the correct name turns up trade name filings). Section 9–503(d) calms the lawyers' fear that the name of the lead creditor as a representative of other secured parties in a loan participation arrangement might not be adequate as the "name of the secured party." In a transaction in which one

---

[80] UCC § 9–503(a)(2) (2010).

[81] UCC § 9–503(a)(2) (2010).

[82] UCC §§ 9–503(a)(3)(A)(i), (B)(i) (2010).

[83] UCC §§ 9–503(a)(3)(A)(ii), (B)(ii) (2010).

creditor makes the initial loan and then sells parts of it to other banks, it makes sense to recognize the name of the lead bank on the financing statement as adequate to perfect the claims of all the banks. Subsection (b) makes clear that certain additional information such as "the trade name or other name of the debtor" is not necessary—even in circumstances where it might be useful.

To understand the difficulty of filing and searching, consider several hypothetical cases. Assume for example the debtor is John P. Christensen, a name that might be spelled "Christiansen," "Christensen" or "Christenson." A reasonable searcher of paper records would be obliged by the ancient doctrine of *idem sonans* to search under names that might be spelled differently but sound the same. But what if the search is by computer and Christensen lives in a county in western Iowa where there are 100 Christxxxns, some with a Danish spelling, some with a Norwegian spelling and some with neither? If the secured creditor enters the name incorrectly, and if the "search logic" of the Iowa computer does not bring up that filing when the correct debtor's name is inserted, the filing does not satisfy 9–503(a) and it would not be saved by 9–506(c) since using the filing office's "standard search logic" does not disclose the financing statement. On the other hand, section 9–506(c) states that if the filing office's standard search logic finds the financing statement, searching under the debtor's correct name, this cures the problem. We suspect the opposite inference is intended as well, namely that if the standard search logic (when instructed to use the correct name) fails to find a financing statement because the name is incorrect, that renders the financing statement not only non-compliant with 9–502 and 9–503, but also means that it fails "substantially" to satisfy the "requirements of this part" under 9–506 and so is "seriously misleading."

Of course an upgrade in Iowa's search logic that makes its computer clever enough to search under all of the Scandinavian variations of Christensen would render the filing effective under 9–506 and so sufficient for 9–502 and 9–503. Likewise, the 2010 Amendments, at least where the debtor has either a public organic record or an unexpired driver's license issued by the filing State, will likely go far toward channeling secured creditors to favor consistent use of either of those records and searchers to begin their search with the names shown on those records.

To see how the same problem can arise in other settings, consider the possibility of filing in the name of the Central Wisconsin Agricultural Cooperative, Inc. There are almost limitless ways in which the name could be abbreviated: Cent. Wisc. Ag. Coop, Central Wisconsin Ag. Co-op, or Central Wisc. Agricultural Co, and on and on. Presumably the Co-op is an organization and has a precise name stated in its organizational documents. The 2010 Amendments finally resolve this issue in favor of the registered organization's name as shown in the most recent public organic record of that organization. By limiting the universe of possible debtor names significantly, we can easily imagine search software that would find most of the erroneous variations, such as those caused by typographical errors, and so validate the financing statement under 9–506(c).

The use of trade names has been a recurring and troublesome problem. Prior to 1999, the text of section 9–402(7) appeared to permit the use of trade names, but Comment 7 to 9–402 appeared to say that a filing in the trade name was never proper. Subsection 9–503(c) explicitly adopts the position that trade names are not enough. What if Harry Platt, a sole proprietor, does business under the name "Platt Fur Company" and a creditor files under the trade name? Assume a search under the name of "Platt, Harry" turns up the Platt Fur Co. filing. Is the secured creditor unperfected because of the provisions in 9–503? No. Because the search logic turned up the filing when there was a search done in the proper name (Platt, Harry), 9–506(c) directs that the mistake in the name, "does not make the financing statement seriously misleading" and, we would argue, the financing statement *ipso facto* "substantially satisfies" the name requirements of Part 5 notwithstanding the explicit prohibition in 9–503(c). So trade name filings live on and if the trade name is close enough to the true name of the debtor, and the search logic of the filing office is clever enough, filings in trade names will sometimes be effective.

To summarize, Revised Article 9 (including the 2010 Amendments) is quite friendly to a filer. It minimizes the necessary data; it gives explicit instruction about things that should and should not be done; and it directs the filing officer to refuse to accept financing statements that contain errors which are likely to result in problems in the future (9–516(b)). By blessing any filing that can be found by searching under the correct name (using the filing office's standard search logic), the Code will save many creditors from the hell of imperfection. Finally, Revised Article 9 continues the protection of former Article 9 in providing that filing occurs upon presentation of the fee and proper documents, irrespective of a subsequent error by the filing officer. Section 9–516(d) buttresses that position by stating that documents are treated as filed even if they are clearly refused, if the refusal is for reasons not specified under 9–516(b) and the requirements of 9–502 are met.

A creditor who is anxious about its filing should adopt the conservative practice of having a person (who did not do the filing) find the correct name of the debtor and conduct a search under that name. If that search does not turn up the filing, something further needs to be done.

b. Addresses

Inaccuracy in, or omission of, the addresses of the debtor and the secured party caused few problems under the Code as it existed prior to 1999. Because 9–516(b), not section 9–502, requires such addresses, these issues will shrink yet further. Under section 9–502 the financing statement is sufficient if it indicates the collateral and gives the name of the debtor and secured party, even though it states no addresses. Recall that 9–520 directs the filing officer to refuse financing statements that omit addresses (because they fail to comply with 9–516(b)), but, 9–520 notwithstanding, if the filing officer takes a financing statement without addresses or one with improper addresses, there still is an effective filing, provided 9–502 is satisfied. The omission of addresses from 9–502 is a statement by the drafters that 9 times out of 10, or perhaps 999 out of 1000, no diligent searcher needs this information.

c. Description of Collateral

Section 9–504 on descriptions in financing statements adopts the standards in 9–108 (for security agreements) as standards for the adequacy of descriptions in financing statements. In general, the standards for the security agreement and the financing statement are the same, namely those specified in 9–108:

(a) [Sufficiency of description.] Except as otherwise provided in subsections (c), (d), and (e), a description of personal or real property is sufficient, whether or not it is specific, if it reasonably identifies what is described.

(b) [Examples of reasonable identification.] Except as otherwise provided in subsection (d), a description of collateral reasonably identifies the collateral if it identifies the collateral by:

(1) specific listing;

(2) category;

(3) except as otherwise provided in subsection (e), a type of collateral defined in [the Uniform Commercial Code];

(4) quantity;

(5) computational or allocational formula or procedure; or

(6) except as otherwise provided in subsection (c), any other method, if the identity of the collateral is objectively determinable.

(c) [Supergeneric description not sufficient.] A description of collateral as "all the debtor's assets" or "all the debtor's personal property" or using words of similar import does not reasonably identify the collateral.

(d) [Investment property.] Except as otherwise provided in subsection (e), a description of a security entitlement, securities account, or commodity account is sufficient if it describes:

(1) the collateral by those terms or as investment property; or

(2) the underlying financial asset or commodity contract.

(e) [When description by type insufficient.] A description only by type of collateral defined in [the Uniform Commercial Code] is an insufficient description of:

(1) a commercial tort claim; or

(2) in a consumer transaction, consumer goods, a security entitlement, a securities account, or a commodity account.

In one respect 9–504 goes beyond 9–108; it accepts super-generic descriptions for financing statements. Thus, in the words of 9–504(2), an indication that the financing statement "covers all assets" or "all personal property" is permissible. As we point out above, 9–108 invalidates such a super-generic description for security agreements.

So, section 9–504 on descriptions in financing statements takes us back to the language of 9–108 which states that a description is adequate if it "reasonably identifies what is described." Subsection 9–108(b) blesses the following descriptions:

(b) [Examples of reasonable identification.] Except as otherwise provided in subsection (d), a description of collateral reasonably identifies the collateral if it identifies the collateral by:

(1) specific listing;

(2) category;

(3) except as otherwise provided in subsection (e), a type of collateral defined in [the Uniform Commercial Code];

(4) quantity;

(5) computational or allocational formula or procedure; or

(6) except as otherwise provided in subsection (c), any other method, if the identity of the collateral is objectively determinable.

Section 9–108(e) invalidates a description by "type" when the collateral is a commercial tort claim, and, "in a consumer transaction, consumer goods, a security entitlement, a securities account or a commodity account."[84] A creditor perfecting a security interest in a consumer's securities account in connection with a consumer transaction would have to use some additional terms beyond "security entitlement," such as "the securities in my account at Merrill Lynch," and in a consumer transaction involving consumer goods, presumably the goods would have to be identified, as for example, "my 5-carat diamond ring" or the like.

Section 9–108(e)(2) applies only if two conditions are met: the transaction is both "a consumer transaction" *and* the collateral is of a type described in the section, namely "consumer goods," "security entitlement," etc. The definition of consumer transaction in 9–102(a)(26) contains two conditions: the obligation must be for personal, family or household purposes *and* the collateral must actually be held for personal, family or household purposes. Thus: 1) if the security entitlement is not held for personal, family or household purposes, or 2) if the securities are personal but the loan is a business loan, (e)(2) does not invalidate a description by "type."

Exactly how section 9–108(b) has changed pre-1999 Code law is unclear because the six examples of "reasonable identification" in 9–108(b) (quoted above) are not parallel. Some of the examples in (b), such as subsection (b)(4)'s "quantity," must certainly be intended only as a partial identification while others such as subsection (2) "category," or subsection (3) "type of collateral defined" in the Code could be a complete identification. It is unclear exactly how the list of examples will affect the cases. Forty years of cases under the old Code have told us that the creditors will make mistakes here.

Does the use of a code category, such as "equipment," necessarily include "equipment" even if after-acquired? Section 9–108(b)(3) blesses the Code's use of these categories, and cases are divided on the question whether a code category such as accounts, inventory or equipment includes after-acquired property of the same type.[85]

---

[84]   It is also unlikely that a commercial tort claim could be rolled into an existing security interest even where the security agreement contains an after-acquired collateral clause covering general intangibles. See Bayer Cropscience, LLC v. Stearns Bank National Assoc., 837 F.3d 911 (8th Cir. 2016).

[85]   White Motor Credit Corp. v. Euclid Nat'l Bank, 1980 WL 98401, 30 UCC 331 (Ohio App.1980) (after-acquired property clause in security agreement implied where collateral is inventory); In re Shenandoah Warehouse Co., 202 B.R. 871, 32 UCC2d 573 (Bankr.W.D.Va.1996) (security agreement describing collateral as "accounts

Comment 3 tells us that the drafters take no position on the coverage of after-acquired property where after-acquired property is not explicitly identified.[86] Presumably that means that the courts are free to find that use of terms such as "inventory" are intended to include after-acquired property. We see no statutory or policy basis for requiring a reference to after-acquired collateral in the financing statement. Because the Code authorizes a filing under "types" it already imposes the burden on the searcher to determine exactly which property of the identified "type" is covered.

d.   Some Collateral Description Cases Prior to the 1999 Code

Frequently, the secured creditor will not describe the collateral in the financing statement by Code category, i.e., by type, but will describe the collateral "by item." When in error, the error may not be fatal. It may only be minor, and the description will still reasonably identify the collateral. Best known here are the cases upholding descriptions by serial number even though mistaken.

Where a description combines Code type and item, and item is erroneous in some major respect, we believe courts should still uphold the description if the collateral nonetheless falls under the Code type designation. In the case of In re Tebbs Construction Co., Inc.,[87] a Code type was used in the description along with a purported but nonexistent itemization. The description read: "those items of machinery and equipment, with replacements thereof, as set forth in the attached security agreement." The security agreement was not attached. The court held that where an existing description as to Code type is sufficient to create a valid financing statement (as it was here), failure to attach a further description of the collateral does not render the statement invalid.

Sometimes the description fails because it is too vague. In one case the description used the word "premises."[88] In another it used

---

receivable" implicitly includes after-acquired accounts); In re GEM Refrigerator Co., 512 B.R. 194 (Bankr. E.D. Pa. 2014) (after-acquired collateral clause referring to "personal property, . . . whether now owned or hereafter acquired" and financing statements referring to collateral as including "investment property. . .whether now existing or hereafter arising" applied to brokerage sub-accounts created by debtor).

[86]   It is unlikely that these issues will be finally resolved. Comment 3 to § 9–108 notes: "Much litigation has arisen over whether a description in a security agreement is sufficient to include after-acquired collateral if the agreement does not explicitly so provide. This question is one of contract interpretation and is not susceptible to a statutory rule. . . . Accordingly, this section contains no reference to descriptions of after-acquired collateral."

[87]   39 B.R. 742, 38 UCC 1400 (Bankr.E.D.Va.1984).

[88]   In re Weiner's Men's Apparel, Inc., 1970 WL 12549, 8 UCC 104 (Bankr.S.D.N.Y.1970).

the word "equity."[89] The courts in both cases found the words inadequate. We agree. On still other occasions ambiguity is the problem. Thus, in Interstate Steel Co. v. Ramm Mfg. Corp.[90] the words "steel inventory" did not reasonably identify the collateral because the debtor owned both sheets of steel and steel utensils. The 1999 and 2010 revisions have not changed the outcomes in these cases, nor could any revision draw clear lines here.

Under former section 9–501(a)(1), a real estate description was required when the collateral is timber to be cut, as-extracted minerals, or for fixture filings. The courts here do not require a legal metes and bounds description. It should be enough if the description reasonably identifies the collateral. Thus, in the case of In re Law,[91] the court upheld a description covering "crops growing or to be grown on real estate located in Chapman Township, Clay County, Kansas." The court pointed out that a searching creditor could reasonably identify the collateral here because "describing the land as being in Chapman Township is tantamount to stating that it is within five miles of Longford," the only town in the Township. On the other hand, not just any description will do. In Gold Kist, Inc. v. Farmers & Merchants Bank[92] the Alabama Supreme Court invalidated a description covering "all crops grown or harvested in 1982 on land rented or leased in Baldwin County, Alabama."

In First National Bank in Creston v. Francis,[93] the description covered growing crops on land described as the "southeast one-quarter of section 24, township 71 north, range 32 in Grant Township, Adams County, Iowa." This description was erroneous in that the reference should have been to section 25, not section 24. The Iowa Supreme Court split 5–4 and invalidated the description. We agree with Judge Larson who dissented as follows: "It is important to note that filings . . . are by name, not land description. Armed with the knowledge that [debtor] had encumbered grain, the . . . next step would be to ascertain whether the grain [that debtor] was offering to sell came off the described land . . . . Such inquiry would have revealed immediately the error, enabling an accurate identification."[94]

---

[89]   Sannerud v. First Nat'l Bank, 708 P.2d 1236, 42 UCC 751 (Wyo.1985).

[90]   108 Ill.App.3d 404, 64 Ill.Dec. 62, 438 N.E.2d 1381, 34 UCC 989 (1982).

[91]   54 B.R. 434, 42 UCC 307 (Bankr.D.Kan.1985).

[92]   425 So.2d 452, 35 UCC 637 (Ala.1983). See also, Chanute Production Credit Ass'n v. Weir Grain & Supply, Inc., 210 Kan. 181, 499 P.2d 517, 10 UCC 1351 (1972) ("land owned or leased by the debtor in Cherokee County, Kansas," invalid).

[93]   342 N.W.2d 468, 37 UCC 1400 (Iowa 1984).

[94]   342 N.W.2d at 472, 37 UCC at 1405.

Section 9–502(b)(3) in Revised Article 9 contains an optional provision that a description of real property should be "sufficient to give constructive notice of a mortgage under the law of this State if the description were contained in a record of the mortgage of the real property." The optional provision may be more restrictive than is necessary or desirable. Consider the *Francis* case where Judge Larson noted these filings are by name and, unlike the real estate filings, are intended only to put one on notice that one must do investigation elsewhere.

2–13 DEFECTIVE—SERIOUSLY MISLEADING?

The requirements of 9–502 et seq. must be read with 9–506 (effect of errors or omissions); it has language similar to that formerly appearing in 9–402(8). Subsection 9–506(a) provides:

> (a) [Minor errors and omissions.] A financing statement substantially satisfying the requirements of this part is effective, even if it has minor errors or omissions, unless the errors or omissions make the financing statement seriously misleading.

The sentence seems to contain two conditions. First, the financing statement must "substantially satisfy" the requirements of Part 5, and second, it must not contain errors or omissions that make it "seriously misleading." Can a court properly conclude that a financing statement that is not "seriously misleading" still fails "substantially to satisfy" the requirements of Part 5? We do not think so, but the drafters have left that possibility open. In our view, the question whether the financing statement should be effective is the same as the question whether the omissions make it "seriously misleading" and that also should be the test of the question whether it "substantially satisfies." In short, we find one, not two conditions in 9–506.

Recall that under section 9–506(c) a statement with a defective debtor's name is valid if the filing office's "standard search logic" can find it in a search under the correct name. This leaves open the possibility that the same financing statement might be effective in one place but not in another. In a state with sophisticated search programs, searching under the proper name might disclose the improper filing when a search in a state with a more brittle search program would not. This is a sensible result and it means, of course, that creditors who do not get it right initially, will sometimes be saved by new and more imaginative programs that can get into the filer's mind and so find its erroneous financing statement.

The second paragraph of Comment 2 to 9–506 states flatly that "an error in the name of the secured party or its representative will not be seriously misleading." Does this mean that a creditor who gets its name on a financing statement has rendered its own successor perfected (e.g., filing as "Nations Bank" perfects a security interest held by its successor "Bank of America")? We think so; there is no reason for any other outcome.

2–14 THE EFFECTS OF POST-FILING CHANGES ON PERFECTION

After a security interest is perfected by filing, changes may occur in the name of the debtor, the nature of its collateral, or the name of the secured party. We draw most of these changes together here and discuss the Article 9 rules and the case law bearing on them:

9–507(b):[Information becoming seriously misleading.] Except as otherwise provided in subsection (c) and section 9–508, a financing statement is not rendered ineffective if, after the financing statement is filed, the information provided in the financing statement becomes seriously misleading under section 9–506.

PROBLEM

Suppose debtor named Jupiter, LLC gave a perfected security interest in its equipment and inventory to Bank on October 31. Jupiter changes its name to Zeus, LLC on November 1. Five months later Zeus continues to own the original equipment, but all of its inventory held on April 1 was acquired in March. During the period from October 31 to April 1, Bank has filed no new financing statement in the debtor's new name, Zeus, LLC. Is Bank perfected? The answer is "yes" as to the equipment, but "no" as to the inventory. Had Bank filed an amendment under "Zeus, LLC" within four months of the November 1st name change, it would have enjoyed continued perfection as to the inventory as well.[95]

These results are dictated by section 9–507(c):

(c) [Change in debtor's name.] If the name that a filed financing statement provides for a debtor becomes insufficient as the name of the debtor under Section 9–503(a) so that the financing statement becomes seriously misleading under section 9–506:

_____

[95]   On what is or is not a seriously misleading name change, see, e.g., In re Paramount Int'l, Inc., 154 B.R. 712, 21 UCC2d 181 (Bankr.N.D.Ill.1993) ("Paramount Attractions, Inc." to "Paramount International, Inc." not seriously misleading); In re SpecialCare, Inc., 209 B.R. 13, 34 UCC2d 857 (Bankr.N.D.Ga.1997) ("Davidson Therapeutic Services, Inc." to "SpecialCare, Inc." seriously misleading because names are "completely dissimilar").

(1) the financing statement is effective to perfect a security interest in collateral acquired by the debtor before, or within four months after, the filed financing statement becomes seriously misleading; and

(2) the financing statement is not effective to perfect a security interest in collateral acquired by the debtor more than four months after the filed financing statement becomes seriously misleading, unless an amendment to the financing statement which renders the financing statement not seriously misleading is filed within four months after the financing statement became seriously misleading.

In our hypothetical case, it is evident that the debtor name Jupiter LLC in the original financing statement has become "insufficient as the name of the debtor under Section 9–503(a) so that the financing statement" has become seriously misleading. No reasonably diligent searcher looking under the new name of the debtor, Zeus LLC, would be likely to find the financing statement showing Bank's interest in equipment and inventory of "Jupiter LLC." Bank's amendment within the four-month period would render the financing statement "not seriously misleading" and so continue its effect. Thus 9–502(c) imposes a duty to refile after a "seriously misleading" name change to preserve perfection with respect to property acquired more than four months after the name change, though not as to collateral owned by the debtor (here equipment) prior to the name change or acquired within four months after the change.

Now suppose that debtor, Jupiter LLC, does not change its name; it ceases to be a limited liability company and incorporates as "Jupiter Co." Assume the LLC's equipment, inventory and contract obligations are all transferred to the new corporation. What is the status of the bank's security interest? Revised Article 9 deals with this question comprehensively. Subsections 9–203(d) and (e) generally make the security agreement of the predecessor effective against the successor:

(d) [When person becomes bound by another person's security agreement.] A person becomes bound as debtor by a security agreement entered into by another person if, by operation of law other than this article or by contract:

(1) the security agreement becomes effective to create a security interest in the person's property; or

(2) the person becomes generally obligated for the obligations of the other person, including the obligation secured

under the security agreement, and acquires or succeeds to all or substantially all of the assets of the other person.

(e) [Effect of new debtor becoming bound.] If a new debtor becomes bound as debtor by a security agreement entered into by another person:

(1) the agreement satisfies subsection (b)(3) with respect to existing or after-acquired property of the new debtor to the extent the property is described in the agreement; and

(2) another agreement is not necessary to make a security interest in the property enforceable.

The new debtor becomes bound if, as in our case, the obligations to the predecessor are assumed by contract or, as in many other cases, they are successors rendered liable by the state corporation law on mergers. It would also be true according to 9–203(d)(2) any time the successor became "generally obligated for the obligations of the other person ... and acquire[d] or succeed[ed] to all ... [or] substantially all of the assets of the other person." So even where the local corporate law, or the contract the parties had drafted, might arguably be deficient, one who generally takes over the liabilities of the predecessor and gets all of that person's assets will (by the terms of 9–203(d)) "become bound as debtor" on the security agreement. Section 9–203(e) makes clear that a successor who is so bound under (d) need not sign a new security agreement. Thus, Revised Article 9 makes plain what was uncertain under the former law, namely that conventional rules which in most circumstances would bind a successor to a predecessor's liabilities do the same things (and more) for the security agreement between the secured creditor and the debtor.

Is the old financing statement still good? By hypothesis, there is a "new debtor" and thus no financing statement that lists "that debtor's" name. Section 9–508(a) solves that problem:

(a) [Financing statement naming original debtor.] Except as otherwise provided in this section, a filed financing statement naming an original debtor is effective to perfect a security interest in collateral in which a new debtor has or acquires rights to the extent that the financing statement would have been effective had the original debtor acquired rights in the collateral.

In general it applies the same rules that were discussed above under 9–507. If "Jupiter LLC," describing the limited liability company, adequately describes "Jupiter Co.," the corporation, the filing remains effective under 9–508. (Effectiveness is likely but uncertain; careful creditors will seldom rely on 9–508.) If, on the other hand, Zeus LLC becomes Jupiter Co., a corporation, section 9–508(b) applies the same four month rule described above. In that case the bank would have to file a new financing statement identifying the successor, Jupiter Co., as the debtor.

Assume now that the secured creditor's name changes, or the address of the secured creditor or debtor changes. These do not render the filing ineffective; section 9–507(b) tells us to ignore all of these changes:

> (b) [Information becoming seriously misleading.] Except as otherwise provided in subsection (c) and section 9–508, a financing statement is not rendered ineffective if, after the financing statement is filed, the information provided in the financing statement becomes seriously misleading under section 9–506.

Are there any changes—except for changes in the debtor's name—that would render the financing statement ineffective under Revised Article 9? Assume that the financing statement identified the debtor's goods as "inventory of rental cars." If debtor went out of the short-term rental business and commenced the sale of new cars and ostrich meat, would the bank continue to be perfected under the terms of 9–507(b)? One can argue that the broad statement in 9–507(b) continues the perfection and one might even justify that conclusion by pointing out that any searcher would have to contact the bank. But we have our doubts. This financing statement once "indicated the collateral," as required by 9–502(a)(3), but it does so no more. We doubt that 9–507(b) covers this case. Surely a trustee in bankruptcy would argue this is not merely a case where the financing statement has become "seriously misleading." It is a case in which the debtor has now acquired collateral that was never covered by any financing statement. For example, no one would argue that a financing statement covering "inventory of automobiles" would also cover an inventory of appliances when the debtor acquired a new business and retained his current inventory of automobiles.

The drafters of Revised Article 9 (1999) and the 2010 Amendments did an admirable job of eliminating the uncertainties surrounding name changes and corporate restructurings. They also took a large and appropriate step in the direction of protecting financing statements that under the former law could have been challenged as "seriously misleading," particularly those having to do with name changes of secured creditors and the like. They may even have protected the secured creditor whose debtor's collateral has changed.

2–15   PERFECTION IN MULTIPLE STATE TRANSACTIONS, SECTIONS 9–301 THROUGH 9–307

Sections 9–301 through 9–307 deal with choice of law—transactions somehow associated with more than one jurisdiction. Although it is technically correct to regard these sections as full-fledged choice of law provisions on perfection and priority, their principal function is to answer a single question: where to file? Since the 1999 revision (including the 2010 Amendments), Article 9 has been adopted by every state. So every state now has nearly identical statutory law on how one takes and perfects a security interest, on the rights of the creditor on default and on rules of priority. Usually there will be no need for choice of law rules to determine, for example, whether the rules of priority in Illinois or those in Ohio govern a particular transaction. Nor will we have to ask whether repossession was proper under the law of Illinois versus the law of Ohio. In all of these cases every state's law will be the same.

That is not true of the place of filing, however. When the law of Ohio controls, it will tell one to file a financing statement in Columbus, but when the law of Illinois controls, one must file in Springfield. Because most perfection is accomplished by filing, and because a filing in the wrong place is no filing at all, the "choice of law" on place of filing is as important as choice of law on other Article 9 questions is unimportant.

a.   Pre-1999 Rules

Prior to Revised Article 9, former section 9–103 contained a comprehensive and complicated set of rules about place of perfection. These rules were built upon the premise that filing with respect to goods should normally be at the place where the goods are located and that filing with respect to intangibles should normally be at the place where the debtor is located. The drafters classified some goods as "mobile"; these they treated like intangibles. Filing for mobile goods was at the debtor's location, not at the location of the goods themselves. Former 9–103 also had a separate rule for purchase money security interests where goods purchased in one state were to be shipped to the debtor in another. In the prior Code, a debtor's location was at its chief place of business, usually the place of the chief executive office.

Each of these rules had a perfectly understandable, rational basis, and, in theory, the rules were easy to understand and apply. In practice, the pre-1999 rules presented considerable difficulty. First, one needed to understand whether the goods were mobile goods or not. If they were mobile, the filing was where the debtor was located; if they were not mobile, the filing was where the goods were located. Second, one needed a rule for the case where goods were moved from one state to another. Since the perfection depended upon the location of the goods in a particular state, a security interest perfected by filing at the original location would necessarily become unperfected at some point after the goods were moved from that state, for the person in the new state would expect to search in the new state. Thus, former 9–103 had a four month "grace period" in which perfection would continue in the new state despite the movement of the goods. If the creditor did not catch up with the goods before the end of the four months and file in the new state, generally it was rendered unperfected. Finally, the question of where a debtor's "chief place of business" is located, was not always clear. This was particularly true with respect to modern companies that have businesses in many states where the chief executive officer might be in one location part of the week, and in another location the other part of the week, and where the remaining members of the executive staff might be in yet a third place. Of all the problems in the pre-1999 Article 9, those presented by the multi-state rules in former 9–103 were the easiest to see and, we hope, the easiest to resolve.

b.   General Rule—1999 Revision

With exceptions we will discuss elsewhere, section 9–301 directs that the law of the debtor's location "governs perfection." Section 9–301(2) excludes possessory security interests from that rule and 9–301(3) excludes fixture filings and security interests in timber to be cut, but the general rule applicable to 99% of all filing is that one perfects by filing at the debtor's location. This means the distinction that formerly had to be recognized between tangible and intangible collateral is gone; the distinction that had to be drawn between mobile and non-mobile goods is not necessary; and rules about continued perfection after goods are moved from one state to another are also not needed.

Section 9–307, on location of debtor, makes a second important change in the law. Subsection (b) adopts the conventional rules about the location of an individual (individual's principal residence), of an organization with only one place of business (place of business), and of an organization with more than one place of business (chief executive office). But the major change comes in 9–307(e) where corporations and other organizations that qualify as "registered organizations" are considered to be located in the state where they are organized. Thus a corporation incorporated under Illinois law is located in Illinois, even if its principal office and all of its business is in California, and a business incorporated in Ohio is located there, even if 90% of its business is in states other than Ohio and even if its chief executive office is located in Chicago. This means that for all corporate debtors and for certain other entities that qualify as "registered organizations" (such as limited liability companies and certain partnerships), all the ambiguity about location will be gone. The messy, practical question about where the CEO goes to work and whether that is the chief executive office will not be relevant. For this important insight, we thank Professor Lynn LoPucki.[96]

The choice of "debtor's location"—particularly in the case of corporate debtors, of their place of incorporation—brings a bonus. We believe the movement of a corporation from one place to another by reincorporation in a new place is far less common than movement of goods from one state to another. Presumably the change of incorporation is also less frequent than the moving of a chief executive office or other indicia of business affairs. Thus, while the law still has to have a provision for change of the debtor's location, the particular indicia of "location" are less likely to change than the former indicia, and debtor's location is far less likely to change than is the location of the goods. Moreover, the change of state of incorporation (or organization in the case of registered organizations other than corporations) is likely to leave a trail of public notices alerting secured creditors and searchers to the change. The movement of goods and other moveable collateral from state to state generally requires no public notice and will be known only to the debtor in most circumstances.

The drafters have done us a favor that is hard to exaggerate. Under Revised Article 9, it is far easier to determine where to file than under the pre-1999 law. It is also less likely that a security interest once perfected will become unperfected because of a change in location of goods or the like, and it is less likely that someone who does a diligent search will fail to find a properly filed financing statement.

To understand the rules we have just described, consider 9–301 which reads in full below:

LAW GOVERNING PERFECTION AND PRIORITY OF SECURITY INTERESTS. Except as otherwise provided in Sections 9–303 through 9–306, the following rules determine the law governing perfection, the effect of perfection or nonperfection, and the priority of a security interest in collateral:

---

[96]   Lynn M. LoPucki, *Why the Debtor's State of Incorporation Should be the Proper Place for Article 9 Filing: A Systems Analysis*, 79 Minn. L. Rev. 577 (1995).

(1) Except as otherwise provided in this section, while a debtor is located in a jurisdiction, the local law of that jurisdiction governs perfection, the effect of perfection or nonperfection, and the priority of a security interest in collateral.

(2) While collateral is located in a jurisdiction, the local law of that jurisdiction governs perfection, the effect of perfection or nonperfection, and the priority of a possessory security interest in that collateral.

(3) Except as otherwise provided in paragraph (4), while negotiable documents, goods, instruments, money, or tangible chattel paper is located in a jurisdiction, the local law of that jurisdiction governs:

(A) perfection of a security interest in the goods by filing a fixture filing;

(B) perfection of a security interest in timber to be cut; and

(C) the effect of perfection or nonperfection and the priority of a nonpossessory security interest in the collateral.

(4) The local law of the jurisdiction in which the wellhead or minehead is located governs perfection, the effect of perfection or nonperfection, and the priority of a security interest in as-extracted collateral.

Having read 9–301, you might doubt what we have said above. Restrain your impulse to call us liars. We said that perfection by filing is at the debtor's location, yet subsection (2) adopts the law of the place where the collateral is located and (3)(C) applies the law where the goods are located on the "effect of perfection." Actually, that is not so. Section 9–301 requires careful, patient reading. First, 9–301(2) does choose the law where the goods are located but only in the case of a *possessory security* interest. Thus if perfection depends on filing or control or if the security interest attaches automatically, subsection (2) does not apply. Moreover, that subsection has become irrelevant or nearly so since Revised Article 9 has been adopted in every jurisdiction; what is sufficient to perfect by possession in one state will not differ significantly from what is sufficient to perfect in another state.

But what is the distinction between 9–301(1) that directs one to the debtor's location and 9–301(3)(C) that directs one to the location of the collateral? Compare the phrase in (1): "perfection, the effect of perfection or nonperfection and the priority" with the phrase in

(3)(C): "the effect of perfection or nonperfection and the priority . . . ."
The distinction is between "perfection" on the one hand and "the *effect*
of perfection" on the other.

Assume a court sitting in Ohio is determining the right of a
secured creditor against goods located in Ohio belonging to a
company doing business in Ohio but incorporated in Illinois. The
Ohio court should look at 9–301(1) and 9–307; these two provisions
of Ohio law will direct the court to look to Illinois law to see whether
the secured creditor has filed the proper documents in the proper
place, in this case, Springfield. If the secured creditor has properly
filed in Illinois, section 9–301(3)(C) instructs the Ohio Court to grant
the secured creditor the rights and priority of a perfected secured
creditor under Ohio law. If the secured creditor is being challenged
by a second creditor or by a judicial lien holder in Ohio or by any other
claimant, 9–301(3) directs the court to determine the *priority dispute*
by reference to Ohio law. In most priority disputes and in most other
cases, the "effect of perfection" will be the same under every state's
law since every state has adopted 1999 Article 9.[97]

Finally, observe that neither section 9–301 nor any of the other
choice of law provisions in Article 9 purports to choose the law for
questions such as attachment or characterization of the transaction
(lease vs. security agreement). These issues are left to the choice of
law rules in section 1–105. Comment 2 to 9–301 makes the point as
follows:

> **Scope of This Subpart**. Part 3, Subpart 1 (sections 9–301
> through 9–307) contains choice-of-law rules similar to those
> of former section 9–103. Former section 9–103 generally
> addresses which State's law governs "perfection and the
> effect of perfection or non-perfection of" security interests.
> See, e.g., former section 9–103(1)(b). This Article follows the
> broader and more precise formulation in former section 9–
> 103(6)(b), which was revised in connection with the
> promulgation of Revised Article 8 in 1994: "perfection, the
> effect of perfection or non-perfection, and the priority of"
> security interests. Priority, in this context, subsumes all of
> the rules in Part 3, including "cut off" or "take free" rules
> such as sections 9–317(b), (c), and (d), 9–320(a), (b), and (d),
> and 9–332. This subpart does not address choice of law for
> other purposes. For example, the law applicable to issues
> such as attachment, validity, characterization (e.g., true
> lease or security interest), and enforcement is governed by

---

[97]   One place where that might not be true would be in competition between a
secured creditor and a statutory lien holder. Statutory liens are not uniform and the
"effect of possession" vis-à-vis a statutory lien holder is likely to be idiosyncratic.

the rules in section 1–301; that governing law typically is specified in the same agreement that contains the security agreement. And, another jurisdiction's law may govern other third-party matters addressed in this Article. See section 9–401, Comment 3.

But never fear; with the adoption of 1999 Article 9, these issues too have shrunk to insignificance.

PROBLEM

Debtor is incorporated in Virginia, has its headquarters in North Carolina, and does business in both North Carolina and Georgia. Bank takes a security interest in its inventory and equipment, and bank perfects its security interest by filing in Richmond, Virginia. Assume that Georgia has a unique and unusual priority rule that applies to some of debtor's collateral.

When debtor files bankruptcy, the trustee makes several arguments. First he argues that the debtor is really "located" in North Carolina, because that is where its chief place of business is. Trustee loses this argument. See 9–308.

Second, he argues that Georgia and North Carolina law governs perfection because of section 9–301(2). He loses this argument also because that subsection applies only to a "possessory security interest."

Third, he claims that the law of Georgia and North Carolina determine perfection (and therefore requires a filing in Atlanta and Raleigh) under 9–301(3)(C). The trustee loses that argument as well, for the subsection cited deals only with the "effect of perfection" and not with "perfection."

Finally, a competing creditor with a statutory lien argues that the idiosyncratic, Georgia priority law on such liens, allows it to win priority even if it would have been subordinate under Virginia law. The competing creditor wins this argument because of 9–301(3)(C).

c. Exceptions to the General Rule of Section 9–301(1)

Above we describe cases (fixture filing, timber to be cut) where section 9–301 directs one to the location of the goods for rules on perfection, effect of perfection or non-perfection and priority. Sections 9–303, 304, 305 and 306 have special rules for certificates of title, deposit accounts, investment property and letter of credit rights, respectively.

Consider section 9–304 on deposit accounts. First, one should understand that there is less to section 9–304 than meets the eye. Since one can perfect security interests in a deposit account (except as proceeds) only by taking control and since the same acts will constitute control in every jurisdiction, choice of law issues will not present the same kinds of important questions in the case of deposit accounts as it will in the case where the secured creditor has attempted to perfect by filing. The same acts are likely to constitute control under every state's law. Thus, if the secured creditor has performed the acts that grant control, it will likely be perfected under the laws of Texas, New York and Illinois and, if it has not, it will not be perfected under the law of any of those states.

d. Change in Governing Law, Section 9–316

Although the 1999 revision greatly diminished the possibility that the law governing perfection will change during a transaction (mostly because the debtor moves), it does not eliminate that possibility. Subsection 9–316(a) sets out the general rules:

(a) [General rule: effect on perfection of change in governing law.] A security interest perfected pursuant to the law of the jurisdiction designated in section 9–301(1) or 9–305(c) remains perfected until the earliest of:

(1) the time perfection would have ceased under the law of that jurisdiction;

(2) the expiration of four months after a change of the debtor's location to another jurisdiction;

(3) the expiration of one year after a transfer of collateral to a person that thereby becomes a debtor and is located in another jurisdiction. . . .

Upon change of debtor's location—under what appears to be the "normal" rule—a secured creditor would have a four month grace period under (a)(2). This would be true if the debtor were an individual who moved from Michigan to Ohio. But what of the case of a Michigan corporation that reincorporates in Delaware? Does this case fall under 9–316(a)(2) as a simple change of the debtor's location, or 9–316(a)(3) as the transfer of collateral to a person "that thereby becomes a debtor" and is located in another jurisdiction? If the latter rule applies, there is a one year grace period; if the former, there is a four month period. We believe it will be covered by (a)(3) and carry a one year grace period. This is because the Michigan corporation is a different juridical person from the Delaware corporation. There is technically a new debtor even though it has the same name, owns exactly the same assets and has exactly the same liabilities as the old debtor. Under 9–316(b) the creditor has the responsibility of chasing the debtor to the new state and filing or taking whatever action would be appropriate in that state. If the creditor takes that action within the grace period, it remains perfected and holds a continuously perfected security interest.

Even though the creditor is considered to be perfected during the grace period, as against a purchaser of the collateral for value it is "retroactively unperfected" if it fails to perfect by the end of the period. Assume a debtor, who has granted a perfected security interest to an Ohio creditor, changes its location from Ohio to South Carolina. One month after the change, a South Carolina secured creditor takes a security interest in debtor's assets and perfects by a South Carolina filing. The Ohio secured creditor does not file a financing statement in South Carolina but later claims that it has priority over the second creditor because at the time the second creditor's interest attached, it (the Ohio creditor) was still perfected— the grace period had not expired. The last sentence in 9–316(b) means the Ohio creditor loses to the later secured creditor even though the Ohio creditor had the potential—until the end of the grace period—to file in Columbia and so defeat the second secured creditor. Comment 3 describes the workings of subsection (b) as follows:

> Retroactive Unperfection. Subsection (b) sets forth the consequences of the failure to re-perfect before perfection ceases under subsection (a): the security interest becomes unperfected prospectively and, as against purchasers for value, including buyers and secured parties, but not as against donees or lien creditors, retroactively. The rule applies to agricultural liens, as well. See also section 9–515 (taking the same approach with respect to lapse). Although this approach creates the potential for circular priorities, the alternative—retroactive un-perfection against lien creditors—would create substantial and unjustifiable preference risks.

The 2010 Amendments added two new subsections to clarify the secured party's perfection of existing security interests that attach within the four month grace period after a debtor's change of location (9–316(h)) and that attach after a new debtor in another jurisdiction becomes obligated under the old debtor's security agreement (9–316(i)). Comment 7 notes, "[u]nder subsection (h), a filed financing statement that would have been effective to perfect a security interest in the collateral if the debtor had not changed its location is effective to perfect a security interest in collateral acquired within four months after the relocation." Subsection (i) deals with situations such as an original debtor who is subject to a perfected security interest in its original jurisdiction being acquired by a new debtor in a different jurisdiction. The new debtor becomes bound by the old debtor's existing security agreements. "The financing statement filed in [old debtor's jurisdiction] is effective under [9–316(i)] to perfect Lender's security interest in inventory that Survivor acquired before, and within four months after, becoming bound as debtor by Debtor's security agreement."[98]

PROBLEM

Debtor, a Nebraska corporation has granted a security interest to Bank who perfected the interest by filing in Lincoln. Debtor decides to reincorporate in Delaware. Six months after it reincorporates in Delaware it files bankruptcy. Trustee in bankruptcy claims that bank is unperfected because it failed to file within four months, section 9–316(a)(2).

Trustee is wrong. The reincorporation makes the debtor a "new debtor" located in another jurisdiction. See 9–316(a)(3) and example 4 in Comment 2.

2–16 SPECIAL CASES, PROCEEDS AND SUPPORTING OBLIGATIONS

a. Proceeds, Attachment and Definition

Article 9 provides automatic attachment of a security interest to the "rights to proceeds provided by section 9–315," 9–203(f). This rule, codified for the first time in 1972, presumes that the parties intend the security interest to attach to proceeds of the collateral even where their agreement is silent. To understand the effect of section 9–203, one must understand the meaning of "proceeds" and the reach of section 9–315. Proceeds are defined as follows in section 9–102(a)(64):

(A) whatever is acquired upon the sale, lease, license, exchange, or other disposition of collateral;

(B) whatever is collected on, or distributed on account of, collateral;

(C) rights arising out of collateral;

(D) to the extent of the value of collateral, claims arising out of the loss, non-conformity, or interference with the use of, defects or infringement of rights in, or damage to, the collateral; or

(E) to the extent of the value of collateral and to the extent payable to the debtor or the secured party, insurance payable by reason of the loss or non-conformity of, defects or infringement of rights in or damage to, the collateral.

With experience under the 1962 and 1972 versions of Article 9, the definition of proceeds has gradually changed and expanded. For example, subsection (E) clearly covers insurance proceeds that are payable on injury to, or destruction of, collateral. Likewise,

---

[98]   UCC § 9–316(i), cmt. 8 (2010).

subsection (B) covers distributions such as cash and stock dividends. Both of these provisions reverse court decisions under the former Code.[99] Under the 1972 version of Article 9, the debtor apparently had to "receive" personal property for that property to be "proceeds." There was no reason for the requirement and the drafters of the 1999 Code have omitted the word "receive."

What if the debtor *sells* collateral but denominates the transaction a "lease"? In that case the "lease" is a security agreement taken by the debtor and is chattel paper. According to PEB Commentary No. 9, the chattel paper itself constitutes proceeds. The same commentary states that payments to the debtor under true leases are proceeds. We do not understand why even a true lease itself should not be considered proceeds. One can argue that a lessor of goods for a limited time does not "dispose" of the collateral. We think there is a disposition. Even though only a portion of the debtor's rights are disposed of (for example, a two-year right to use out of a ten-year useful life of a commodity), we would argue that the lease itself is a disposition and that both the lease and the payments under the lease are proceeds.

There are other transactions that look like sales or dispositions, but are not. What if a cow gives milk or bears a calf? There is, of course, no sale or other disposition of the cow, but the production of the milk or a calf looks like a stock dividend—something that now constitutes proceeds under the new third sentence. Until the drafters expand the definition, and notwithstanding the third sentence, such natural production and reproduction are still not proceeds. Presumably that is the reason why many security interests dealing with animals include the term "product," i.e., milk, eggs and young.

Further to test the boundaries of "disposition" under 9–102(a)(64), assume a debtor has given a security interest in a valuable piece of industrial machinery. Because the debtor wishes to sell the machinery or move it to another location, the debtor proposes that the creditor's security interest be transferred from that machine to another. The other machine becomes subject to the security interest not because it is proceeds of the first, but because of the agreement of the parties. The second machine is not proceeds of the first. We think that "exchange," "disposition" and the like contemplate a transfer by the debtor to a *third party*, not the transfer of a security interest from one asset of the debtor to another asset of the debtor.

---

[99]   For general discussion of proceeds under former Article 9, see, Freyermuth, Rethinking Proceeds: The History, Misinterpretation and Revision of U.C.C. Section 9–306, 69 Tul. L. Rev. 645 (1995).

Under section 9–315(a)(2) the security interest attaches only to "identifiable" proceeds. In most cases proceeds will be easily identifiable as having come from particular collateral. For example, if a secured creditor had a security interest in an automobile that was sold and if the purchaser gave the seller a security interest and a note, the security interest would make a specific reference to the automobile and would be directly traceable to that particular piece of collateral.

By far the most common trouble comes when collateral is sold for cash, for a check or for some other form of payment, and the proceeds of that payment or the payment itself are deposited into a bank account. If there are other funds in that account, one will need some accounting fiction to determine which part of the account should be regarded as proceeds and which part as something else. Prior to 1999 the courts allowed creditors to use various tracing methods to identify their collateral in deposit accounts. A common method was the "lowest intermediate balance." Assume a secured creditor could prove the debtor had deposited $10,000 of proceeds into its bank account, and that thereafter the lowest balance in the account was $8,000. In that case, the lowest intermediate balance fiction would treat the remaining $8,000 as identifiable proceeds of the secured creditor. Revised 9–315(b)(2) blesses such fictional tracing doctrines:

> [I]f the proceeds are not goods, to the extent that the secured party identifies the proceeds by a method of tracing, including application of equitable principles, that is permitted under law other than this article with respect to commingled property of the type involved.

Subsection 9–315(b)(1) allows a secured creditor to claim commingled goods to the extent provided by section 9–336, a provision that deals explicitly with commingled collateral such as grain and the like.

b.   Proceeds, Perfection

Subsections (c) and (d) of 9–315 state the rules for perfection of proceeds:

> (c) [Perfection of security interest in proceeds.] A security interest in proceeds is a perfected security interest if the security interest in the original collateral was perfected.

> (d) [Continuation of perfection.] A perfected security interest in proceeds becomes unperfected on the 21st day after the security interest attaches to the proceeds unless:

> (1) the following conditions are satisfied:

(A) a filed financing statement covers the original collateral;

(B) the proceeds are collateral in which a security interest may be perfected by filing in the office in which the financing statement has been filed; and

(C) the proceeds are not acquired with cash proceeds;

(2) the proceeds are identifiable cash proceeds; or

(3) the security interest in the proceeds is perfected other than under subsection (c) when the security interest attaches to the proceeds or within 20 days thereafter.

The reassuring starting point is that the interest in the proceeds is automatically perfected if the security interest "in the original collateral was perfected." Under subsection (d) that perfection continues for 20 days; if the creditor wishes to continue its perfection beyond 20 days, it must either satisfy one of the other subsections or take whatever action would be necessary to perfect a security interest in the particular assets involved.

Consider two cases where perfection continues without any act on the part of the secured creditor. First are the cases in 9–315(d)(1): the creditor has filed as to the original collateral at the same office where one would file with respect to these proceeds if one were perfecting an original security interest in them. There is an additional condition that these proceeds cannot have been purchased with earlier cash proceeds. To see how this provision might work and how pervasive its reach, consider an example. Assume the debtor is a Kentucky corporation and the secured creditor has filed a financing statement covering the debtor's inventory at the state capital in Frankfort. Assume further that the financing statement covers only "debtor's inventory of used automobiles" and the proceeds are chattel paper received on the sale of some of those automobiles. Since one originally perfecting as to the debtor's chattel paper would file a financing statement in the "same office" and since the proceeds have not been acquired with "cash proceeds," the secured creditor is perfected as to the chattel paper without any action by the creditor and despite the fact its financing statement does not list chattel paper. Since almost all filings under Article 9 are at the place of a corporate debtor's incorporation, the most common result is that perfection will continue as to proceeds without any action by the secured creditor. Presumably the drafters assumed that any search in the name of the debtor will find the filing as to inventory and will understand that the prior secured creditor likely claimed proceeds as well.

The second indefinite extension of perfection covers "identifiable cash proceeds," 9–315(d)(2). Section 9–102(a)(9) defines cash proceeds as "money, checks, deposit accounts, or the like." The good news is that the secured creditor is indefinitely perfected with respect to these identifiable cash proceeds; the bad news is that money, checks, and the like are seldom long in the hands of a troubled debtor. Of course, this section does mean that our secured creditor has a continuously perfected security interest in the debtor's bank account, at least if the secured creditor can "identify" the proceeds portion of that account.

Before the adoption of the 1962 Code, the idea that a secured creditor would have a right to things we now call "proceeds" was foreign to commercial law. Each year since the adoption of the 1962 Code, we have learned new things about proceeds, things never contemplated by the original drafters. Notwithstanding the incorporation of this learning into the 1999 Code, we suspect there are more surprises to come.

c. Supporting Obligations

Section 9–102(a)(78) defines supporting obligation as follows:

[A] letter-of-credit right or secondary obligation that supports the payment or performance of an account, chattel paper, a document, a general intangible, an instrument, or investment property.

Comment 5(f) states that the most common supporting obligations are "suretyship obligations (including guarantees) and letter-of-credit rights that support one of the types of collateral" in Article 9. Assume, for example, that debtor granted a security interest in its accounts receivable and the parent corporation of the debtor guarantees payment of those accounts. That guarantee would be a supporting obligation.

Under section 9–203(f) the security interest automatically attaches to the supporting obligation. Under section 9–308(d) perfection of a security interest in the collateral "also perfects a security interest in a supporting obligation for the collateral." Section 9–310(b)(1) confirms that no separate filing is necessary, and section 9–322(b) essentially grants the same priority as to the supporting obligation as a secured creditor enjoys with respect to the original collateral.

The idea of supporting obligations involves some interpretive difficulties. Comment 5f to section 9–102(78) hints that certain obligations of insurance companies could be supporting obligations despite section 9–109's exclusion of insurance from Article 9. The

Comment is quite coy; it stops short of stating that something recognized as "insurance" can be a supporting obligation. We suspect that imaginative lawyers will offer things as "supporting obligations" that may fit within the definition but were never contemplated by the drafters.

Comment 8 to 9–203 recognizes but does not resolve the problems that might arise if a "supporting obligation" supported multiple secured interests. What, for example, if Company A had guaranteed only $200,000 of Company Y's $1 million debt? If the $1 million debt is owed to more than one creditor and if there is a default as to one creditor only, does that creditor take the entire $200,000 of guarantee, or is it distributed pro rata among all of the debts—those currently in default and those who may be in default in the future? One must look to the law of suretyship for an answer to these questions; Article 9 does not give one.

We doubt support obligations will play a big role in the cases to come, but we are even more confident we have not foreseen all or even most of the issues that will be presented in the limited number of cases where the right to support obligations is an issue.

PROBLEM

Assume that Creditor has a perfected security interest in Debtor's inventory and equipment. At the time Debtor files bankruptcy, it is discovered that some of the inventory has been sold to customers who paid by charging their credit cards. Other inventory has been sold for cash and the cash has been used to purchase new inventory. Yet other inventory has been sold for cash and the cash has been used to buy equipment.

The accounts that arise from the credit card sales are proceeds and Creditor's security interest is perfected under 9–315(d).

The new inventory purchased with cash does not enjoy perfection beyond 20 days, see section (d)(1)(C). Since almost all security agreements covering inventory have after-acquired property clauses, Creditor's security interest will attach under that clause to the new inventory—at least to the extent that it is acquired before the bankruptcy filing.

Since there may be no after-acquired property clause with respect to the equipment, Creditor's interest in the newly purchased equipment will be unperfected at the end of 20 days, unless Creditor takes some action.

Chapter 3

THE BANKRUPTCY TRUSTEE VS. THE ARTICLE 9 CLAIMANT

Analysis

3–1 INTRODUCTION

Bankruptcy is, of course, a remedy of the federal law. Since this is a book about the Uniform Commercial Code and not about bankruptcy, we focus here only on a small part of the bankruptcy law, principally on the avoidance powers of the trustee in bankruptcy.

In general, a perfected secured creditor is entitled to his collateral or the value of his collateral in a debtor's bankruptcy. Unsecured creditors, on the other hand, generally share pro rata in the non-exempt assets that are not subject to perfected security interests. That is not to say that the secured creditor is happy to see his debtor go into bankruptcy. While the debtor must often give his

131

secured creditors "adequate protection" against the decline in value of their collateral during the bankruptcy, secured creditors generally earn no interest during the pendency of the bankruptcy and they often complain that the "protection" offered by the debtor is truly not adequate to maintain the value of their collateral.

If a debtor files under Chapter 7 of the Bankruptcy Code, a trustee will be appointed and that trustee will exercise the avoidance powers that are discussed below. If, on the other hand, the debtor files a Chapter 11 case, the debtor will almost always become a "debtor in possession" (DIP) and—in that status—exercise the avoidance powers that would otherwise belong to the trustee. The consequence of the individual debtor's Chapter 7 is that the debtor gets a "discharge," a defense against any pre-bankruptcy creditor's attempt to collect a debt personally against the debtor. The consequence of a Chapter 11 proceeding for a corporation is quite different. Typically, a corporation is not seeking to be discharged from its liabilities upon liquidation (in fact that could not be done under the Bankruptcy Code), rather the corporation is seeking to reorganize itself by reducing its debt, trading equity for debt and otherwise by manipulating its capital structure and legal obligations with an eye to emerging from bankruptcy as a leaner but more sound business organization. Notwithstanding that attempt by a corporate debtor, Chapter 11 proceedings often end up in the same place as the Chapter 7 proceedings. Many Chapter 11 cases are converted to Chapter 7 for liquidation; other Chapter 11 cases suffer the same consequence through a "liquidating" Chapter 11 plan. The Bankruptcy Code gives special rights to the trustee (wherever we say trustee, read DIP, too)[1] to defeat and otherwise affect the interests of Article 9 secured creditors in ways that are unknown outside of bankruptcy.

The trustee and, to a lesser extent, the debtor in possession have every incentive to set aside a claimed Article 9 security interest. The former earns more money when he does and the latter earns more elbow room by turning a powerful secured creditor into a weaker unsecured creditor. We concentrate here on these attempts by the trustee or debtor in possession to turn secured creditors into unsecured creditors by use of the various avoidance powers. It is often said that the "acid test" of an Article 9 security interest is its capacity to survive a trustee's attack. Under sections 541 and 558 the trustee steps into the legal shoes of the debtor, becomes the owner of the debtor's assets and acquires the various defenses the debtor might assert against the parties with whom he previously dealt.

---

[1]   *See* 11 U.S.C. § 1107(a).

Under section 558 the trustee may claim that the Article 9 security interest is invalid because the parties did not comply with 9–203 or other law, and therefore did not effectively create an Article 9 security interest in the first place. The trustee's more important rights are the rights of a lien creditor under section 544(a) (exercised against unperfected parties by using the priority rights in 9–317(a)(2)), the right to avoid preferences under 547, and the rights to be subrogated to claims of certain specific parties under section 544(b) and state law. Still in its infancy, the Bankruptcy Code of 1978 has undergone several amendments, most recently in 2005. This is not the place to consider those revisions but one should understand that the rules in a number of the cases cited and discussed below may have been modified by subsequent amendments to the Code.

A final and important aspect of bankruptcy law is not explicitly stated in any of the avoidance or other powers of the trustee. This aspect is the fact that bankruptcy cases and controversies in bankruptcies are heard in a particular federal court presided over by a federal judge known as a bankruptcy judge. Appeals from these courts go to the federal district courts (and in some cases to a Bankruptcy Appellate Panel) and then to a federal Circuit Court of Appeals. The fact that bankruptcy cases are seldom appealed and are heard by judges whose sole judicial function is to hear bankruptcy cases is an important structural aspect of the system. Of all judges, bankruptcy judges are the most likely to have experience with Article 9 and to be the most facile with its operation. They also are more likely to understand how a debtor might cheat and how a creditor might overreach than are judges who are not involved day-to-day with creditors and debtors.

In the sections that follow we distinguish between unassailable security interests and those that can somehow be struck down or can otherwise be impeded by the trustee in bankruptcy. In general, the bankruptcy law provides that a secured creditor that has crossed its *t*'s and dotted its *i*'s has a right to take his collateral or the value of his collateral out of the hands of the trustee in bankruptcy, but the law would have been simpler had it said so.

3–2   FAILURE TO CREATE A SECURITY INTEREST THAT IS ENFORCEABLE AGAINST THE DEBTOR—THE TRUSTEE'S RIGHTS UNDER SUBSECTION 541(a) AND SECTION 558

The most basic failure of a security interest is its failure to become enforceable against even the debtor for want of fulfillment of one of the conditions of 9–203. If, for example, the debtor inadvertently fails to sign a written security agreement and the collateral is not in the possession of the secured party, section 9–203 makes the security agreement unenforceable even against the debtor. If the security agreement is unenforceable against the debtor it would seem self-evident that the trustee in bankruptcy, who is a representative of a group of other creditors, would also be able to strike it down. Section 541 gives the trustee the debtor's property rights and 558 gives the trustee the debtor's defenses against third parties. Under those provisions the trustee in bankruptcy can simply assert the debtor's claim under 9–203 to the effect that the creditor's security interest was not effective and so deprive the secured creditor of the collateral.

Even though a security interest is enforceable against the debtor under Article 9, it still may be unenforceable against the debtor under other state law. Thus, it is elementary that one party to a consensual transaction may rescind for fraud, for mutual mistake, for duress, or for undue influence.[2] The trustee succeeds to powers of rescission that the debtor has against a secured creditor upon bankruptcy.[3] The trustee similarly succeeds to any defenses or rights that the debtor may have against the secured creditor under the doctrine of unconscionability or under the expanding reach of consumer credit protection acts.[4]

3–3 LACK OF PERFECTION AS OF DATE OF BANKRUPTCY—TRUSTEE'S RIGHTS UNDER SUBSECTION 544(a)

By far the most common and most simple clash is between the bankruptcy trustee and the Article 9 claimant who either fails to perfect or lets its perfection lapse. As you see below the federal law gives the trustee, as of the date of the filing of the bankruptcy petition, the rights of a state law lien creditor; under section 9–317 a lien creditor has priority over an unperfected security interest. Thus, the trustee prevails under a blend of federal and state law by applying section 544(a) which states:

(a) The trustee shall have, as of the commencement of the case, and without regard to any knowledge of the trustee or of any creditor, the rights and powers of, or may avoid any transfer of property of the debtor or any obligation incurred by the debtor that is voidable by:

(1) a creditor that extends credit to the debtor at the time of the commencement of the case, and that obtains, at such time

---

2   Restatement (Second) of Contracts § 7 (1981).

3   11 U.S.C. § 558.

4   *Id.*

and with respect to such credit, a judicial lien on all property on which a creditor on a simple contract could have obtained such a judicial lien, whether or not such a creditor exists;

(2) a creditor that extends credit to the debtor at the time of the commencement of the case, and obtains, at such time and with respect to such credit, an execution against the debtor that is returned unsatisfied at such time, whether or not such a creditor exists; or

(3) a bona fide purchaser of real property, other than fixtures, from the debtor, against whom applicable law permits such transfer to be perfected, that obtains the status of a bona fide purchaser and has perfected such transfer at the time of the commencement of the case, whether or not such a purchaser exists.[5]

Under section 544(a), the trustee gets all the rights under state law of a hypothetical creditor with a judicial lien on all property of the debtor. For our purposes, the relevant state law is Article 9, and the relevant provision is 9–317(a)(2), doubtless the most important provision in the entire Article to bankruptcy trustees. Subsection 9–317(a)(2) reads as follows, in pertinent part:

(a)(2) A security interest . . . is subordinate to the rights of: . . . a person that becomes a lien creditor before the earlier of the time:

(A) the security interest . . . is perfected; or

(B) one of the conditions specified in Section 9–203(b)(3) is met and a financing statement covering the collateral is filed.

By the terms of section 544(a), the trustee may assert the rights of a hypothetical lien creditor under 9–317(a)(2), and accordingly prevails over most Article 9 claimants whose interests are unperfected at the date the petition is filed. Stated conversely, the way for an Article 9 claimant to be protected against the trustee's section 544(a) avoidance power is to either: (1) be perfected at the time of the bankruptcy filing, or (2) have filed a financing statement and also met a 9–302(b)(3) condition, the most common of which is to have obtained a valid written security agreement authenticated (i.e., usually signed) by the debtor. If the Article 9 creditor has not satisfied either of these conditions, it is in danger of the trustee's avoidance powers. Article 9's perfection requirements here reflect a Code policy against secret security.

---

[5] For a discussion of § 544(a)(3) and its effect on fixture security interests, see The Practitioner's Edition.

Before it can prevail under sections 544(a), 9–102, 9–317, or 9–323, must the trustee identify at least one actual creditor who could have prevailed against the secured creditor if that creditor had acquired a lien? No. This section is not designed to be "subrogational," but to give the trustee rights on its own behalf. It explicitly states that the "knowledge" of the trustee or of any creditor is to be disregarded and it speaks not of the rights of any actual creditor but of an entirely hypothetical creditor with particular attributes.

Section 544(a)(3) gives the trustee in bankruptcy the rights of a "bona fide purchaser of real property, other than fixtures . . . ." The reference to fixtures makes it clear that if the secured creditor has perfected an interest in a fixture in such a way as to defeat a lien creditor, the secured creditor also defeats the trustee in bankruptcy even though it might not defeat a subsequent purchaser of the real estate. *Compare* section 9–334(e)(3).

Note that there are some cases (involving particularly purchase money security interests) in which the creditor will be unperfected at the time the petition is filed and yet able to achieve priority over the trustee, despite the trustee's rights under section 544. Assume, for example, that a secured creditor makes a purchase money loan to the debtor on day one, that the debtor files a petition on day three and that the creditor perfects its security interest on day seven by an appropriate filing. Under 9–317(e) the creditor's security interest would relate back and so take priority over a lien creditor whose interests intervene between the taking of a security interest and the filing of the financing statement. Since subsection 544(a) does nothing more than give the trustee the rights that the lien creditor would have under state law as of the date of the petition, the trustee also loses in that circumstance. This outcome is made explicit by subsection 546(b).

A trustee may also recover property transferred from the estate in an apparent outright sale if that transfer may be classified as the creation of a security interest. For example, in Octagon Gas Systems, Inc. v. Rimmer,[6] Rimmer purchased rights to 5% of all proceeds payable to the debtor from a natural gas gathering system. The court found that this interest was an account and that under Article 9, Rimmer's interest as a buyer of the account was a security interest, even though the transaction giving rise to the account was not designed to secure a debt. The court also concluded that the account was a part of the bankruptcy estate under section 541 and if Rimmer had not perfected, the trustee could defeat this interest. This case

---

[6]   995 F.2d 948, 20 UCC2d 1330 (10th Cir.1993), cert. denied, 510 U.S. 993, 114 S.Ct. 554, 126 L.Ed.2d 455 (1993).

upset the "securitization" process by apparently making such absolute transfers of a debtor's intangible rights subject to a trustee's reach. Promptly after Rimmer, the Permanent Editorial Board issued Commentary 14 in an effort to nullify Rimmer. The drafters of the 1999 Code made a more elaborate attempt to protect securitization from the trustee's interference in section 9–318(a):

> (a) [Seller retains no interest.] A debtor that has sold an account, chattel paper, payment intangible, or promissory note does not retain a legal or equitable interest in the collateral sold.

Reading that, one might think that no property interest remained in the hands of the seller of an intangible under the 1999 provision of Article 9. Unfortunately, subsection (b) muddies the water; it says that the seller of an account or chattel paper to one who does not perfect, is "deemed" to retain "rights and title" identical to those the debtor sold.

The drafters are squirming to make inconsistent positions appear to be consistent. On the one hand, the drafters tell the trustee in bankruptcy "keep your hands off money attributable to intangibles that have been sold; the seller has no claim to them." On the other hand, they recognize that the seller (debtor) still has enough title to pass "good title" to "creditors" and "purchasers for value" where the earlier buyer of the intangibles has failed to perfect. Apparently, the drafters are afraid the trustee will interfere with the payments from the account debtors to the buyers/assignees or claim that the seller retains some interest which becomes part of the bankruptcy estate. Only time will tell whether the drafters can simultaneously divest the seller of all its rights, yet still recognize a residual right in that same seller when the buyer did not perfect. A recent case reached the same result in *Rimmer*, observing: "When [9–318(a)] is read together with [9–318(b)], the meaning of [9–318] becomes clear: a debtor who sells an account retains no interest in it. Section [9–318(b)] is not to the contrary. It only applies to resolve disputes between competing creditors or purchasers for value regarding a debtor's accounts, and it does so by creating a legal fiction—something completely hypothetical—that the debtor has rights and title to the account. Section [9–318(b)] does not actually revest rights and title to accounts in the debtor."[7]

Finally, the trustee's rights as a hypothetical lien creditor arise only upon the "commencement of the case"—as of the filing of the petition. Therefore, even a perfection that occurs seconds before the petition will frustrate the trustee's 544(a) claims. Of course, the

---

[7]   In re C.W. Mining Co., 530 B.R. 878, 886 (Bankr. D. Utah 2015).

trustee may be able to avoid the transfer under another section, such as 547 or 548.

Consider the following cases:

PROBLEM

1.   Bank holds a perfected security interest in debtor's inventory. Upon debtor's bankruptcy, the trustee claims priority over Bank on the ground that a buyer in the ordinary course would take free of Bank's interest under section 9–320.

Trustee loses. With respect to personal property, trustee is merely a lien creditor and not even a purchaser much less a buyer in the ordinary course.

2.   Bank holds a security interest in debtor's fixtures; Bank has perfected by a filing at the state capital, but not by a fixture filing. On debtor's bankruptcy trustee claims priority on the ground that it is a buyer of real estate and that a buyer would prevail over Bank under section 9–334(e).

Trustee loses. Although the trustee is a buyer with respect to real estate in general, there is an exception for fixtures. As to fixtures, the trustee is treated merely as a lien creditor. Because of that, trustee is subordinated by 9–334(e)(3).

3.   Bank makes a loan, obtains a signed security agreement and files a financing statement two days before debtor files bankruptcy and with knowledge of debtor's intention to file. Trustee challenges Bank's security agreement under section 544a.

Trustee loses. Trustee does not become a lien creditor until the moment of filing and filing occurred two days after the transaction. (As we will see below the trustee has other avoidance powers that it will attempt to use in this case. Those powers allow it to reach back beyond the date of filing, but, as we will see, none of them will work in this case.)

3–4   VOIDABLE PREFERENCES, SECTION 547

Although the trustee will not find as many opportunities for the use of section 547 as for section 544, section 547 is at least as important. Of the important avoidance provisions in the Bankruptcy Code, it is the most complex and subtle. If the trustee is able to prove a series of facts, the section authorizes the trustee to strike down even perfected security interests and to recover payments and other transfers to secured creditors and other third parties in the 90 days, and, in some cases, in the year preceding the filing of the petition.

Initially, one should understand the most frequent voidable preferences. The most common is the payment of a debt within the 90 days preceding the filing of a petition in bankruptcy. Many of these payments will be saved from avoidance by the exceptions under

547(c); however, almost all of them will be subject to scrutiny and some will be voidable preferences.

Of greater importance for one interested in the rights of a secured creditor is the second common form of preference, the transfer of security in the debtor's property within the 90 days prior to the petition. In some instances, the time of perfection is the "time of the transfer." Thus, if one gives a security interest to a creditor outside the 90 days, and the creditor perfects within 90 days, the transfer will sometimes constitute a voidable preference. Below we deal at length with the question of when the transfer occurs.

Broadly, the policies behind the preference rules are twofold. First is the policy that on the eve of bankruptcy (now 90 days) the debtor should be required to treat similarly-situated creditors equally. We do not permit the insolvent debtor to pay one particularly favored creditor while failing to pay others. So we have the rule that authorizes the trustee to reach back 90 days to recapture certain transfers made within that period.

We also wish to forestall particularly aggressive creditors from dismembering the debtor (by use of liens and repossession) in the days running up to bankruptcy. In theory, preference rules protect the debtor's "good will" by keeping its business intact and operating, something not possible if creditors are free to seize individual assets.

The second policy is to discourage secret liens. But for the presence of section 547, a secured creditor could take a security interest in the debtor's collateral and decline to file a financing statement in reliance upon the debtor's promise to let the creditor know if and when the debtor planned to file a petition in bankruptcy (so that the favored creditor could then perfect). The presence of section 547 makes that procedure more risky than would otherwise be true. Since the trustee will be able to reach back 90 days, the creditor who takes a secret lien and files on notice of impending bankruptcy, must keep the debtor out of bankruptcy for at least 90 days after the filing to protect its security from challenge under section 547.

The two policies are independently significant. The actions of a given creditor may bring one into play but not the other, or one into play far more strongly than the other. Thus, for example, a creditor who actually achieves a secured position outside the 90 day period but stays "off record" until warned by his debtor offends the first policy (equity) far less than the second (anti-secrecy).

The following example illustrates the equity rationale. Assume that Debtor owes 10 unsecured creditors $1,000 each, a total liability of $10,000. Assume further that its total assets are worth only

$1,000. On January 10, Debtor gives C, one of the preexisting unsecured creditors, an enforceable and perfected security interest in all of its assets. On February 1, Debtor files a voluntary petition in bankruptcy. The trustee could not invalidate the security interest through section 544(a) since it was perfected before the petition was filed. However, the trustee could avoid the interest as a preferential transfer pursuant to section 547(b).

If C were allowed to walk off with $1,000 in full satisfaction of its debt, the other nine creditors would receive nothing and C would receive full payment, yet all 10 were similarly situated as unsecured creditors of Debtor when Debtor made its transfer to C. Each should receive the same percentage of its debt out of Debtor's $1,000 of assets. The drafters of section 547 therefore gave the trustee the power to take the $1,000 away from C and to divide it among all of the unsecured creditors. Note that as between Debtor and C, C has done nothing untoward. A creditor is entitled to payment and a debtor ought to pay his creditors in full. However, section 547 is activated when payments to a particular creditor infringe on the perceived equities of other creditors of the debtor.

To illustrate the anti-secret security policy, assume that the security agreement had been signed in May of the prior year but perfection did not occur until January 10, twenty-one days before the date of bankruptcy. If the Article 9 claimant were permitted to perfect on the eve of bankruptcy and walk off with the collateral, this would reward secrecy and defeat other creditors who may have believed that the collateral was free and clear.

Of course, one can take issue with the policies discussed above. Some might argue that until the debtor is in bankruptcy, whom he pays and when is his own business. Except for fraudulent conveyance law, state law does not prohibit favoring one creditor over another for the silliest or most selfish reason. Why is equal treatment so obviously correct in and on the verge of bankruptcy but not prior to that time? Conceivably the expansive reading that many courts are giving to the 547(c) exceptions arises from skepticism about the policy in favor of equal treatment.

In response to the anti-secret security policy argument, one might note that many secret liens are recognized in today's law. Among them are purchase money liens that relate back, judicial liens that do the same, certain mechanic liens, and a variety of claims arising out of federal law. As long as the secret lien is subordinated to actual lien creditors and to perfected secured creditors, what is the need for further subordination? Invariably many, perhaps most, beneficiaries of preference rules are unsecured creditors who were never injured by the secrecy of a lien, and who lent without reliance upon, or even knowledge of, the public filing system.

In summary, you should examine the policies that support preferences. For too long, these policies have been treated as icons of commercial law. At least they should be subjected to critical examination; perhaps the policies do not justify the trustee's grand and subtle powers under 547(b).[8]

One of the costs of preference law is the time and money spent by trustees, trustees' lawyers and creditors' lawyers in unsuccessful challenges to transfers that do not violate 547. If the transaction costs of such failed preference challenges outweigh the modest benefit then—even conceding some power to the policies discussed above— preference law may be a net waste. We do not argue that section 547 should be repealed; we offer this caveat as a brake on those who extol section 547 as virtuous, efficacious and entitled to even broader reading.

Turn now to the statute. To establish a voidable preference, the trustee must prove each of the conditions of section 547(b) that are applicable to the particular. In the typical case, the trustee must prove seven factors:

(1) A transfer

(2) of the debtor's property

(3) to or for the benefit of a creditor

(4) for or on account of an antecedent debt

(5) made while the debtor was insolvent

(6) within 90 days before the original filing of the petition

(7) which enables the creditor to receive more than it would receive under a Chapter 7 liquidation.

The trustee's burden under section 547 is considerably lighter than it was under the predecessor, section 60 of the Bankruptcy Act of 1898. Under the old Act the trustee had to prove not only that the debtor was insolvent, but also that the offending creditor had "reasonable cause to believe" that the debtor was insolvent.

Subsection (f) of 547 establishes a rebuttable presumption that the debtor was insolvent during the entire 90 days prior to the filing

---

[8]   For discussion of policy reasons favoring the debtor over the trustee as better placed to dispose of assets upon financial distress, see, Bowers, Groping and Coping in the Shadow of Murphy's Law: Bankruptcy Theory and the Elementary Economics of Failure, 88 Mich. L. Rev. 2097 (1990).

of the petition.[9] The reasonable cause to believe standard has been abolished. The practical consequence of these changes is that all payments and other transfers to creditors within the 90 days preceding the filing of the petition are potentially vulnerable.

PROBLEM

1.   Creditor lends, takes, and perfects a security interest 10 days before debtor files for bankruptcy. Trustee challenges the transfer as a preference.

Trustee loses. To win a preference claim the trustee must demonstrate each of the conditions listed above. In this case the transfer was not "for or on account of an antecedent debt." (The transaction does not violate the policy underlying preference rules. Because the creditor made a contemporaneous loan, the transaction left just as many assets available to the unsecured creditors as had been available before the transaction occurred.)

2.   Bank has a fully secured perfected security interest in debtor's inventory. The debt is $1 million and the value of the collateral is $1,500,000. Thirty days before bankruptcy debtor makes a $300,000 payment to Bank. Trustee challenges the payment as a preference.

Trustee loses. In this case trustee loses because the payment did not "enable the creditor to receive more than it would receive under a Chapter 7 liquidation." Since the value of the collateral exceeded the amount of the debt, upon liquidation the creditor would have been paid 100% of its $1 million debt. Thus this early payment does not take money from unsecured creditors that would otherwise go to them.

a.   Transfer

The first element of a voidable preference is that a "transfer" be made. Since the creation and perfection of a security interest is a conveyance of rights in the debtor's property to the creditor in the most basic sense, these acts are a "transfer" of the debtor's property and the creditor will seldom argue otherwise.[10]

The critical issue in most cases involving grants of security is to determine the time of the transfer. Does the transfer occur when the security interest is created or when the security interest is perfected? A moment's thought will reveal how important this question might be. Assume, for example, that in January a secured creditor takes a security interest valid under 9–203. Creditor does not file a financing statement to perfect it until September and the debtor files for

---

[9]   Proof of a debtor's insolvency may be difficult and expensive. If one believes, as we do, that most who file petitions have long since passed over the brink of solvency, it makes sense to throw the burden on the creditor.

[10]   A secured creditor's foreclosure on property may be a preference if the interest is not properly perfected. See In re Balcain Equip. Co., 80 B.R. 461, 5 UCC2d 766 (Bankr.C.D.Ill.1987).

bankruptcy in October. If the transfer occurred when the security interest was created in January, the creditor's interest is unassailable for the transfer occurred more than 90 days prior to the filing of the petition. If, on the other hand, the transfer occurred at the time of perfection in September, the trustee can attack under section 547.

As a general rule, section 547 chooses the time of perfection as the time of transfer. In the case of personal property, subsection (e)(1)(B) fixes perfection "when a creditor on a simple contract cannot acquire a judicial lien that is superior to the interest of the transferee." This definition of perfection conforms generally to the definition which one would get from Article 9 by reading the perfection provisions and sections 9–102, 9–317 and 9–323 on the rights of lien creditors.

Before going on, understand why the drafters have chosen the time of perfection as opposed to the time of creation as the time of transfer. Had they chosen the time of creation, they would have greatly diminished section 547's capacity to strike down secret liens. In our example in which the creditor creates a security interest in January, the transfer would have become unassailable in April despite the fact that it remained a secret lien until it filed a financing statement in September. To combat just such creditor inaction the drafters selected the time of perfection as the time when the transfer occurs.

Subsection (e)(2)(A) contains an important exception to the rule discussed above. It provides that the transfer occurs at the time it "takes effect between the transferor and the transferee, if such transfer is perfected at, or within 30 days after, such time; . . . ." Thus, if one perfects a security interest within 30 days after its creation under 9–203, the transfer is considered to have occurred when the security interest was created. Note the significance of this rule. It means that if one perfects within 30 days, the security interest can never be challenged under section 547 even if bankruptcy occurs within 90 days of its creation; that is so because the transfer is deemed to have occurred simultaneously with the creation and is therefore not for an *antecedent* debt.

b. The Debtor's Property

The second requirement in section 547(b) is that the transfer be of the "debtor's property." The usual preference is a direct transfer from the debtor to the creditor in the form of the payment of a debt, transfer of a security interest in the debtor's property or the transfer of some other property interest.[11] When the issuer of a letter of credit or a guarantor pays, the transfer will not be a transfer of the debtor's property. But, a transfer of the debtor's property (i.e., granting of a security interest) to the issuer of the letter of credit at the time the letter was issued may have been a preference.

c.   For the Benefit of

When is the payment or grant of security to one person a preference to another? This issue comes up most frequently when there is an unsecured debt that is supported by a guarantee or by a letter of credit.

The issue achieved notoriety in the 1989 Seventh Circuit case, Levit v. Ingersoll Rand Financial Corp.,[12] commonly known as the *Deprizio* case. In that case debtor made a series of payments to secured and unsecured lenders whose debts were guaranteed by officers of the debtor. The trustee argued that these payments were preferences to the *guarantors* because they relieved the guarantors of contingent liability. Asserting the claim against the guarantors was critical in *Deprizio* because the payments were made outside the 90 day preference period and the guarantors—but not the creditors who received the payments—were insiders. The point was pertinent because while the preferential lookback period is generally 90 days before the filing of the bankruptcy petition, with respect to insiders the period is extended to one year before the filing. Holding that there was "one transfer" and not two, Judge Easterbrook concluded that these payments were preferential to the insider guarantors and furthermore that they could be recovered from the creditors—as to whom no preference was alleged—under the provisions of section 550(a) that allows recovery from the initial transferee.

In 1994 Congress amended section 550 to prohibit recovery in a case like *Deprizio*—where transfers were made for the benefit of someone between 90 days and one year before bankruptcy—from anyone other than the "insider."[13] If *Deprizio* arose today there would still be a preference to the *Deprizio* guarantors and that preference could be recovered from them (except, of course, for the fact that Richard had been shot dead pending trial), but it could not be

---

[11]   In re Antinarelli Enterprises, Inc., 107 B.R. 410, 10 UCC2d 1006 (D.Mass.1989).

[12]   874 F.2d 1186 (7th Cir.1989).

[13]   § 550(c) now reads:

"If a transfer made between 90 days and one year before the filing of the petition:

(1) is avoided under section 547(b) of this title; and

(2) was made for the benefit of a creditor that at the time of such transfer was an insider; the trustee may not recover under subsection (a) from a transferee that is not an insider."

recovered from the initial creditors who received the payments more than 90 days before bankruptcy. Thus, the 1994 amendment removed the concern of cautious creditors who routinely seek guarantees that they could be punished for those guarantees by being made to give back payment received beyond 90 days, but within one year. The amendment was buttressed by further amendments in 2005 to section 547, adding subsection (i) which provides a bookending clarification to the preference provision to the effect that any avoidances of transfers to insiders more than 90 days but less than one year before filing, are considered avoided as to the insider only.[14]

These revisions, however, do nothing to resolve the many issues that exist in a three-party transaction where the challenged transfer occurs within the 90 day preference period. First, one must determine whether the payment was "to or for the benefit of a creditor." In *Deprizio*, Judge Easterbrook struggled to determine that the guarantors were themselves "creditors." Because they had subrogation and other contingent rights against the debtor who made the payment to the creditor, they were. One response of many creditors to *Deprizio* was to have guarantors sign waivers of those rights so depriving them of "creditor" status against the debtor and so rendering payments for their benefit, *not* for the benefit of "a creditor." For example, a shareholder who controls a corporate debtor and who causes that debtor to pay one of the shareholder's creditors has not caused a preference since the payment would not be to a creditor of or for the benefit of a creditor of the debtor, but rather to a creditor of the shareholder. Since the shareholder himself is not a creditor of the corporation, there would be no payment for the benefit of a creditor.[15] This approach has now apparently divided the courts, with some holding that such a structure keeps the guarantor from being a "creditor" of the debtor as discussed above, while other decisions ignore the form and focus on the reality that the guarantor could, at any moment, decide to purchase the debt and re-insert himself as a creditor, thus deeming the waivers invalid.[16]

If one assumes that the beneficiary of a payment is a creditor and the payment is made within the preference period, it can be recovered from the beneficiary as a preference. But what if the trustee seeks to recover the payment from the creditor who received it on the ground

---

[14]   11 U.S.C. § 547(i). *See also* H.R. Rep. No. 109–131, 109th Cong., 1st Sess. 143–144 (2005). ("Thus both the previous amendment to section 550 and the perfecting amendment to section 547 protect the noninsider from the avoiding powers of the trustee exercised with respect to transfers made during the 90-day period to one year pre-filing period.")

[15]   The payment we have described probably would be a fraudulent conveyance avoidable under § 548, but it would not be a preference.

[16]   *See* In re Adamson Apparel, Inc., 785 F.3d 1285, 1293 (9th Cir. 2015) (citing cases on both sides of the issue).

that the creditor is "an initial transferee" under section 550? Under the reasoning of *Deprizio*, recovery would be permissible since there was but one transfer and the initial transferee of that transfer was the creditor. Of course, in our hypothetical case the payment to the creditor might itself be a direct preference (without considering the "to or for the benefit of" language); if so, we need never reach the question whether section 550 would allow a recovery from an initial transferee who is not himself the beneficiary of a preference.

Let us turn to some cases where a transfer is claimed to be for the benefit of a creditor. The simplest case is one in which a guarantor or issuer of a letter of credit pays a creditor shortly before bankruptcy. Where the guarantor has not taken security in any of the debtor's assets, there is no preference. This is because the guarantor is transferring its own property, not that of the debtor, and there is no transfer of the property of the debtor.

But what if the guarantor has a security interest in the debtor's assets? Now the payment will affect the property of the estate and will conceivably reduce the amount available to the general creditors. The person making the payment might be a guarantor, the bank on a letter of credit, or simply another creditor. In all of these cases, the court will have to answer the question whether the transfer of the security to the one making payment should be regarded in effect as a preference to the other creditor who receives the payment. Under pre-Code law this was characterized as the Dean v. Davis[17] problem (a case that held the payor guilty of a fraudulent conveyance).

An early case, In re Twist Cap, Inc.,[18] illustrates the no preference case. In *Twist Cap*, the court enjoined payment under a letter of credit on the ground it might constitute a preference since the bank had a perfected security interest in the assets of the debtor. That case caused chaos in markets where the parties depend upon letters of credit. For example, the credit rating of bond issues sometimes depends upon a letter of credit backing those bonds from a bank with stronger credit standing than the issuer. After *Twist Cap*, issuers had difficulty getting a favorable rating for fear that a bankruptcy court might enjoin the bank from paying. If the bank could be enjoined, potential bondholders could not rely upon the letter of credit to establish the credit rating. Elements of that problem have persisted despite the fact that nearly every court that has since considered the issue has held there is no preference (at least if the letter of credit arose and the issuing bank's security interest was perfected prior to the 90 day period) and thus no basis for

---

[17]   242 U.S. 438, 37 S.Ct. 130, 61 L.Ed. 419 (1917).
[18]   1 B.R. 284 (Bankr.M.D.Fla.1979).

injunction.[19] As one court described it, "the grant by a debtor to the issuing bank of a security interest in such debtor's property so as to obtain a letter of credit in favor of such debtor's creditor, is preferential only if such security interest is granted within the 90-day preference period."[20]

Courts have come to a different conclusion when the entire transaction occurs within the 90-day period. In American Bank of Martin County v. Leasing Service Corp. (In re Air Conditioning, Inc. of Stuart),[21] a creditor leasing service obtained a judgment against the debtor for $40,447. Creditor and debtor then agreed to free assets of the debtor (that had been subject to the writs of replevin issued under the judgment) in return for a letter of credit issued June 15, 1984 by the bank, a third party. As consideration for the issuance of the letter of credit, the bank took and perfected a security interest in a $20,000 certificate of deposit owned by the debtor. On July 25, 1984 debtor filed a petition in bankruptcy.

The court rejected the creditor's argument that, in receiving money under the letter of credit, it was receiving no property that belonged to the debtor. Although the creditor had a perfected security interest in the debtor's goods, the goods proved to be of little value and the creditor's interest was subordinate to others' interests. The court concluded that the transfer of the security interest to the issuing bank was a preference since it met all elements of 547(b). This seems a correct outcome when the entire transaction occurs within 90 days of bankruptcy; it differs from *Twist Cap* in that respect. The transaction in *American Bank of Martin County* is tantamount to a debtor's granting security to a preexisting unsecured creditor within the preference period. That this was done in a roundabout way, i.e., security to a new issuing bank whose promise secures the existing creditor, does not render it any less a preference.

Assume that the letter is issued and secured within the 90 day period, the beneficiary presents appropriate documents, and the issuer pays. From whom can and should the trustee recover? Quite clearly the trustee may recover from the beneficiary under the letter of credit (original creditor) who is the "entity for whose benefit such transfer was made" under section 550(a)(1).

---

[19]   See In re Clothes, Inc., 35 B.R. 487 (Bankr.D.N.D.1983); In re Leisure Dynamics, Inc., 33 B.R. 171 (Bankr.D.Minn.1983); In re North Shore & Central Illinois Freight Co., 30 B.R. 377 (Bankr.N.D.Ill.1983); In re M.J. Sales & Distrib. Co., 25 B.R. 608 (Bankr.S.D.N.Y.1982).

[20]   In re ITXS, Inc., 318 B.R. 85, 88 (Bankr. W.D. Pa. 2004) (citing In re Metro Communications, Inc., 115 B.R. 849, 857 (Bankr.W.D.Pa.1990); In re Compton Corp., 831 F.2d 586, 595 (5th Cir.1987)).

[21]   845 F.2d 293 (11th Cir.1988). See also Kellogg v. Blue Quail Energy, Inc. (In re Compton Corp.), 831 F.2d 586 (5th Cir.1987).

The trustee may also be able to recover from the bank as an initial transferee under section 550(a)(1). Arguably (and contrary to *Deprizio*) section 550(a)(1) may refer only to a case where there is a payment made to one person that is then *passed on* to another, not to the case where there is a direct transfer to one *on behalf* of another.[22]

In *American Bank*, the trustee sought recovery from the beneficiary. There is language in the opinion, however, that suggests that the trustee could have recovered from the bank.[23] Given many courts' willingness to allow recoveries from creditors in the insider guarantee context, it is likely that the banks will be found to be initial transferees.[24]

It is possible, too, that an issuing bank may receive a preference in a letter of credit. In the case of In re Security Services, Inc.,[25] an unsecured creditor was the beneficiary of the letter of credit. The letter of credit had an "extend or pay" clause, i.e., the beneficiary had a right to draw on the letter of credit within a certain window of time unless the issuer extended the letter of credit for an additional period. Apparently, the end of the window was within the 90 day preference period. The beneficiary presented a sight draft and demanded that the issuer either extend the letter or pay the sight draft of $1,500,000. The bank extended the letter of credit, but insisted upon a grant of security from the debtor (applicant) to do so. The debtor granted the security interest, the bank extended the letter of credit, and the beneficiary took back its sight draft. Within 90 days of the extension, the debtor declared bankruptcy and ultimately the beneficiary drew the full amount of $1,500,000.

The trustee sued the beneficiary, but the court found that there was no preference as to the beneficiary (creditor) because it was as well off before the renewal as after (since it would have been paid on the letter of credit whether or not the bank was granted security).

The trustee may have been able to recover a preference from the bank had the letter of credit been drawn on before the grant of the security interest (during the preference period), the bank would have been an unsecured creditor of the bankruptcy estate (its customer). Because of the grant of security, the bank wound up as a secured creditor of the estate. While the bank may argue that it gave new

---

[22]   See discussion of the *Deprizio* rule, *supra*.

[23]   845 F.2d at 299.

[24]   Another issue that may arise involving letters of credit and preferences is the case in which an existing unsecured creditor insists upon receiving a letter of credit to support its claim if it is to abstain from foreclosure. If the letter of credit is unsecured, there should be no preference. In this case, there has been no transfer of the debtor's property, but merely a substitution of one unsecured creditor for another.

[25]   132 B.R. 411 (Bankr.W.D.Mo.1991). See also In re Auto Specialties Mfg. Co., 153 B.R. 510 (Bankr.W.D.Mich.1993).

value to the debtor by extending the letter of credit (and thus the transfer was not a preference under 547(b)(2) or (c)(1)), the mere extension of the time of payment on a debt is not new value and that is all the bank did.

In a similar case, one court has found that direct payments from the debtor to a creditor within 90 days of bankruptcy were not a preference where the debtor had provided a *secured* standby letter of credit to the creditor.[26] In *Fuel Oil Supply*, the debtor signed an agreement whereby Gulf transferred 200,000 barrels of gasoline to the debtor. The debtor agreed to return the gasoline in June and July, 1981 together with a $0.01 per gallon "handling differential" for each 30 day period the debtor had the gasoline. The debtor provided Gulf two irrevocable fully secured standby letters of credit. Between July 24 and August 6, the debtor returned the gasoline to Gulf, and the letters of credit were canceled or allowed to expire. On September 4, 1981, an involuntary petition was filed against the debtor.

Seeking to recover the value of the gasoline transferred from Gulf, the DIP alleged that the transfer was a preference. The court found that the transfer was not a preference because the release of the letters of credit was a substantially contemporaneous exchange for new value to the debtor. Since the letters of credit were fully secured, the release of the letters released the bank's security interest on the property. Under section 547(a)(2), the release of property previously transferred by the debtor may constitute new value. Thus, the transfer flunked section 547(b)(2). Note that if the letters of credit had been unsecured, the debtor's shipment of gasoline would have been a preference to the bank. Although Gulf would not receive more through the shipment than it would have in a hypothetical liquidation (since it would have been paid under the letter of credit), the bank would receive more as a result of this transfer (since it would not have to become an unsecured creditor of the debtor). Then the trustee might have recovered the value of the gasoline from Gulf as an "immediate transferee" under 550(a). It is likely that Gulf would be liable under the *Deprizio* line of cases. Contrary to the *Deprizio* holding, we would argue that Gulf should not be considered an "initial transferee" here.

Similar issues may arise outside of the letter of credit context. In the case of In re Hartley,[27] Emory, who had been doing business

---

26   In re Fuel Oil Supply & Terminaling, Inc., 837 F.2d 224, 5 UCC2d 1446 (5th Cir.1988). See also In re Microwave Products of America, Inc., 118 B.R. 566 (Bankr.W.D.Tenn.1990); In re Powerine Oil Co., 59 F.3d 969, 33 Collier Bankr. Cas. 2d 1778 (9th Cir.1995). Another court has found that a creditor's draws on letter of credit count as payments of the debtor to the creditor for purposes of the new value exception. In re Lease-A-Fleet, Inc., 155 B.R. 666 (Bankr.E.D.Pa.1993).

27   55 B.R. 770 (Bankr.N.D.Ohio 1985).

with the debtor, agreed to pay the debtor's bank $500,000 to reduce the amount of the debtor's overdraft. Simultaneously the creditor took a security interest in debtor's various assets. The trustee ultimately challenged the transfer as preferential and recovered the $500,000 payment from the bank. The court rejected the argument that there was no transfer of the debtor's property. Here we believe the court was wrong. The additional security interest given by the debtor to Emory was not like the certificate of deposit in *American Bank*. Rather it was a security interest in various assets that were subject to prior perfected interests of other parties. It turned out the debtor had little or no equity in those assets because of the prior interests. It turns out that the Sixth Circuit agreed with us, reversing and remanding for a determination of the value of the assets in which a security interest was granted.[28] The Sixth Circuit found that "the only depletion of the debtor's estate resulted from his transfer of security interests to" the creditor. Assuming that the value of such security interests indeed proved to be nominal, it seems to us that there was no transfer of property of the debtor and no preference.

d. For or on Account of an Antecedent Debt

The fourth requirement of a preferential transfer—"for or on account of an antecedent debt owed by the debtor before such transfer was made . . . "—is at least theoretically, if not practically, troublesome. Recognizing the difficulty in defining "antecedency," the Federal Bankruptcy Commission proposed that an antecedent debt be "any debt incurred more than five days before a transfer paying or securing the debt." Congress rejected such an explicit definition; the meager help that section 547 gives is to be found in (a)(2) where there is the following definition of "new value:"

> (a)(2) "new value" means money or money's worth in goods, services, or new credit, or release by a transferee of property previously transferred to such transferee in a transaction that is neither void nor voidable by the debtor or the trustee under any applicable law, including proceeds of such property, but does not include an obligation substituted for an existing obligation; . . . .

Presumably if the creditor gave new value concurrent with the transfer in the form of money or the release of property, the transfer is not on account of antecedent debt. Unfortunately, the definition of new value does not touch upon the question how much time can pass between the incurring of the debt and the transfer without the debt's being antecedent. By means other than defining antecedency, the drafters have minimized the problems that otherwise would be presented. First, as indicated above, they have allowed a thirty-day

---

28   In re Hartley, 825 F.2d 1067 (6th Cir 1987).

grace period for perfection and so have removed the antecedency question for any secured creditor who perfects within 30 days of the creation of a security interest. Second, by subsections 547(c)(1) and (2), discussed in Chapter 3–5 below, the drafters have legitimized certain close at hand and ordinary course transactions that would otherwise be subject to attack under section 547(b).

e. Insolvency

The presumption of insolvency in subsection 547(f) will effectively eliminate this issue from the usual voidable preference case. Only in the case of insider preferences that occur more than 90 days prior to the petition will the trustee in bankruptcy have to prove insolvency without benefit of the presumption.

In Chapter 11 cases parties often argue the solvency issue with one another, but that issue is seldom litigated. We suspect that the absence of litigation is attributable to the cost and uncertainty involved in determining whether a large publicly held corporation is solvent or not. We know of cases where, after many expensive hours of work, accounting experts for the competing sides have come to radically different conclusions about the debtor's solvency. These differences of opinion arise from conflicting conclusions about the potential value of the debtor's assets under varying prospective business and industry scenarios.

f. Ninety Days

The sixth requirement of a voidable preference is that the transfer (for or on account of an antecedent debt) occur within the 90-day period immediately preceding bankruptcy. The 90-day period is as arbitrary as was the four-month rule of old section 60(a); the reduction of the time period may have been an attempt to balance the effects of eliminating the "reasonable cause to believe" requirement and of establishing the presumption of insolvency.

Several issues lurk in the 90-day computation. For example, does one count the days from the date of the petition backwards or from the date of the transfer forward? Students of the new math might wonder why it matters whether one counts forward or backward. To understand, consider the case In re J.A.S. Markets, Inc.[29] In that case the transfer occurred on Friday, November 15. If one counted from that day forward and treated November 15 as the first day, day 90 would be the day before the petition, so no transfer within 90 days. If, on the other hand, one counted backward, using the day before the petition as Day 1, November 16 is day 90, but because November 16 was a Saturday, Bankruptcy Rule 9006(a)

---

[29]   113 B.R. 193 (Bankr.W.D.Pa.1990).

extends the period for one more day, so includes Friday, November 15, and makes the transfer challengeable as a preference. In that case, counting backward turned 90 days into 91 days. Most courts count backward beginning with the day before the petition as Day 1.[30] The courts should apply the extending rule of Bankruptcy Rule 9006(a) in calculating the 90-day period under section 547, especially since the 2009 amendments to the rule (and its Federal Rules counterpart Fed.R.Civ.6) clarified that statutory periods falling on Saturdays, Sundays or legal holidays were to be extended "in any statute that does not specify a method of computing time" (which section 547 does not).[31]

In 1992 the Supreme Court settled a recurring issue on when a debtor's check causes a transfer of property: at the creditor's receipt of the check or at final payment by the payor bank. It held that a transfer by conventional check occurs when the check is paid by the payor bank.[32] In *Barnhill*, the debtor delivered a check to the creditor 92 days before bankruptcy. The payor bank honored the check 90 days before bankruptcy. The Court found that the transfer of the debtor's property occurred at the time the bank honored the check.[33] The Court rejected the creditor's argument that the transfer of the check was a conditional transfer under 101(54).[34] The Court found that all that is transferred with a check is a chose in action against the debtor, which cannot be characterized as a conditional right to "property or an interest in property." The Court carefully noted that it did not decide whether its rule would apply to the section 547(c) exceptions as well.[35]

PROBLEM

1.   Creditor tells debtor that it will not lend any more money and that it plans to initiate collection action on the money already outstanding. To mollify creditor, debtor proposes a letter of credit under which a large and reliable bank would pay off creditor if debtor defaults. Creditor agrees and a letter of credit is issued. Assume that bank, foolishly, did not ask for collateral to support its letter of credit obligation. Ten days before

---

[30]   Most of the cases hold that the time period runs backwards from the date the petition is filed and excludes the date of filing. See, e.g., In re Nelson Co., 959 F.2d 1260 (3d Cir.1992); In re Carl Subler Trucking, Inc., 122 B.R. 318 (Bankr.S.D.Ohio 1990).

[31]   *See* In re Jesup & Lamont, Inc., 507 B.R. 452, 464–65 (Bankr. S.D.N.Y. 2014) (citing Fed.R. Bankr. P. 9006).

[32]   Barnhill v. Johnson, 503 U.S. 393, 112 S.Ct. 1386, 118 L.Ed.2d 39, 17 UCC2d 1 (1992).

[33]   *Id.* at 399.

[34]   *Id.* at 402.

[35]   Under the old Act, all creditors of the same "class" had to receive an equal percentage of their claims, or payment would constitute a preference. The new Act decrees equal treatment (by the debtor) of all unsecured creditors.

bankruptcy, debtor defaults and bank pays creditor under the letter of credit. Trustee maintains that creditor has received a preference.

Trustee loses. Payment by bank did not diminish the assets of the debtor. The other creditors of debtor may be suffering envy but they have no legitimate complaint, for they are in the same position as before the transaction occurred. The only change is that bank is now subrogated to creditor's claim, and creditor has left the stage with his money. Technically the transfer is not preferential, for there was no "transfer of an interest in the debtor's property."

2.   Assume now that the bank agrees to issue a letter of credit but that bank takes a security interest in debtor's assets. Trustee now claims that creditor has received a preference.

Trustee wins. Now there is a transfer of the debtor's properties (in the form of the security interest) to the bank and the transfer is "for the benefit of" creditor. So, creditor is clearly guilty of a preference and can be made to return the money. (What about the bank? The bank gave new value, but it might be an "initial" transferee who will have to give up the transferred assets under section 550 (a).)

g.   "Hypothetical Liquidation" Under Section 547(b)(5)

A seventh and final element of a voidable preference is that the transfer must "enable the creditor to receive more than it would receive under a Chapter 7 liquidation" without the transfer. A principal consequence of the seventh condition is that it will protect fully secured creditors—i.e., those whose interests are fully perfected in collateral which equals or exceeds the amount of outstanding debt—who receive payments within the 90-day period. Assume, for example, that a secured creditor has collateral of $200,000 securing a debt of $100,000. If it receives a $25,000 payment on that debt within the 90-day period, it has received the transfer of the debtor's property on behalf of an antecedent debt while the debtor was insolvent, but this is not a transfer that enables the creditor to receive more than it would have on liquidation if the transfer had not been made. A fully secured creditor would have received its entire $100,000 in liquidation if the liquidation had occurred at the time of the transfer. Thus, the seventh condition has not been met and no voidable preference has occurred.

It is important to understand how condition seven might relate to the after-acquired property clause of a security agreement. Assume, for example, that the debtor owes $100,000 and the value of its collateral is also $100,000. Thirty days prior to the filing of the petition, debtor acquires an additional $30,000 of collateral that "feeds" the after-acquired property clause. If the value of the collateral declines over the succeeding 30 days because of depreciation (or for other reasons) by an amount greater than $30,000, how does one apply the seventh criterion to the $30,000 transfer? If it speaks at, and only at, the time of transfer, the transfer does not enable the creditor to receive more than it would have on liquidation at that moment, for, by hypothesis, the collateral equaled the amount of the debt even before the transfer. If the seventh criterion speaks at the time of the filing of the petition, there is a different result. Because of the intervening depreciation in the value of the collateral, the secured creditor now needs all of the $30,000 of after-acquired property to receive full satisfaction. We believe the section speaks at the time of the transfer, not at the time of the filing of the petition.

We regret to report that several courts in quite different settings have found that 547(b)(5) should be applied not at the time of transfer but at the time of the petition, or possibly later.[36] One of us has argued in print that the liquidation test should be applied at the time of the transfer.[37] Had our secured creditor above deemed itself insecure and repossessed in lieu of taking the transfer of additional collateral, presumably there would be no voidable preference. (No one could then prove the collateral depreciated in value.) Why then should there be a voidable preference because the creditor is more patient and waits 90 days, at the end of which time the collateral has declined in value?

h.   Insiders

Before we turn to the exceptions in subsection 547(c), consider the insider preference, a creation of the 1978 Act. If the trustee is able to prove the basic elements, including insolvency (without the benefit of the presumption of insolvency of 547(f)), he can strike down transfers that occurred more than 90 days prior to, but within one year of, the petition. These transfers are avoidable only if they are made "to insiders."

Insiders are defined at length in section 101(31).[38] In general, an insider is a relative of the debtor, an influential or controlling party of the debtor, or a corporate affiliate of the debtor. In some cases, the trustee argues that the extended preference period applies to a particular creditor, usually a bank, because the creditor's relationship with the debtor was close enough to make the creditor a "controlling party" of the debtor. Courts have focused on two factors: the closeness of the relationship between the transferee and the

---

[36]   In re Sufolla, Inc., 2 F.3d 977 (9th Cir.1993); In re Castletons, Inc., 990 F.2d 551, 21 UCC2d 1062 (10th Cir.1993).

[37]   See J. White & D. Israel, Preference Conundrums, 98 Com. L.J. 1 (1993).

[38]   Formerly 11 U.S.C.A. § 101(25).

debtor; and whether the transactions between the transferee and the debtor were conducted at arm's length.[39] A lender is not an insider unless it is able to "exercise actual managerial control over the debtor or has some special affinity with the debtor that extends beyond a business relationship."[40] A creditor does not become an insider merely because it has financial leverage over the debtor, nor does it become an insider because it has a long-term relationship with the debtor.[41] We applaud these courts' reluctance to characterize lenders as insiders. All creditors exercise some influence over their debtor and it is right and proper that they should. This diligence doubtless is good not only for the creditor, but also for society, for it can minimize fraud, bankruptcy and costly default. Nor should long-term business relationships with the debtor raise a presumption of insider status. Lenders should be encouraged to know their debtors and to pursue their rights by informal means, rather than through expensive formal means.

3–5 EXCEPTIONS TO THE PREFERENCE RULES, SECTION 547(c)

Subsection 547(c) contains seven exceptions to the voidable preference rules of subsection (b). Several of these exceptions, and particularly subsection (c)(2), are important. Those who need to know every detail should consult the practitioner's edition; here we outline the issues. The first exception is for transfers that the parties intended to be contemporaneous and which, in fact, turn out to be substantially contemporaneous but not exactly contemporaneous. For example, a seller delivers goods to a buyer in return for the buyer's check. When the seller holds the check for several days before presenting it for payment, the trustee might argue that the payment was on an antecedent debt because of the few days intervening between the transfer of title to the goods and final payment on the check. Subsection (c)(1) protects the creditor here.

How far (c)(1) reaches beyond checks is unclear. The term "substantially contemporaneous" is not precise; it could conceivably validate the perfection of a security interest more than 30 days after its attachment or permit the repayment of a loan that was

---

[39]   In re Murchison, 154 B.R. 909, 911–12 (Bankr.N.D.Tex.1993); Badger Freightways, Inc. v. Continental Illinois Nat'l Bank and Trust Co., 106 B.R. 971, 982 (Bankr.N.D.Ill.1989).

[40]   In re Murchison, 154 B.R. at 913.

[41]   In re Holloway, 955 F.2d 1008 (5th Cir.1992) (ex-wife an insider despite divorce 20 years earlier where the relationship was still close); In re Wescorp, Inc., 148 B.R. 161 (Bankr.D.Conn.1992); In re Torcise, 146 B.R. 303 (Bankr.S.D.Fla.1992); In re Friedman, 126 B.R. 63, 69–70 (B.A.P. 9th Cir.1991) (real estate brokers not insiders where they did not exercise control of debtor's business affairs); In re Octagon Roofing, 124 B.R. 522 (Bankr.N.D.Ill.1991).

outstanding for a week or 10 days. Most courts have concluded that (c)(1) is not intended to protect a secured creditor who has failed to perfect within the perfection window (formerly 10 days, now 30).[42] We agree with those cases. While the courts have recognized the check cases described above as within the subsection, they have denied protection for checks dishonored and later paid.[43] Nor have the drawee banks fared any better in arguing that their extension of provisional and overdraft credit to debtors writing checks with insufficient funds, constitutes a contemporaneous exchange of new value, given that the exchange was not intended at the inception of the events.[44]

The second exception, protecting ordinary course payments, is the most important. Arising from humble beginnings before 1978, later modified and molded by court interpretation, the ordinary course rule in (c)(2) now validates a large percentage of all transactions that would otherwise be regarded as preferences under subsection (b).

Subsection (c)(2) springs from a rule of convenience practiced under the Bankruptcy Act of 1898 that disregarded small payments as *de minimis*. In its original form in the 1978 Act, subsection (c)(2) protected only payments made within 45 days after the debt was incurred; in that format, it appeared to be aimed at routine, small payments such as those to utilities, mortgagees, and the like. After the 45-day limit was removed in 1984 and the Supreme Court in 1991 interpreted the section to apply not merely to short-term payments, but to any ordinary course payment,[45] the exception has assumed grand proportions. It now applies not only to consumers' utility payments and to routine payments to trade creditors, but also to payments of tens of thousands and perhaps millions of dollars to conventional and long-term lenders such as banks. The subsection was made even more generous in 2005 when subsections (A) and (B) were made alternative; now the creditor need only satisfy one **or** the other.

There are now hundreds of cases on the question of what is an ordinary course payment. Note that there are a series of adjectives and phrases that limit the ordinary course transaction. The debt must have been incurred in the ordinary course of business or

---

[42]   In re Walker, 161 B.R. 484 (Bankr.D.Idaho 1993); In re Holder, 892 F.2d 29 (4th Cir.1989); In re Davis, 734 F.2d 604 (11th Cir.1984); In re Arnett, 731 F.2d 358 (6th Cir.1984). But see Pine Top Ins. Co. v. Bank of America Nat'l Trust and Sav. Ass'n, 969 F.2d 321 (7th Cir.1992); In re Telecash Industries, Inc., 104 B.R. 401 (Bankr.D.Utah 1989).

[43]   In re Barefoot, 952 F.2d 795, 16 UCC2d 417 (4th Cir.1991).

[44]   In re AgriProcessors, Inc., 859 F.3d 599 (8th Cir. 2017).

[45]   Union Bank v. Wolas, 502 U.S. 151, 112 S.Ct. 527, 116 L.Ed.2d 514 (1991).

financial affairs of both the debtor and the transferee. In addition, the payment must have been made in the ordinary course, or according to ordinary business terms. Examples of things not in the ordinary course are easy to imagine. Payments made in direct response to creditor pressure stimulated by the deteriorating financial condition of the debtor are not ordinary course payments.[46] On the other hand, when creditor pressure and other forms of deviance shade off into what is common or expected, even payments that are not utterly common and mundane may be regarded as ordinary course. Even late payments may be in the ordinary course where the debtor is habitually late and the industry tolerates late payments.[47] The "ordinariness" of the payment activity can be viewed from the parties' own history if such exists; otherwise, the court may consider the debtor's and transferee's respective historical practices, if such practices involved similarly situated parties.[48]

To determine whether a payment was according to ordinary business terms, most courts look both to the practice between the particular creditor and the particular debtor, and to practice in the trade.[49] We have trouble understanding what "according to ordinary business terms" adds to the "ordinary course" language. Courts have given conflicting, and not always persuasive, explanations. Since, after 2005, a creditor needs to satisfy only one of these formulations ((A) or (B)), the problem may go away.

In short, it is hard to exaggerate the importance of subsection (c)(2). The tiny leak in the Act of 1898—that *de minimis* payments should not be set aside—grew in 1978 to a trickle of utility payments and has now exploded into a torrent of payments of every conceivable kind. With the blessing of the Supreme Court in *Union Bank*, the

---

[46] See, e.g., In re Production Steel, Inc., 54 B.R. 417, 42 UCC 1285 (Bankr.M.D.Tenn.1985); In re Tennessee Chem. Co., 159 B.R. 501, 511 (Bankr.E.D.Tenn.1993), aff'd in part, rev'd in part, 112 F.3d 234 (6th Cir. 1997); In re Craig Oil Co., 785 F.2d 1563 (11th Cir.1986). See also In re Colonial Discount Corp., 807 F.2d 594 (7th Cir.1986), cert. denied 481 U.S. 1029, 107 S.Ct. 1954, 95 L.Ed.2d 526 (1987); In re Seawinds Ltd., 888 F.2d 640 (9th Cir.1989).

[47] In re U.S.A. Inns of Eureka Springs, Arkansas, Inc., 9 F.3d 680 (8th Cir.1993) (late and irregular payments were in the ordinary course because savings and loans typically accepted late and irregular payments from "real estate trouble loans"); In re Tolona Pizza Products Corp., 3 F.3d 1029, 1033 (7th Cir.1993); Yurika Foods Corp. v. United Parcel Serv., 888 F.2d 42 (6th Cir.1989). But see In re Meridith Hoffman Partners, 12 F.3d 1549 (10th Cir.1993), cert. denied sub nom.; Balcor Real Estate Holdings, Inc. v. Clark, 512 U.S. 1206, 114 S.Ct. 2677, 129 L.Ed.2d 812 (1994) (escrow arrangement not in the ordinary course of business because creditors use such an arrangement only in extraordinary circumstances, when debtors are in trouble).

[48] See In re Ahaza Systems, Inc., 482 F.3d 1118 (9th Cir. 2007).

[49] See, e.g., In re U.S.A. Inns of Eureka Springs, Arkansas, Inc., 9 F.3d 680 (8th Cir.1993).

subsection now protects the high and mighty as well as the petit bourgeois.

The third and fourth exceptions, subsections (c)(3) and (c)(4), apply to purchase money loans and to cases where new value is given by the creditor in the preference period after it has already received a preference. Neither of these subsections contains much mystery. We believe that (c)(3) is self explanatory. The only puzzling part of (c)(4) is that it codifies only one-half of the "net result rule." That is to say, subsection (4) allows value given only "after" a transfer to protect the transferee, not value given in the preference period, but prior to the transfer.[50] The oft-cited reason for the (c)(4) exception is to encourage creditors to continue to deal with a troubled debtor, and to reward subsequent advances of new value which have the effect of replenishing the estate.[51]

Subsection (c)(5) protects the floating lien—the after-acquired clause in inventory and receivables. Prior to 1978, courts had found the time for perfection of an after-acquired property was at the time of filing. Thus, the trustee in bankruptcy could never attack the acquisition of after-acquired property that fattened the belly of the secured creditor even though it occurred within the 90-day period as long, as the secured creditor had filed a financing statement outside that period. Section 547(e)(3) changes that rule by providing that no "transfer" can occur until the after-acquired asset is acquired.

In response to creditor complaints that the normal after-acquired property clause was not preferential in practice or in spirit, the drafters adopted (c)(5). We leave the intricacies of (c)(5) to the practitioner's edition and to books on bankruptcy. Briefly, it provides that a creditor who does not "build up" its collateral-to-debt ratio within the 90-day period prior to bankruptcy will probably be spared a preference attack as to the assets that were acquired by the debtor during that period even though those acquisitions would otherwise be transfers that violate subsection (b). If, on the other hand, the creditor causes the debtor to build the collateral-to-debt ratio from a low level to a high level within the 90-day period, that build up will sometimes be preferential under (b) and, to the extent of the buildup within the 90-day period, will not be saved by (c)(5).

---

[50]   See Note 15, p. 244 of Vol.4 of the 5th ed. of the Practitioner's Edition.

[51]   *See, e.g.,* In re Musicland Holding Corp., 462 B.R. 66 (Bankr. S.D.N.Y. 2011) (citing Jones Truck Lines, Inc. v. Central States, Southeast and Southwest Areas Pension Fund (In re Jones Truck Lines), 130 F.3d 323, 326 (8th Cir.1997); Southern Technical Coll., Inc. v. Hood, 89 F.3d 1381, 1384 (8th Cir.1996); Kroh Bros. Dev. Co. v. Cont'l Constr. Eng'rs, Inc. (In re Kroh Bros. Dev. Co.), 930 F.2d 648, 651 (8th Cir.1991)).

Subsection (c)(6) is merely a housekeeping detail included in section 547 to insure that the section does not overturn the generous treatment granted to statutory lienors under section 545. Under the terms of 545 many statutory liens can be perfected within the 90-day period and even in some cases beyond the filing of the petition, and yet will be invulnerable to the trustee's attack. But for (c)(6), some of those transfers could be attacked as preferences under 547.[52]

Subsection (c)(7) protects spouses or ex-spouses from avoidance of any payments in satisfaction of a "domestic support obligation."

Subsection (c)(8) protects transfers by "an individual debtor" whose debts are "primarily consumer debts" to the extent such transfer is less than $600. In effect, this will protect conventional and modest payments by consumer debtors to banks, finance companies, utilities, and many others. It will also protect certain wage and bank account garnishments done within 90 days of bankruptcy.

Subsection (c)(9) is in effect a de minimis rule of $6,425 per transfer for a debtor whose debts are not "primarily consumer debts." This means that a small business' payments of under $6,425 to various creditors are not voidable.[53]

PROBLEM

1.   Assume the debtor makes a payment of $1 million to creditor on the 80th day before debtor files for bankruptcy. A week later creditor advances the other $500,000 to debtor. Trustee challenges the entire million-dollar payment as preferential.

Because of section 547(c)(4), only the $500,000 is preferential. The creditor gets a bonus because of the new loan. For reasons that we do not understand, the creditor would not enjoy this benefit if the new loan had preceded the payment by the debtor.

2.   Debtor, a successful retailer before bankruptcy, made several payments in excess of $200,000 each to several trade creditors during the preference period. Creditor One had received $200,000 in payments periodically during the preceding year. Creditor Two had received no payments during the six-months preceding and received this payment in response to an angry confrontation between the chief executive officers. Are the payments to Creditor One or Creditor Two saved by the "ordinary course" exception?

The first case seems easy; since there is a practice on which the creditor is relying, this seems to be an ordinary course payment. The

---

[52]   An IRS tax lien is one example of a statutory lien protected by § 547(c)(6). See In re Rogers Refrigeration, Inc., 33 B.R. 59 (Bankr.D.Or.1983) (properly filed tax lien protected from avoidance); In re PDQ Copy Center, Inc., 26 B.R. 77 (Bankr.S.D.N.Y.1982).

[53]   Note that this dollar amount is adjusted every three years. The current amount of $6,425 was set under 11 U.S.C. § 104; 81 Fed. Reg. 8748 (Feb. 22, 2016).

second case is harder; the creditor might argue that it received a payment according to "ordinary business terms" but it is hard to know what that means. Surely the practice between the parties does not make this solitary payment into an ordinary course payment, quite to the contrary. So we suspect that Creditor Two will not enjoy the exception and that the payment will be found to be preferential.

3.   Assume that creditor has a security interest in debtor's inventory. Ninety days prior to bankruptcy the debt stood at $1 million and the collateral was worth $800,000. During the 90 days prior to bankruptcy the entire $800,000 of collateral was sold to bona fide purchasers and was replaced with collateral that stands at $600,000 at the date the petition is filed. Trustee argues that the property acquired within the 90 days ($600,000) was a preferential transfer to the creditor.

Subsection (c)(5) saves the secured creditor here. The operation of the after-acquired property clause has not caused a "reduction . . . of any amount by which the debt secured by such security interest exceeded the value of all security interests" 90 days before the bankruptcy.

4.   Consumer debtor, hounded by one of his credit card companies, made a $400 payment to the credit card company 50 days before his bankruptcy. Is this a preference?

This payment is saved by subsection (c)(8). If the credit card company had been greedier and gotten a payment of $800, it appears that it would have had to pay back the entire $800 not just the $200 excess. Do you agree with that interpretation of subsection (8)?

3–6   TRUSTEE'S SUBROGATION TO THE CLAIMS OF OTHERS, SECTION 544(b)

The enactment of the Uniform Commercial Code radically reduced the importance of section 544(b).[54] To understand the question one should go back to Moore v. Bay,[55] the seed which produced a flourishing academic debate. That case, a two-paragraph opinion by Justice Oliver Wendell Holmes in his dotage, held that a trustee standing in the shoes of a "gap" creditor with only a modest claim could entirely avoid the claim of the secured creditor under the law of California. A "gap" creditor is one who makes its loan after a secured creditor's interest attaches but before it is perfected. In theory, the gap creditor is misled, for it makes its loan in ignorance of the security interest and in theoretical reliance upon the freedom of the debtor's assets from the claims of the secured creditor.

---

[54]   The attraction to § 70(e) for the trustee was that he was not limited in his avoidance power by the amount of the lien to which he was subrogated. The trustee could use a $50 claim to defeat a $1,000 security interest and thereby avoid the interest for the benefit of all unsecured creditors. This differed substantially from the preservation clauses of §§ 60(b), 67(a)(3), 67(c)(2) and 67(d) which confined the trustee's power to the amount of the lien to which he was subrogated.

[55]   284 U.S. 4, 52 S.Ct. 3, 76 L.Ed. 133 (1931).

First, one should understand how the enactment of the Uniform Commercial Code has rendered *Moore* and section 544(b) less important than 70(e) was in a different regime. Under the pre-Code law of some states, an unsecured creditor who lent in the gap could avoid the security interest in whose gap he lent. Note well, this was a state law right brought to bankruptcy by 544(b)'s predecessor.

By the enactment of the predecessors of sections 9–102, 9–201, 9–317 and 9–323, the Code changed the relevant state law. Under 9–201 an unperfected security interest is valid against all parties, except those who are explicitly given priority. Gap creditors do not get priority unless they acquire judicial liens within that gap. That is to say, if A grants a security interest that is perfected 30 days later and B lends in the 30-day gap, B, the gap creditor is subordinate to the secured creditor's interest under the UCC, unless the gap creditor procures a lien within the gap, a most unlikely event. Since the trustee merely steps into the shoes of the actual creditor under 544(b), those rights of the trustee rise and fall with the state law rights of the actual creditor. In modern practice, judicial liens are more scarce than hen's teeth. For these reasons, section 544(b) has been shrunk by the enactment of the UCC.

The Bankruptcy Reform Act of 1978 resolved the few remaining issues. Assume, for example, that our gap creditor was a lien creditor. Alternatively, assume that a second secured creditor lent and perfected in the gap. These present several additional issues. First, they present the *Moore* question: does the trustee upset the secured creditor's rights entirely or does the trustee merely take priority over the secured creditor to the extent of the claim of the one represented? As enacted, and contrary to the Bankruptcy Commission's initial proposal, section 544(b) leaves us with the old rule, namely, that the trustee upsets the security interest entirely. That is the significance of the language in 544(b); the trustee may "avoid" any transfer. "Avoid" is carefully chosen, and the fact that it does not say "is prior to" or "avoid to a limited extent" or language of that sort, shows that Congress intended to upset the interest entirely Moreover, the legislative reports at the time of the enactment of the 1978 Code confirmed such intention evidenced by the language of the text.[56] Second, is the trustee subrogated under section 544(b) only to the rights of unsecured creditors or also to the rights of lien creditors and other secured creditors whose interests the trustee could not strike

---

[56]   H. Rep. No. 95–595, 95th Cong., 1st Sess. 370 (1977); S. Rep. No. 95–989, 95th Cong., 2d Sess. 85 (1978).

down? Here it limits subrogation to the claims of unsecured creditors. Subsection (b) reads in pertinent part[57] as follows:

> (b) . . . the trustee may avoid any transfer of an interest of the debtor in property or any obligation incurred by the debtor that is voidable under applicable law by a creditor holding an *unsecured claim* that is allowable under section 502 of this title or that is not allowable only under section 502(e) of this title (emphasis added).

To the extent that the trustee can strike down security interests or liens under section 547 or under other avoidance sections, section 551, not section 544(b), preserves those rights and subrogates the trustee to those claims. The trustee may use only those claims which he can strike down. Thus, if we have a case with two secured creditors, one junior to the other, but neither of which may be challenged under any of the avoidance provisions, it is clear under the Bankruptcy Reform Act of 1978 that the trustee may not subrogate himself to the senior creditor's rights in order to avoid the junior creditor's claims.[58]

PROBLEM

1.   Lender 1 lends money to debtor and takes a security interest, then files a financing statement 30 days later. In the 30-day period between the granting of the security interest and perfection by Lender 1, Lender 2 makes an unsecured loan to the same debtor. Assume the debtor falsely claims that there are no security interests in any of his assets. Can debtor's bankruptcy trustee claim to be subrogated to the claim of Lender 2 and defeat Lender 1?

---

[57]   The preamble to subsection 544(b)(1) refers to subsection (b)(2), which protects certain charitable contributions from avoidance, in the context of the trustee seeking to invoke 544(b) to recover fraudulent transfers.

[58]   Could a trustee use section 544(b) and state fraudulent conveyance law to upset a foreclosure? Until the *BFP* case (BFP v. Resolution Trust Corp., 511 U.S. 531, 114 S.Ct. 1757, 128 L.Ed.2d 556 (1994)) held otherwise, federal courts had sometimes recognized a right of the trustee to upset a foreclosure sale under the provisions of section 548. *BFP* closes that avenue. Could a clever trustee now use 544(b) and the state fraudulent conveyance law to the same effect? We doubt it. In using section 544(b), the trustee would be subrogating himself to the rights of a creditor and that creditor would be asserting that a state foreclosure sale proper under one state law would nevertheless be a fraudulent conveyance under another law of the same state. To say that Congress' enacting 548 shows an intention to overturn properly conducted state-law foreclosure proceedings may be plausible; to say that a state legislature intended the same thing about its own law is not plausible. One would be arguing that the state legislature intended to condemn as fraudulent the acts of one who complied with complex, time-consuming and expensive foreclosure procedures designed by the same legislature explicitly to protect the debtor's interest. A court should be hesitant to find such an intent in the state's adoption of two statutes. To the extent of conflict, the more particular (foreclosure laws) should govern the more general (fraudulent conveyance laws).

Despite the fact the trustee is subrogated to Lender 2, he loses. He loses because Lender 2 is subordinate to the unperfected security interest of Lender 1. Under section 9–201, Lender 1 has priority. Read the section.

2.   Parent has two subsidiaries, Able and Cain. Parent borrows $10 million from bank and directs its subsidiaries to grant bank a security interest in all of their assets to secure the loan. Debtor and both subsidiaries then file for bankruptcy. Trustee uses section 544(b) to subrogate itself to the rights of the other creditors of the two subsidiaries. Trustee will argue that the state fraudulent conveyance laws were violated because the subsidiaries never received reasonable equivalent value for granting security. The value, according to the trustee, went exclusively to the shareholders and perhaps to the creditors of Parent.

Although he has an uphill battle, the trustee might win here. The secured creditor will resort to arguing that value—in the form of new business arising from Parent's business—went to the subsidiaries. In any case these are the circumstances under which section 544(b) will come into play.

3.   Buyers are going to buy "Target." They propose to grant a security interest in all of Target's assets to secure the loan from the bank to buy out the shareholders of Target. When the transaction is completed, the pre-existing creditors of Target will be in a manifestly diminished position. The cumulative effect of the transaction is to take money out of Target and pay it to the shareholders. Thus, in effect, elevating them over the corporation's creditors to whom they should have been subordinate. Assume that Target goes into bankruptcy a year after the transaction. To the bank's argument that it gave value in the form of a loan, the trustee will argue that the bank was a knowing conspirator in a smelly transaction. Will the bank's security interest be avoided?

There are some cases from the leveraged buyouts of the 1980s and 1990s that appear to say so. Those cases carry enough weight that lawyers are hesitant to give assurances to their clients that there is no fraudulent conveyance.

3–7 RECLAMATION RIGHTS VS. THE TRUSTEE IN BANKRUPTCY, SECTIONS 2–702, 546(c)

As a general proposition, an unsecured seller of goods on credit is no better than a general creditor—even as to the very goods it sold to the buyer. Section 2–702 of the UCC is the exception to that general rule. It authorizes the seller to refuse to deliver upon buyer's insolvency and in certain cases permits the unsecured seller to recover goods if a demand is made within 10 days after the buyer's receipt of the goods or over a longer period if buyer has misrepresented its solvency in writing to the seller. In theory, this seller is more deserving than a conventional creditor, for the debtor has committed fraud by buying on credit while insolvent.

In its attempt to reclaim the goods under 2–702, the seller is often confronted with a trustee in bankruptcy who claims competing rights in the goods, with a secured creditor who claims to be a bona fide purchaser, or with another purchaser who claims similar rights. Subsection (3) of 2–702 subordinates the seller to the rights of bona fide purchasers—including the rights of a secured creditor who claims as a bona fide purchaser under its after-acquired property clause.[59] Generally, the section gives the seller superiority over intervening lien creditors of the buyer.

In the 2005 amendments to the Bankruptcy Code, Congress substantially expanded the rights of reclamation that existed in Article 2 of the UCC and in the prior versions of section 546(c). The new version of section 546 grants a freestanding right in the federal law that does not depend upon section 2–702. Here the seller may reclaim goods that were given to an insolvent buyer "within 45 days" of the bankruptcy filing. The seller must reclaim the goods in writing within 45 days after the date of receipt by the debtor; provided, if this 45-day notice period expires post-petition (because the goods were received less than 45 days before the filing of the petition), the deadline cannot extend beyond 20 days after filing.

Section 546(c)(2) references an ancillary right in section 503(b)(9) given to sellers of goods to buyers who slide into bankruptcy. Under section 503(b)(9), the seller is entitled to claim a priority administrative expense claim for the value of any goods received by an ordinary seller in the 20 days before bankruptcy filing. Administrative expense claims are given top priority in the bankruptcy distribution, and are normally reserved only for the debtor's post-filing dealing. The availability of an administrative expense claim is available even if the seller fails to provide proper reclamation notice under section 546(c).[60]

Section 2–702(3) provided that buyers in the ordinary course or other good-faith purchasers for value—presumably those who purchase the goods in the interim (as well as those security interests which include capturing after-acquired clauses) between delivery to the buyer and seller's attempt to reclaim them—would defeat a seller's reclamation effort. Since the reclamation right against a bankrupt debtor is now fully encompassed in section 546, the status of the cases decided under section 2–702(3) are in doubt. Section 546(c)(1) has a mere offhanded reference which notes that the right to reclamation is "subject to the prior rights of a holder of a security

---

[59]   See, e.g., In the Matter of Reliable Drug Stores, Inc., 70 F.3d 948 (7th Cir.1995); In re Pester Ref. Co., 964 F.2d 842 (8th Cir.1992).

[60]   11 U.S.C. § 546(c)(2).

interest." Whether this formulation is intended to carry forward the holdings in the cases under section 2–702 (3), is not clear.

It seems likely that courts interpreting section 546 will find the decisions under section 2–702(3) to be persuasive. Consider some examples. First, the courts have recognized a secured creditor as a good faith purchaser entitled to the protection of 2–702(3). But the courts have disagreed about the consequences when bankruptcy keeps the secured creditor from seizing the collateral. How does the incipient but unexercised right of the secured creditor affect the competition that ensues between the trustee, on the one hand, and the reclaiming buyer, on the other?[61] The secured creditor might not assert its claim for a variety of reasons. It might be fully secured or it might have waived its claim as part of the confirmation of the plan.[62]

In United States v. Westside Bank,[63] a seller of goods asserted reclamation rights to proceeds from the sale of goods delivered just prior to foreclosure. Prior to delivery of goods by seller, Westside Bank had perfected a security interest in after-acquired property of Texas Electronics Mart, Inc. (TEMI) in order to secure a loan. Upon default by TEMI, all assets of TEMI were sold at foreclosure and the funds, less Westside's interest, were deposited with the district court for distribution among TEMI's creditors. Reasoning that foreclosure by a prior secured lender cuts short a seller's right to reclamation, the district court held the seller of goods had no right to proceeds from the sale of assets. Judge Brown reversed, in part, holding that a seller of goods in the setting of foreclosure maintains priority status against a buyer's unsecured creditors and foreclosure by a prior secured lender does not terminate a reclaiming seller's right to remaining proceeds. Hence, a seller of goods in compliance with statutory requirements for reclamation of goods retains priority status to the traceable proceeds from the sale of goods seller seeks to reclaim, but takes subject to the rights of prior perfected secured lenders.

Particularly in its current form, section 546(c) is important for many parties in bankruptcy cases. Many companies that file Chapter 11 cases will have purchased goods within the 45 days prior to the petition. The expanded reclamation right, as well as the new administrative claim will, at the very least, strengthen the bargaining position of the sellers of those goods. For the unusual case

---

[61]   See In re Samuels & Co., 510 F.2d 139, 16 UCC 577 (5th Cir.1975), rev'd, 526 F.2d 1238, 18 UCC 545 (1976), cert. denied sub nom., Stowers v. Mahon, 429 U.S. 834, 97 S.Ct. 98, 50 L.Ed.2d 99 (1976).

[62]   In re Pester Refining Co., 964 F.2d 842, 17 UCC2d 1138 (8th Cir.1992).

[63]   732 F.2d 1258 (5th Cir.1984).

where the harried debtor does not go into bankruptcy, section 2–702 remains important.

Chapter 4

PRIORITY CONFLICTS

Analysis

4–1 INTRODUCTION

Some rules of priority are exquisitely complicated, while others are quite straightforward and easy to understand. Behind each rule is a policy and so a reason. You will understand the rules more fully, remember them more accurately, and think about them more clearly if you try to understand the policy behind each rule. Here we deal with Article 9's most basic priority disputes—those between bankruptcy trustee and creditor—and with the most sophisticated— those involving priority of fixture claimants and buyers of chattel paper.

As a starting point, you should think of these rules as serial competitions pitting the secured creditor against a series of opponents. In each case one competitor is a secured creditor; the other competitor changes with each section. Thus section 9–317 covers a secured creditor vs. a lien creditor (as well as buyers and lessees); 9–322 covers the case of a secured creditor vs. other secured creditors. Because the sections are intricate, interrelated, and logical, we suspect they get more consideration in law school than they deserve. Of course, Article 9 has no corner on the priority conflict market. Some of the most ancient priority rules are set down in American real property law; others appear in Article 4, Article 7 and elsewhere in the UCC. In this Chapter, we deal exclusively with cases where one of the claimants is an Article 9 secured creditor.

Consider first the most important sections and their coverage: section 9–201—the secured creditor wins unless the competitor finds a rule that says otherwise; section 9–317—secured creditors vs. lien creditors (as well as buyers and lessees); section 9–322—secured creditors vs. secured creditors; section 9–324—purchase money secured creditors vs. other secured creditors (see also section 9–317, purchase money secured creditors vs. lien creditors, buyers and lessees); section 9–334—security interests in fixtures and crops; and section 9–320—secured creditor vs. buyer of goods from the debtor in the ordinary course. Most of the remaining priority rules are particular applications of those listed above or, in some cases, deal with quite narrow areas. We cover most of them in this Chapter.

4–2   RIGHTS OF UNPERFECTED SECURED CREDITORS VS. UNSECURED CREDITORS WITH AND WITHOUT JUDICIAL LIENS

Section 9–201 states the basic right of the secured creditor vs. other competitors. Subsection (a) reads as follows:

> Except as otherwise provided in the Uniform Commercial Code, a security agreement is effective according to its terms between the parties, against purchasers of the collateral, and against creditors.

The sentence means what it says; a secured creditor, even an unperfected secured creditor, has greater rights in its collateral than any other creditor unless the Code provides otherwise. Of course, a creditor without a security interest or a lien has no claim on any specific collateral and the principal consequence of 9–201 is to give an unperfected but *secured* creditor rights superior to the rights of that *unsecured* creditor.

Section 9–317 subordinates an unperfected secured creditor to a lien creditor and, by negative implication, says that a perfected secured creditor beats a lien creditor (assuming, generally, that the secured creditor has acted to protect its rights under the section prior to the judgment creditor's acquisition of a lien). The most important part of 9–317 is (a)(2) which renders a security interest subordinate to the rights of one who "becomes a lien creditor before the earlier of the time: (A) the security interest or agricultural lien is perfected; or (B) one of the conditions specified in Section 9–203(b)(3) is met [usually obtaining a signed security agreement] and a financing statement covering the collateral is filed." Thus, if a bank takes a security interest in the debtor's equipment but fails to file a financing statement or to take possession, and an unsecured creditor levies against the property and so procures a judicial lien on it, this formerly unsecured creditor (now a "lien creditor") will defeat the prior unperfected secured creditor. Subsection (e) states an exception to this rule for purchase money claims; the holder of a purchase money security interest has 20 days after the debtor receives delivery of the collateral in which to file. If that secured creditor files within such 20-day period, the security interest takes priority over the rights of a lien creditor that attaches to the collateral between the time the security interest arose and the time of the filing.

Subsections (b), (c), and (d) give priority to a variety of buyers, lessees, and licensees over unperfected secured creditors. Under these provisions, these parties "take free" of the security interest. The rules in the various subsections are somewhat different but all require that the party who is to defeat the secured creditor must give "value" and, in the case of tangibles (or as to intangible collateral represented by an indispensable "res" like an instrument), "receive delivery," all "without knowledge of the security interest."

In section 9–317, the drafters have chosen the language "takes free" in lieu of "is subordinate to." And the statute provides that all buyers meeting the qualifications take free, not just "buyers not in ordinary course of business". As stated earlier, the basic rule in (a)(2) no longer requires the victorious secured creditor to be perfected before the lien becomes effective as a means to achieve priority over a lien creditor; it is alternatively sufficient that a written security agreement is signed by the debtor, along with a financing statement filed before that time. In that sense, section 9–317 follows the basic rule always applied in competition between secured creditors— priority dates from the earlier of filing or perfection.

What is implicit in the drafters' decisions here? In some cases, a "gap" creditor who lends money in the "gap" after another creditor's security interest attached, but before it was perfected, can make a plausible claim that he has been injured. Prior to the adoption of Article 9, a few states gave priority to gap creditors over unperfected secured creditors even though the gap creditors had no lien. By generally subordinating creditors without liens to unperfected security interests, 9–201 makes a conscious judgment that those "gap" creditors and others like them are not entitled to protection. As we point out in Chapter 3, this decision means that section 544(b) of the Bankruptcy Code has much less significance than it would otherwise have.

In general, the secured creditor has claims on the collateral superior to those of any unsecured creditor who has no lien. A secured but unperfected creditor will usually be subordinate to lien creditors and to all buyers who give value and take without knowledge.

PROBLEM

To understand how section 9–317 works, consider three hypothetical cases.

1.   Bank takes a security interest in debtor's equipment on March 1. On that day, the parties sign a security agreement and the bank advances funds to the debtor. A week later, on March 8, a third party gets a lien. Are the lien holder's rights superior to the bank's rights?

Unless the secured creditor, Bank, is a purchase money lender and files in time, the lien creditor defeats it.

2.   Instead of a lien holder, assume that a buyer purchases the debtor's equipment on March 8. Since the purchaser is buying equipment and not inventory, the purchaser cannot be a buyer in the ordinary course that would be entitled, under section 9–320, to defeat even a perfected security interest. Instead, the buyer must claim that he defeats the unperfected secured creditor under section 9–317(b).

What if the buyer had knowledge of bank's security interest at the time of his purchase? Then he is subordinated. Read subsection (b) carefully. You will note the buyer is subordinated if he has knowledge (meaning actual knowledge not merely notice) or if he does not take "delivery" before perfection.

3.   Change the facts so that the parties sign a security agreement and the secured creditor files a financing statement on March 1. Because the bank has not yet given value, its security interest has not attached and therefore is not perfected. Does that subordinate the bank to a lien creditor who gets his lien eight days later?

The answer is no. Read subsection (a)(2) carefully; it elevates secured creditors over the lien creditor despite the absence of perfection, so long as a financing statement had been filed and the debtor has signed a written security agreement. What is the justification for this outcome? Presumably this outcome is justified by the presence of a public notice (the filing of the financing statement) at the time the competing claim arose. Note the same rule applies with respect to competing secured creditors under section 9–322.

4–3   BASIC PRIORITIES AMONG CONFLICTING SECURITY INTERESTS: FIRST IN TIME, FIRST IN RIGHT, SECTIONS 9–322, 9–323

Section 9–322(a) states the basic priorities among certain secured creditors concisely and precisely:

[General priority rules.] Except as otherwise provided in this section, priority among conflicting security interests and agricultural liens in the same collateral is determined according to the following rules:

(1) Conflicting perfected security interests and agricultural liens rank according to priority in time of filing or perfection.

Priority dates from the earlier of the time a filing covering the collateral is first made or the security interest or agricultural lien is first perfected, if there is no period thereafter when there is neither filing nor perfection.

(2) A perfected security interest or agricultural lien has priority over a conflicting unperfected security interest or agricultural lien.

(3) The first security interest or agricultural lien to attach or become effective has priority if conflicting security interests and agricultural liens are unperfected.

Section 9–322 replaces a multitude of unclear and inconsistent state laws that existed prior to the adoption of the Uniform Commercial Code. First in time, first in right—that general rule runs like a thread through virtually all priority schemes and 9–322 is no exception. However, the Code is uniquely precise. The drafters of the Code well appreciated the ambiguity inherent in "the first in time" slogan; namely, first what? Does the person who makes a first loan have priority? Or is it the first to file? Or the one who first procures the debtor's signature on a security agreement? Particularly where a creditor will make repeated advances (for example, lines of credit secured by inventory or accounts receivable where there might be repayments and new extensions of credit daily), pre-Code law was in conflict. Some rules gave the lender priority from the time it filed or did some other perfecting act; others measured the priority only from the time of the advance (the time the loan was actually made). The drafters of 9–322 and its predecessor (9–312) chose the former approach and have stated all the rules with precision.

Observe first that subsection (a) is a "pure race" statute as opposed to a "notice-race" statute. That is, the one who wins the "race" to the courthouse to file is superior even if that one had "notice" or "knowledge" of an earlier claim. The section nowhere requires that the victor be without knowledge of its competitor's claim. Example 1 of Comment 4 illustrates both the unimportance of knowledge and the fact that one who is perfected second may be prior if first to file. One justification for the rule is certainty. Under 9–322 no disappointed secured creditor can assert trumped up (or true) facts from which a compassionate court might find sufficient knowledge to subordinate the winner of the race. If the competitor filed first or perfected first, as the case may be, that is the end of it; that party wins even if aware of the other party's prior but unperfected claim.

Because the drafters chose to permit perfection by possession and by certain other non-filing acts, they could not simply give priority to the first to file. However, they went as far as possible in that direction and 9–322(a) is the result: the first to file wins if both competitors perfect by filing. Since filing is a public act, the timing of which can be proved with accuracy from public record, it is the most certain and satisfactory of the measuring points for priority.

Determining priority by order of filing protects the filing system—that is, allowing the first secured party who has filed to make subsequent advances without each time having to check for subsequent filings as a condition of protection. Both as to future advances and to after-acquired collateral, a lender's priority generally dates back to the time of filing.

The guiding principle of section 9–322(a) is that the secured party who either files or otherwise perfects before the other person, wins. If both parties perfect by filing, priority goes to the person who filed first. Likewise, if one or both parties perfect by means other than filing, priority goes to the one who first perfected or filed, whichever was the first to do either one of those things before the other did either one of them.

In the sections that follow we will also encounter important exceptions in which a person who perfects only after another has filed or perfected nevertheless has priority. The most important example of "second in time, first in right" is the purchase money lender discussed in chapter 4–4; other examples are secured creditors who perfect interests in investment property, or in deposit accounts, by taking control and so prevail over perfected security interests perfected earlier by other means.

PROBLEM

On March 1, Bank 1 commences negotiation with debtor and, expecting to make a loan, files a financing statement. On March 8, Bank 2 signs a security agreement with debtor, advances funds to debtor and files a financing statement. A week later, on March 15, Bank 1 advances funds and signs a security agreement with debtor.

Which Bank was the first perfected? Because Bank 1 did not give value until March 15, Bank 2 was the first perfected. Which bank has priority? Bank 1 has priority under section 9–322 because priority dates from the earlier of filing or perfection.

What justifies giving priority to the first to file even though that person does not hold a perfected security interest? Think about it; the rule makes sense. The rule seeks to encourage Bank 2 to check the records before making a loan to the debtor. Had it done so in this instance, it would have discovered Bank 1's filing and would have prevented the debtor's fraud. Since the negotiation of a significant secured transaction may take days or weeks, it makes sense to allow the secured creditor to examine the files at the outset and to make its own filing even before it advances money.

a. After-Acquired Property

Section 9–204 states that a security agreement "may create or provide for a security interest in after-acquired collateral." This rule does not extend to commercial tort claims or, with limitations, to consumer goods, but in general a debtor and creditor may agree that a security interest automatically attaches to after-acquired collateral. The section adopts the principle of a "continuing general lien" or "floating lien" and it does that even though the debtor "has liberty to use or dispose of collateral without being required to account for proceeds or substitute new collateral." It is clear from the words of subsection (a) that the priority in after-acquired collateral relates back to the time of priority as to the original collateral (filing or other method of perfection). The point is made explicitly by Comment 5 and example 4 to section 9–322.

b. Future Advances

Future advances have earned an entire section, 9–323. The language of subsection (a) does its best to obscure the general rule of priority as to future advances. It appears, on first reading, to say that priority as to a future advance dates from the time of that advance not from the time of an earlier filing or perfection.[1] Of course, that is not what subsection (a) *really* says; the drafters state the rule much more clearly in Comment 3 as follows:

> Under a proper reading of the first-to-file-or perfect rule of section 9–322(a)(1) (and former section 9–312(5)), it is abundantly clear that the time when an advance is made plays no role in determining priorities among conflicting security interests except when a financing statement was not filed and the advance is the giving of value as the last step for attachment and perfection. Thus, a secured party takes subject to all advances secured by a competing security interest having priority under section 9–322(a)(1).

To understand the general rule, assume the secured creditor takes a security interest and perfects it by filing a financing

---

[1]   "(a) **[When priority based on time of advance.]** Except as otherwise provided in subsection (c), for purposes of determining the priority of a perfected security interest under Section 9–322(a)(1), perfection of the security interest dates from the time an advance is made to the extent that the security interest secures an advance that:

(1) is made while the security interest is perfected only:

(A) under section 9–309 when it attaches; or

(B) temporarily under section 9–312(e), (f), or (g); and

(2) is not made pursuant to a commitment entered into before or while the security interest is perfected by a method other than under section 9–309 or 9–312(e), (f), or (g)."

statement. Assume further that the debtor makes periodic payments and that the creditor allows the debtor to make periodic draws on the underlying line of credit. These draws are "future advances." Under section 9–322, the secured creditor's priority as to each advance relates back to the time of the original filing. Section 9–323(a) will not apply to these advances because they have been perfected by a prior filing. As we explain below, in rare circumstances a lien creditor under subsection 9–323(b) or a buyer of goods under subsection 9–323(d), might achieve priority over the secured creditor as to some of these future advances.

The real role of section 9–323 is to state several intricate—but rather unimportant—*exceptions* to the general rule. First, consider those cases in which a secured creditor who would likely enjoy priority from the time of filing or first perfection is nevertheless considered to be perfected only when it makes a subsequent advance. The case is illustrated by example 2 in Comment 3. Sometime when one has an hour or so to waste, one might look at example 2 to try to understand it or the policy behind it. The statute seems to say that a secured creditor who is automatically perfected, or who has temporary perfection without filing, and who would enjoy priority as to its first advance because of that perfection, may in some cases, be subordinated as to advances made during such nondisclosed perfection. (The drafting committee listened too closely to someone who was impossibly tied up in the details of Article 9.) To take a simple but improbable case where section 9–323(a) might apply, consider a creditor who takes a security interest in debtor's certificated securities on day one. Assume that creditor advances $10,000 on day two and an additional $10,000 on day seven. Under the provisions of 9–312(e), the secured creditor would have a perfected security interest for 20 days without filing or the taking of possession. On day five a second creditor takes and perfects a security interest in the same collateral. The first secured creditor will have priority as to the loan made on day two but not to the loan made on day seven.

More important, but only slightly so, is the case of the lien creditor or buyer who intervenes between a secured creditor's perfection and a later advance by that secured creditor. The rules having to do with buyers on the one hand and lien creditors on the other, are similar but different.[2] Consider this example: Assume a secured creditor has a perfected security interest in debtor's machine worth $1 million and that the creditor has extended only $10,000 to

---

[2]   As Official Comment 4 points out, the 45-day rule for lien creditors in 9–323(b) also interrelates to some degree with similar rules in Section 6323 of the Internal Revenue Code, which govern priority between a secured creditor making future advances and a tax lien obtained by the IRS.

debtor when a lien creditor's lien attaches to the machine. The secured creditor is informed of the lien but nevertheless decides to advance another $900,000 to the common debtor. The secured creditor does this even though it has no binding commitment to do so (the creditor might choose to do this because the creditor was the parent of the debtor corporation and because the competing lien arose out of a $2 million judgment). If the secured creditor were able to push the lien creditor out of the nest, the lien creditor would be justifiably upset, correct? We can see that examples like this one must be exceedingly rare; the drafters have nevertheless given a rule to determine the priority in such a case. Under 9–323(b) the lien creditor will take priority over the later advance only if a series of conditions has been met. First, the advance must occur more than 45 days after the competing creditor became a lien creditor. Even if the advance was made more than 45 days after the lien arose, the secured creditor still has priority over the lien creditor if the advance was made "without knowledge of the lien" or pursuant to a "commitment." We suspect that it will be a cool day in hell when a secured creditor makes an advance that is subordinate to a lien creditor's claim.

Assume now that the secured creditor takes a security interest in a piece of equipment and that a buyer purchases that equipment from the debtor after the secured creditor has perfected. If the buyer is not a buyer in the ordinary course (he probably would not be since this is equipment, not inventory which the debtor is in the business of selling), the buyer takes subject to the security interest under the terms of 9–315, 9–317, and 9–201. But what if the secured creditor makes a new advance after its collateral has been sold? Under (d) (and assuming no commitment to make the advance under (e)) the buyer takes free if the advance was made more than 45 days after the purchase *or* was made after the secured party learned of the purchase. Thus, for understandable reasons, the buyer is given greater protection than the lien creditor. Subsections (f) and (g) have similar rules for lessees.

What justifies the more generous treatment that is given to a buyer than is given to a lien creditor? In several places in Article 9 "purchasers" or "buyers" are favored over lien creditors. This is because the former are presumed to have put out money in reliance upon the state of the public record or other circumstances. Lien creditors, on the other hand, are not "reliance creditors"; they are presumed to have begun life as unsecured creditors without any claim against any particular asset of the debtor and to have given no new value at the time they acquire their liens.

4–4 PURCHASE MONEY SECURITY INTEREST: SECOND IN TIME, FIRST IN RIGHT, SECTION 9–324

a. In General

Section 9–324 grants priority to purchase money security interests over prior conflicting security interests even though the purchase money security interest is later perfected; we sometimes call this "super priority." The purchase money secured creditor is often the seller of a product who has retained a security interest to secure its purchase price; however, a bank or other financing agency can also be a purchase money secured creditor. The priority of purchase money secured creditors has long been recognized in real estate transactions and in pre-Code rules for personal property. What is the justification for this special priority?

First, one might argue that a seller of goods (who is going to retain a security interest) should not be obliged to inspect public filings (with respect to its purchaser) in order for the seller to maintain priority in goods which it owns and proposes to sell. By hypothesis a seller starts out with the interest in the goods to be sold, and does not transfer it to the buyer. A careful student of property doctrine might favor the seller on the ground that he never transferred that part of his title which represents the security interest. This rationale stems from the "derivative title" rule in property, such that the purchaser cannot obtain any greater title than his seller had, and the purchaser's lenders should also thereby be subject to such title.[3] The problem with that argument is that the Code does not consistently follow any such principle. For example, a purchase money secured creditor claiming inventory (including a seller) must inspect the files to be sure of priority under section 9–324.

A second possible justification for purchase money priority is that the debtor needs some protection from an earlier secured creditor who may have filed a financing statement with respect to many of debtor's assets (including after-acquired), but who is unwilling to advance additional funds. Absent purchase money priority, an earlier filing with broad after-acquired coverage would give the prior creditor priority over other lenders. This scenario would leave the debtor unable to borrow despite the fact that other lenders might be willing to finance new purchases, if they could have priority as to the goods purchased. The possibility of priority for

---

[3]   See Juliet M. Moringiello, (Mis)use of State Law in Bankruptcy: The Hanging Paragraph Story, 2012 Wis. L. Rev. 963, 1005 (2012).

purchase money lenders gets the debtor out from under the thumb of an original creditor; it may enable the debtor to borrow notwithstanding the reluctance of the original lender.

Finally, law and economics scholars maintain that purchase money lenders should be permitted to go to the head of the line because they do not threaten preceding creditors in ways that general creditors might.[4]

b. Purchase Money

In section 6 of Chapter 2, we discussed the establishment of purchase money status in the consumer context. That discussion dealt with the situation in which a creditor finances several purchases for the debtor and the case in which a purchase money security interest is refinanced or rewritten. Section 9–103 explicitly *does not* provide rules for those issues in the consumer context; that is left to the case law. With respect to business loans, the drafters were more bold. For the questions addressed in this Chapter (mainly priority of purchase money claims against business debtors), the drafters have given concrete direction.

The starting point for determining purchase money status is section 9–103(a)(1) and (2). That section contemplates a seller as a purchase money lender and, more frequently, a lender who gives "value . . . to enable the debtor to acquire rights in or of the use of the collateral if the value is in fact so used." Courts will still have to answer the question whether the value was "to enable" and whether the value was "in fact so used." Usually, the answer is clear if debtor obtains the loan, and then utilizes it directly to purchase the goods. In rare circumstances the order can be reversed, such as when a car dealer advanced money to obtain cars with the knowledge that a loan advance was forthcoming to cover the purchase in a matter of a few days.[5] The court held that where "the loan transaction appears to be closely allied to the purchase transaction, that should suffice" to establish purchase money status. However, in the ordinary instance, if a debtor actually buys collateral with its own money when expecting a loan, the loan will not be a purchase money loan merely because it replaces monies earlier used to buy the goods.

The definition in 9–103 contemplates as purchase money collateral only "goods or software." Except when they are proceeds, security interests in accounts receivable and other intangibles will

---

[4] See Hidecki Kanda & Saul Levmore, Symposium on the Revision of Article 9 of the Uniform Commercial Code: Explaining Creditor Priorities, 80 Va. L. Rev. 2103 (1994).

[5] See GE Capital Commer. Auto. Fin. v. Spartan Motors, Ltd., 246 A.D.2d 41 (N.Y. App. Div. 1998).

not enjoy purchase money status. In the business context, subsection 9–103(f) makes it clear that a single security agreement can give rise to a purchase money security interest and also to a non-purchase money security interest. Subsection (b) even elevates certain inventory purchases to purchase money status despite the fact they do not themselves secure a "purchase money obligation." To understand how these sections might work, consider a hypothetical case. Assume that debtor, a John Deere farm implement dealer, buys ten tractors in a sequence of individual transactions each of which is financed by the bank and each of which includes a cross-collateral clause (a clause that makes every individual item collateral, not only for its own purchase price, but also for the purchase price of the other nine tractors). Assume that debtor sells the tenth tractor and remits the proceeds to the bank whose FIFO accounting system treats the payment for this sale as the payoff for the loan on the *first* tractor. In that circumstance, one could argue that the remaining "cross-collateral" claim against the first tractor (securing the obligations to pay for the nine remaining tractors) is not a purchase money obligation and therefore does not enjoy the super priority of a purchase money obligation. Section 9–103(b)(2) rules otherwise and provides as follows:

(b) A security interest in goods is a purchase-money security interest:

(2) if the security interest is in inventory that is or was purchase-money collateral, also to the extent that the security interest secures a purchase-money obligation incurred with respect to other inventory in which the secured party holds or held a purchase-money security interest[.]

The section thus makes clear that the entire security interest on all the tractors, including the first, remains a purchase money security interest. In this case the first tractor, by virtue of the cross-collateral clause, secures a "purchase money obligation incurred with respect to other inventory." So, at least with respect to inventory, all of the theoretical problems about allocation of payments and the like are greatly diminished.

Now change the hypothetical case to a construction company that owns the tractors and the tractors are equipment, not inventory. In this case, subsection 9–103(b)(2) does not apply, but 9–103(f)(1) still recognizes that "dual security interests" could (and presumably would) be created by a single security agreement.

(f) . . . a purchase-money security interest does not lose its status as such, even if:

> (1) the purchase-money collateral also secures an obligation that is not a purchase-money obligation[.]

Thus, one security interest (securing the price of *this* unit) will enjoy the super priority accorded to purchase money and the second (securing the price of *other* units) will have only the priority given to mine-run interests. Accordingly, the secured creditor will need a method of allocation to determine what part of each debt (purchase money or non-purchase money) has been paid off by the debtor's payments that are themselves undifferentiated. Subsection (e) invites the parties to make this allocation by agreement, and, if there is none, gives the creditor the right to allocate unilaterally in some cases, or, failing all else, to allocate according to subsection 9–103(e)(3):

> (e)(3) in the absence of an agreement to a reasonable method and a timely manifestation of the obligor's intention, [payments are allocated] in the following order:

>> (A) to obligations that are not secured; and

>> (B) if more than one obligation is secured, to obligations secured by purchase-money security interests in the order in which those obligations were incurred.

Assume the construction company had borrowed $1 million in ten consecutive transactions of $100,000 each and had granted a purchase money security interest in each case to the bank. Assume further that the construction company makes a $200,000 payment against the $1 million principal obligation and so reduces it to $800,000. If the parties' agreement had a FIFO clause so that the first purchased was the first released, this payment of $200,000 would pay off the purchase money loan against the first two tractors. Nevertheless, the cross-collateral clause in the security agreement would make these two tractors subject to the security interest against the purchase price of the eight remaining tractors. This latter security interest is not a purchase money interest and would not be entitled to the super priority in 9–324, but it would still be perfected and sufficient to defeat the trustee in bankruptcy, for example.

Finally subsection (f)(3) states that a purchase money security interest does not lose its status even if "the purchase money obligation has been renewed, refinanced, consolidated, or restructured." *Quaere* whether there is any novation that could deprive a purchase money lender its purchase money status because the loan was in some way new or rewritten? Under subsection (f)(3) it looks as though a creditor would always be able to trace its money into a current loan, no matter how frequently renewed or restructured. Assume, for example, that Creditor lends $1 million for the purchase of medical equipment; Creditor takes and perfects a purchase money security interest. In the succeeding year Creditor rewrites the loan three times and on each occasion, advances new money. At the end of two years the outstanding debt is $2.5 million. Is any part of that debt still "purchase money"? Ignoring the allocation problem that might arise if the debtor had made payments on the debt, does the "rewriting" and execution of new documents constitute a completely new loan so that the secured creditor no longer has purchase money status? We read 9–103(f)(3) to say no. Presumably the creditor could explicitly renounce its purchase money status, but, short of that, we believe the creditor retains its purchase money status as to principal amounts that can be traced by some allocation scheme to the original purchase money loan.

PROBLEM

Assume that Bank has a prior existing and perfected security interest in all of car dealer's assets. Finance Company has agreed to make a purchase money loan to enable dealer to buy an inventory of Chevrolets and Toyotas. Finance Company lends $3 million to car dealer and car dealer buys the cars. All of the Chevrolets are purchased before any of the Toyotas.

1.   Assume that the Toyotas are in great demand and that all of them are sold before any of the Chevrolets. At that point debtor goes into bankruptcy and is confronted with challenges from the trustee in bankruptcy and from Bank.

Since dealer's method of accounting is first in first out, trustee claims that the loans against the Chevrolets were satisfied by the payments on the Toyotas. Trustee will lose this argument because the security agreement will provide otherwise and because of the inferences drawn from 9–103(b).

Bank argues that the remaining claim against the Chevrolets is a non-purchase money security interest because the loans against the Chevrolets have been satisfied under dealer's method of accounting. Bank loses because subsection (b) provides that the loan against the Chevrolets (other inventory) remains a purchase money loan.

2.   Dealer falls on hard times and has to renegotiate his loan. As part of the renegotiation, dealer and Finance Company changed the terms of the loan and Finance Company adds another million dollars to the loan on a non-purchase money basis.

Over the next several months dealer makes payments of $1 million on the reworked loan. He then files bankruptcy and Bank argues that the $1 million should be treated as a payment on the purchase money part of the loan, to which its loan is inferior, and not on the non-purchase money loan to which it is superior. Bank will probably lose. Subsection (e) allows Finance Company and debtor to agree to any allocation method that is reasonable. One would expect them to agree that payments should go first to the inferior loan and second to the purchase money loan.

c. Rules of Priority

For collateral other than inventory and livestock the rules are quite straightforward. Under subsection 9–324(a), the purchase money secured creditor need only perfect within 20 days after the debtor receives possession. Although possession is generally straightforward, issues can sometimes arise as to the exact moment debtor is considered to have obtained possession.[6] Nevertheless, proper compliance with the rule of perfection within 20 days entitles the purchase money lender not only to priority in the collateral but also to priority in "its identifiable proceeds" (subject to some caveats discussed below). Most of the action here will be in the definition of the type and scope of the purchase money claim—issues discussed earlier.

When the collateral is inventory, the debtor's right to proceeds is more limited and the conditions to achieving priority are extensive. Subsection (b) to 9–324 reads as follows:

(b) [Inventory purchase-money priority.] Subject to subsection (c) and except as otherwise provided in subsection (g), a perfected purchase-money security interest in inventory has priority over a conflicting security interest in the same inventory, has priority over a conflicting security interest in chattel paper or an instrument constituting proceeds of the inventory and in proceeds of the chattel paper, if so provided in section 9–330, and, except as otherwise provided in section 9–327, also has priority in identifiable cash proceeds of the inventory to the extent the identifiable cash proceeds are received on or before the delivery of the inventory to a buyer, if:

(1) the purchase-money security interest is perfected when the debtor receives possession of the inventory;

(2) the purchase-money secured party sends an authenticated notification to the holder of the conflicting security interest;

---

[6]   See, e.g., In re Piknik Products Co., Inc., 346 B.R. 863, (Bankr. M.D.Ala.2006) (buyer was to have received possession of machine when it was installed in plant and bolted to floor, even though seller still had to bring it online and operational afterwards). See also § 9–324 cmt. 3 ("sometimes a buyer buys goods and takes possession of them in stages, and then assembly and testing are completed . . . at the debtor's location. Under those circumstances, the buyer 'takes possession' within the meaning of subsection (a) when, after an inspection of the portion of the goods in the debtor's possession, it would be apparent to a potential lender to the debtor that the debtor has acquired an interest in the goods taken as a whole.").

(3) the holder of the conflicting security interest receives the notification within five years before the debtor receives possession of the inventory; and

(4) the notification states that the person sending the notification has or expects to acquire a purchase-money security interest in inventory of the debtor and describes the inventory.

What is the justification for requiring the purchase money secured creditor, who is financing inventory purchases made by the debtor, to search the files and, upon finding an earlier security interest, to make an "authenticated notification"? The answer lies in the commercial practices of creditors and debtors. In inventory finance, the "revolving loan" or "line of credit," is common and the debtor comes to the general financier periodically asking for new extensions and offering new collateral. It was feared that an unscrupulous debtor might take advantage of the ignorance of his original secured inventory financier by procuring a secured loan against new inventory from the original general financier when he had already granted a purchase money interest to another creditor. The obligation to notify earlier creditors of purchase money security interests on inventory makes that kind of fraud difficult. On the other hand, the practice with respect to equipment is for the secured creditor to make a single loan against a single piece of equipment and for the loan to be paid down without additional related extensions of credit. Because of that practice the drafters believed that there was no need for a notice to a prior lender against equipment.

Two things may not be obvious about the conditions in subsection 9–324(b). The first is that the purchase money creditor is not forever condemned by failure to perfect before the debtor possessed the first item of inventory. The words "the inventory" in subsection (1) refer to the inventory in dispute, not to the very first inventory the debtor may have acquired (and long since sold). The fact that the debtor held one item of inventory before the filing and the notice does not subordinate the purchase money creditor as to inventory that the debtor acquired after the filing and the notice. Assume that Creditor One has a perfected security interest in debtor's inventory. Assume that Creditor Two wishes to finance a new line of inventory and to achieve priority over Creditor One. Assume further that Creditor Two goes through the ritual in 9–324(b); the debtor receives possession of some of the inventory before Creditor Two perfects and before Creditor Two sends notification to Creditor One. As to the inventory received before the perfection or before the notice, Creditor Two will not enjoy priority. Because inventory will be sold and replaced periodically, usually this subordination will not last long. If Creditor Two perfects and sends notice one month after the first inventory is delivered to the debtor, Creditor Two will enjoy priority as to covered inventory that is received thereafter. Note also that under 9–324(b)(3), the notification is effective for five years. So, the statement in subsection (3) that the notification be received "within five years" really means only that a notice is good for five years.

d. Proceeds of Purchase Money Secured Creditor

The rules concerning the purchase money secured creditor's claim to proceeds have become increasingly more complicated with each major revision of Article 9. The general rule with respect to non-inventory collateral in 9–324(a) is that the purchase money priority carries over into identifiable proceeds. Of course, the purchase money lender can still lose, if, for example, the proceeds are deposited into a bank account and the bank perfects by "control" (which priority rules are contained in 9–327).

By contrast, the purchase money priority against *inventory* carries over only to a limited set of proceeds. The preamble in subsection 9–324(b) states this purchase money priority "in identifiable cash proceeds of the inventory to the extent the identifiable cash proceeds are received on or before the delivery of the inventory to a buyer . . . ."

The complex rules in subsection 9–324(b) boil down to this. First the purchase money priority continues in identifiable cash proceeds. Cash proceeds are defined in 9–102(a)(9) as "money, checks, deposit accounts, or the like." Thus, the purchase money secured creditor has priority in a set of quite transitory assets, and then only if the assets are not put into a bank account and subjected to the superior claim of the bank, via control (and as resolved under the priority rules of 9–327). The section also grants priority in chattel paper or an instrument constituting proceeds of the inventory, but only if the purchase money secured creditor is victorious under section 9–330, against a buyer of the paper. (We consider 9–330 in section 10 of this Chapter.)

Because accounts are not "cash proceeds," the inventory purchase money lender's priority does *not* carry over into accounts that arise on sale of the inventory. What is the purpose of this rule? The rule arises out of the commercial expectations of those who lend against inventory and of others who lend against accounts. Comment 8 describes those expectations as follows:

> many parties financing inventory are quite content to protect their first-priority security interest in the inventory itself. They realize that when the inventory is sold, someone else will be financing the resulting receivables (accounts or

chattel paper), and the priority for inventory will not run forward to the receivables constituting the proceeds. Indeed, the cash supplied by the receivables financier often will be used to pay the inventory financing. In some situations, the party financing the inventory on a purchase money basis makes contractual arrangements that the proceeds from receivables financing by another be devoted to paying off the inventory security interest.

So these apparently inconsistent rules arise from and depend on business practice and expectations.

e.   Other Cases

Subsection (d) has rules for livestock that are similar to the rules for inventory (except that the notice is for six months rather than for five years); subsection (f) suggests that the software follows the collateral at least in this case, and subsection (g) has special rules for cases of conflicting purchase money interests.

In one case subsection (g)(1) grants priority to a seller over a financier where both are purchase money secured creditors with respect to the same collateral. That can happen when the debtor borrows its down payment from a bank (who becomes a purchase money lender to that extent) and borrows a remaining amount from the seller by purchasing "on time." In all other cases—usually lender of part of the price vs. lender of the other part of the price—the rule of (g)(2) resorts to the first-in-time rules of 9–322(a).

4–5   FIXTURES

In general, Article 9 does not deal with real estate security. In fact, it is largely excluded by the provisions of 9–109(d)(11) and left largely to the domain of real property law. The single important exception to that rule is section 9–334 concerning priority of security interests in fixtures. That section governs the conflict between personal property interests in fixtures and real property interest in fixtures.

Typical of the priority conflicts we consider here are those that arise when a real estate mortgagee claims not only the real estate but also all "appurtenances, fixtures, buildings, equipment." After the mortgage is on the property, the debtor purchases a furnace or lathes or some other item of industrial equipment that becomes a fixture on the real property and subject to the real estate mortgage under the state real property law. This single transaction comes in a dozen variants depending on when the interests attach and when they are perfected, and on the identity of the claimant and the mode of perfection. Section 9–334 deals with most of the possible conflicts.

If the collateral in question is not a fixture or if it is "building material" that has become so intimately associated with the real property that it no longer constitutes either personal property or a fixture, other law governs the priority dispute. Article 9 doesn't apply, because subsection (a) specifically provides that a "security interest does not exist under this article in ordinary building materials incorporated into an improvement on land."

The secured creditor with a claim to a fixture has a choice. It can either make a filing in the local real estate records (a fixture filing) or do a regular UCC–1 filing in the personal property records at the state capital. As we will see, the former gives the secured creditor protection against certain real estate claimants, and the latter gives protection only against lien creditors and certain other claimants where the fixture involved is not considered to be important to mortgagees and the like. For example, subsection (e)(3) grants the secured lender who has done only a personal property filing at the state capital priority over the trustee in bankruptcy (lien creditor) on the theory that a lien creditor is not someone who would rely upon the real estate records. Subsection (e)(2) gives priority to the secured creditor who has only done a personal property filing on certain assets such as factory or office machines on the theory that mortgagees or other purchasers of the real estate do not place any reliance upon such machines when they make loans or buy; thus, it is fair and appropriate to grant the secured creditor priority in this case even though the secured creditor does not do a fixture filing.

a. Fixtures and Fixture Filings, Section 9–102(a)(40) and (41)

Section 9–102(a)(41) defines fixtures as "goods that have become so related to particular real property that an interest in them arises under real property law." Broadly, goods can be classified for the purposes of 9–334 into three categories: (1) those that remain "pure goods," (2) those so substantially integrated into real estate as to become real estate themselves, i.e., "pure realty," and (3) those in between that would pass with a deed to the real estate yet remain personal property. The items that fall under the third classification are fixtures. Comment 3 to 9–334 presents this division as follows:

> [T]his section recognizes three categories of goods: (1) those that retain their chattel character entirely and are not part of the real property; (2) ordinary building materials that have become an integral part of the real property and cannot retain their chattel character for purposes of finance; and (3) an intermediate class that has become real

property for certain purposes, but as to which chattel financing may be preserved.

Goods cross the line from pure goods to fixtures when they become sufficiently related to the real estate that they would pass in a deed under the local real estate law. What passes by deed in Minnesota may not pass in Wisconsin, and what is sufficiently related to a real estate interest in New York might not be sufficiently related in Georgia. Thus the general definition in 9–102(a)(41) is no more than a cross reference to state case law and state real estate statutes. What, then, are the state law principles governing when goods become fixtures? We cannot go much beyond posing the question.

Most courts start from the proposition that status of goods as a fixture depends upon the intention of the parties.[7] Of course, "objective manifestations of intention" are the windows through which we view actual intent. One searching for such manifestations might ask:[8] What did the parties say in their agreement? How did they attach the goods to the realty? What is the relation between the parties? How is the operation of the goods related to the use of the real property? For many courts, intent is most clearly manifested by the firmness with which the goods are affixed to the real estate and the amount of sweat that removal would entail.[9] One authority on property states that whether an item becomes a fixture depends on how it was annexed, the type of chattel which is attached, and the parties' intention; and yet, the manner of annexation and the type of chattel are usually regarded as germane to the ultimate question of intention.[10] The American Law of Property puts the matter as follows (emphasis added):

> In the United States, whether a given chattel becomes a fixture is said to depend on intention, but whether it is the

---

[7] 5 American Law of Property § 19.3 at 16–19 (1952). See, e.g., In re Hot Shots Burgers & Fries, Inc., 169 B.R. 920, 24 UCC2d 1289 (Bankr.E.D.Ark.1994) (modular building used as a drive-through restaurant not a fixture; debtor's intention that it not be permanent supported by fact that building could be moved and had twice been moved).

[8] The factors mentioned in the text were first enunciated in the leading case on fixtures, Teaff v. Hewitt, 1 Ohio St. 511 (1853), which is discussed in 5 American Law of Property § 19.3 at 16–19 (1952).

[9] Thoughtful decisions canvassing a variety of factors are Wyoming State Farm Loan Bd. v. Farm Credit System Capital Corp., 759 P.2d 1230, 7 UCC2d 243 (Wyo.1988) (not a fixture) and Lewiston Bottled Gas Co. v. Key Bank, 601 A.2d 91, 17 UCC2d 282 (Me.1992) (fixture). But see, Bank of Valley v. United States Nat'l Bank, 215 Neb. 912, 341 N.W.2d 592, 37 UCC 994 (1983) where the court gave pre-eminence to "intent" and held that a five-bedroom house built by lessee was personalty where the parties to the lease agreed that lessee had the privilege of removing all improvements he made to the premises.

[10] 2 Tiffany, Real Property § 607 (3d edition).

unilateral intention of the annexor at the time of annexation, or the bilateral intention of the parties to some transaction relating to the chattel or to the land, and whether it is the actual intention, or the manifested intention, or the imputed intention, is not always clear.

Part of the confusion comes from the various meanings ascribed to the term "fixture." Under the modern cases no more precise definition is possible than this: a fixture is a former chattel which, while retaining its separate physical identity, *is so connected with the realty that a disinterested observer would consider it a part thereof.*[11]

This is not the place to inject order into this chaotic body of law. We do no more than to warn you that the local cases must be examined with care to arrive at a reasonable guess about what is and what is not a fixture in a particular jurisdiction. And, that analysis of whether an item is a fixture is "fraught with difficulty," such that savvy practitioners will be wise to file in every possible place.[12]

Section 9–102(a)(40) states that a "fixture filing" is "the filing of a financing statement covering goods that are or are to become fixtures and satisfying section 9–502(a) and (b). The term includes the filing of a financing statement covering goods of a transmitting utility which are or are to become fixtures." The concept of a "fixture filing" was introduced in the 1972 revision of Article 9. The drafters concluded that one should be required to file a fixture filing in the office in which a record of a mortgage for the real property would be filed if one seeks priority over subsequent real estate interests who would typically check in the real estate files and only in those files. Comment 4 to revised 9–501 explains the two ways in which a secured party may file a financing statement to perfect a security interest in goods that are or are to become fixtures, depending upon the parties against whom protection is sought. First, a secured party may make a non-fixture filing in Article 9 records, as with goods, in accordance with section 9–501(a)(2). Or, a secured creditor may file a "fixture filing" in the office in which a record of a mortgage on the related real property would be filed; see 9–501(a)(1)(B). Given the uncertainty whether goods are or may become fixtures under applicable real-property law, Comment 3 to 9–334 recognizes that a secured party may make a fixture filing as a precaution. A court may not infer merely from a fixture filing that the secured party concedes that the goods are or will become fixtures.

---

[11]   5 American Law of Property § 19.1 at 3–4 (1952).

[12]   Barbara M. Goodstein and Clint D. Bergstrom, The Wide World of Fixtures, 46 Uniform Com. Code L.J. 225 (2014–2015).

In addition to the normal information under 9–502(a), a financing statement filed as a fixture filing under subsection (b) must include: (1) a showing that it covers goods which are, or are to become, "fixtures"; (2) a recital that the financing statement is to be filed in the real estate records; (3) a description of the real estate; and (4) the name of the record owner if the debtor has no interest of record.[13] Section 9–502(c) states that the recording of a complying mortgage is equivalent to a fixture filing. In the event an actual mortgage contract is filed under subsection (c), in lieu of the form financing statement, the 2010 Amendments clarify a couple of things: (1) that a mortgage form need not indicate that it is to be filed in the real estate records (presumably since it is obvious where mortgages are filed), and (2) the new rules in 9–503(a)(4) regarding the debtor's driver's license name do not apply to a mortgage filing; instead, merely the "individual name of the debtor or the surname and first personal name of the debtor" need be provided.

b. Fixture Priority Rules, Section 9–334(d)–(h)

The priority rules in subsections (d) through (h) look threatening at first, but once one understands the reasons for the rules, they are logical and relatively easy to understand. First is a general rule stated in (c): except as stated in (d) through (h) "a security interest in fixtures is subordinate to a conflicting interest of an encumbrancer or owner of the related real property other than the debtor." So, the default rule is that the real estate mortgagee or buyer of the real estate defeats the personal property secured creditor unless the secured creditor can find an exception that states otherwise.

1. Purchase Money Security Interest, Section 9–334(d), (h)

Subsections (d) and (h) of Section 9–334 provide as follows:

(d) [Fixtures purchase-money priority.] Except as otherwise provided in subsection (h), a perfected security interest in fixtures has priority over a conflicting interest of an encumbrancer or owner of the real property if the debtor has an interest of record in or is in possession of the real property and:

(1) the security interest is a purchase-money security interest;

---

[13] A financing statement with an accurate street address substantially complied with the requirement, under former 9–402(5), that the statement include a legal description of the real estate. In re Mistura, Inc., 13 B.R. 483, 32 UCC 633 (Bankr.D.Ariz.1981). Failure to identify the record owner was fatal in Lewiston Bottled Gas Co. v. Key Bank, 601 A.2d 91, 17 UCC2d 282 (Me.1992).

(2) the interest of the encumbrancer or owner arises before the goods become fixtures; and

(3) the security interest is perfected by a fixture filing before the goods become fixtures or within 20 days thereafter.

. . .

(h) [Priority of construction mortgage.] A mortgage is a construction mortgage to the extent that it secures an obligation incurred for the construction of an improvement on land, including the acquisition cost of the land, if a recorded record of the mortgage so indicates. Except as otherwise provided in subsections (e) and (f), a security interest in fixtures is subordinate to a construction mortgage if a record of the mortgage is recorded before the goods become fixtures and the goods become fixtures before the completion of the construction. A mortgage has this priority to the same extent as a construction mortgage to the extent that it is given to refinance a construction mortgage.

Subsection (d) gives priority over competing real estate claimants to a purchase money secured creditor who complies with 9–334(d), subject to one exception. First the security interest must be a "purchase money security interest" as that term is defined in section 9–103. Second, the security interest must be perfected by a fixture filing no later than 20 days after the goods become fixtures. The secured creditor's claim, though second in time, defeats the prior perfected real estate claim, just as with purchase money security interests in personal property generally under section 9–324. The wording of (d)(2) is somewhat awkward, but it sets up purchase money security interests in fixtures to have priority over prior interests because of the status as purchase money. If the purchase money interest arises before the competing interest, other general first-in-time rules may apply. The debtor must either have an interest "of record" or be in possession of the real property. If neither of those is so, a fixture filing (in the real estate records) will not put third persons on notice.

There is one important exception to the purchase money priority of the secured creditor. Consider a construction mortgagee financing the construction of a building and another lender is financing an important fixture such as a large heating or cooling system. In that case both parties would be purchase money lenders; each would be advancing funds to enable the debtor to construct a functional building. Subsection (h) generally grants priority to the construction mortgagee. And the construction mortgagee's priority carries over even into a refinanced mortgage. In effect, the drafters here have concluded that the construction mortgagee is the more important lender; the rule of (h) requires the purchase money lender against the fixture to go to the construction mortgagee and seek a subordination agreement if the fixture lender wishes to have priority.

Finally, the construction mortgagee does not achieve priority over fixture lenders who claim under subsections (e) and (f). Thus for most of the cases that follow, the fixture lender has priority not only over garden variety mortgagees but also over construction mortgagees.

2. Subsequent Real Estate Interests, Section 9–334(e)(1)

Section 9–334(e)(1) provides as follows:

A perfected security interest in fixtures has priority over a conflicting interest of an encumbrancer or owner of the real property if:

(1) the debtor has an interest of record in the real property or is in possession of the real property and the security interest:

(A) is perfected by a fixture filing before the interest of the encumbrancer or owner is of record; and

(B) has priority over any conflicting interest of a predecessor in title of the encumbrancer or owner[.]

If the debtor is in possession of the real property or has an interest of record, a secured creditor who does a fixture filing generally earns priority over any subsequent mortgagee or buyer of the real estate. (Of course it is also necessary that there *not* be a prior real estate interest that is itself superior to the security interest and that was transferred or assigned to the competing mortgagee or owner.) For a straightforward application of this rule consider a case in which Bank finances a heating system that becomes a fixture in a high-rise building. After the bank has done a fixture filing, Owner sells the building to Third Party. Subsection (e)(1) says the Bank's interest is superior to Third Party's interest. By reading the real estate records, Third Party will find Bank's filing. Of course, if the debtor was neither in possession of the building nor the record title holder, Third Party would not be put on notice by the fixture filing because a search in the name of the record title holder would not turn up the filing in the debtor's name.

3. "Non Fixture" Fixtures, Section 9–334(e)(2)

Some goods that are "fixtures" under state law would nevertheless never be relied upon by a mortgagee. Accordingly, a personal property secured creditor gets priority as to certain "readily removable" machines even though the lender has not done a fixture filing. The subsection now grants priority to a secured creditor who perfects "by any method" as to certain assets that are readily removable. To enjoy the protection of the subsection, the secured creditor must perfect "by any method" (i.e., including a filing in the statewide Secretary of State's office) before the goods become fixtures. Goods covered by 9–334(e)(2) are the following:

(A) factory or office machines;

(B) equipment that is not primarily used or leased for use in the operation of the real property; or

(C) replacements of domestic appliances that are consumer goods[.]

Subsection (e)(2) presents at least two minor interpretive problems. First, not all domestic appliances are covered. Only "replacements" are covered. Thus, if a real estate lender finances the construction of a series of tract houses and if the lender's mortgage covers built-in stoves and ovens, the fixture lender against those stoves and ovens could not gain priority under 9–334(e)(2)(C) for they would be initial items and not the "replacements." In regard to some goods, the line between replacement and repair may be a fine one!

Second, what precisely are "readily removable" factory or office machines and "readily removable" equipment not primarily used or leased for use in the operation of the real property?[14] Surely computers and photocopying machines are covered, but what about typical industrial machinery? The line between what is readily removable and what is not probably should be drawn by asking whether a real estate mortgagee would lend in reliance on such equipment. That means that most industrial equipment should be regarded as readily removable, but that most integral equipment like electrical, heating and cooling apparatus should be treated as not readily removable.

Finally, for a lender to have priority under (e)(2), the lender's security interest must have been perfected before the goods "become fixtures." Put another way, the secured lender in most cases has to be a purchase money lender, for usually that is the only such lender to have a security interest before the goods become affixed. And, such purchase money lender must be sure to have its filing in place before the goods are implemented into the facility (filing before delivering them to the debtor in the first place would be wiser still).

---

[14] See, e.g., Hoyt v. Christoforou, 692 A.2d 217, 32 UCC2d 1208 (Pa.Super.1997) (restaurant equipment such as high chairs, cash registers, broilers, fryers, and other movable items cannot be classified as fixtures).

4. Lien Creditors—The Trustee in Bankruptcy, Section 9–334(e)(3)

Subsection (e) provides as follows:

(e) [Priority of security interest in fixtures over interests in real property.] A perfected security interest in fixtures has priority over a conflicting interest of an encumbrancer or owner of the real property if:

. . .

(3) the conflicting interest is a lien on the real property obtained by legal or equitable proceedings after the security interest was perfected by any method permitted by this article.

If the secured creditor has perfected a security interest "by any method," the creditor defeats a later lien creditor and, most importantly, the lien creditor from hell, the trustee in bankruptcy. Comment 9 explains the rationale as follows:

Such a lien is subordinate to an earlier-perfected security interest, regardless of the method by which the security interest was perfected. Judgment creditors generally are not reliance creditors who search real-property records. Accordingly, a perfected fixture security interest takes priority over a subsequent judgment lien or other lien obtained by legal or equitable proceedings, even if no evidence of the security interest appears in the relevant real-property records. Subsection (e)(3) thus protects a perfected fixture security interest from avoidance by a trustee in bankruptcy under Bankruptcy Code section 544(a).

Since section 544(a)(3) of the Bankruptcy Act gives the trustee in bankruptcy the rights of "a bona fide purchaser of real property from the debtor," what is to keep the trustee from avoiding 9–334(e)(3)'s restriction by asserting rights as a bona fide purchaser under 9–334(c)? The answer is in section 544(a)(3) which makes it clear that the trustee in bankruptcy does not have the rights of a bona fide purchaser, at least when the trustee is making a claim against fixtures. In the words of the Bankruptcy Act, the trustee has the rights of "a bona fide purchaser of real property, *other than fixtures.*"

5. Manufactured Homes, Section 9–334(e)(4)

Subsection (e)(4) provides as follows:

(e) [Priority of security interest in fixtures over interests in real property.] A perfected security interest in fixtures has priority over a conflicting interest of an encumbrancer or owner of the real property if:

. . .

(4) the security interest is:

(A) created in a manufactured home in a manufactured-home transaction; and

(B) perfected pursuant to a statute described in section 9–311(a)(2).

Subsection (e)(4) states a special rule for the perfection and priority of a security interest in fixtures consisting of "manufactured homes." If the fixture qualifies as a manufactured home, as that term is defined in 9–102(a)(53), if the transaction is a "manufactured home transaction" as that term is used in 9–102(a)(54), and if the perfection is by means of compliance with the certificate of title law, the secured creditor enjoys priority over the mortgagee on the real estate (both those who came before and those who come after), over owners, and over buyers.

The term "manufactured home transaction" includes only: 1) purchase money security interests in manufactured homes that are not held as inventory and, 2) secured transactions in which the manufactured home (not as inventory) is the "primary collateral." The definition encompasses both purchase money loans made to a consumer upon the consumer's purchase of the manufactured home and "home-equity loans" against the manufactured home after it has been purchased. The exclusion for inventory will cut out purchase money loans made to dealers in such homes.

The hard part is likely to come now (and later in the courts) in defining exactly the boundaries of "manufactured home." The Uniform Commercial Code definition is borrowed from the federal Manufactured Housing Act, as pointed out in comment 4.b of 9–102. Consider the actual definition in 9–102(a)(53):

"Manufactured home" means a structure, transportable in one or more sections, which, in the traveling mode, is eight body feet or more in width or 40 body feet or more in length, or, when erected on site, is 320 or more square feet, and which is built on a permanent chassis and designed to be used as a dwelling with or without a permanent foundation when connected to the required utilities, and includes the plumbing, heating, air-conditioning, and electrical systems contained therein. The term includes any structure that meets all of the requirements of this paragraph except the size requirements and with respect to which the manufacturer voluntarily files a certification required by the United States Secretary of Housing and Urban Development and complies with the standards established under Title 42 of the United States Code.

Clearly the definition excludes the typical weekend camper or the U-haul moving trailer on the small end, but it is not entirely clear to us what is excluded on the large end. We wonder, for example, about the "double wide" trailers one sees traveling down the interstate preceded by a station wagon, proclaiming "wide load." Is this incipient residence built on a "permanent chassis"? We suppose that someone must understand what that chassis looks like and how a permanent chassis would differ from one that is not permanent, but we can imagine disputes here. Moreover we can imagine the possibility that some lenders would insist that a "permanent chassis" be put on homes against which they are going to lend even though there was no utilitarian purpose—just so they can benefit from the certificate of title filing.

Taking a security interest in mobile homes has been a precarious business. One of the surest ways to provoke a dispute among sophisticated lawyers is to ask how one perfects a security interest in a mobile home. In our experience, a group of lawyers responds to that question with the kind of passionate disagreement one might hear between students discussing their answers to an examination they had just taken. Some claim the only way to perfect a security interest in a mobile home loan is to use a real estate mortgage, others swear by a fixture filing and yet others will claim to use a certificate of title as the best way to perfect a security interest. Since perfection by a notation on a certificate of title does not expire at the end of five years (like most financing statements), the perfection of an interest in a mobile home by listing one's name on the certificate of title will often last well beyond five years, in some cases perhaps indefinitely. (Since the Code recognizes the possibility that a financing statement filed for certain manufactured home transactions will be good for 30 years, there can be long term perfection there too, see 9–515(b).)

But let us do some wicked speculation. Assume Bank gets its name on a certificate of title and so perfects its interest in a "manufactured home." Ten years pass and in the interim a real estate mortgagee takes a mortgage on the (formerly mobile) home. The mortgagee of course, searches the real estate files and finds nothing about Bank and the debtor fails to mention his loan from the Bank. What are the arguments one could make on behalf of the real estate lender? First one might argue that the mobile home is not "a manufactured home" because it was not built on a "permanent" chassis or because it has the wrong dimensions. Second, the competitor will point out that section 9–334 protects the secured creditor only as long as the mobile home is a "fixture." The real estate mortgagee will argue that, notwithstanding the definition of manufactured home, some mobile homes become so permanently and firmly affixed to the real estate that they are no longer fixtures but are part of the real estate as much as the dirt itself. If the court so concludes, Bank that is relying on the certificate of title has problems not only under section 9–334 but also, presumably, under the certificate of title law.

c.   Remedy, Section 9–604(c), (d) and (b)

Under the terms of 9–604(c) the secured creditor "may remove the collateral from the real property" if the secured creditor has priority over all others. Under subsection (d) the secured creditor must "promptly reimburse any encumbrancer or owner who is not the debtor" for damage caused by the removal (gouges on the wall paper, changed doors, holes in the wall), but need not reimburse any encumbrancer or owner (or debtor) for the diminution in value of real property caused by the absence of the goods removed. This is, after all, simply the secured creditor removing its collateral, to which it was entitled to the exclusion of others, in the event of priority.

There may be some hard cases lurking in subsection (d). Consider the case in which an angry creditor rips out the furnace in February in International Falls, Minnesota; the pipes freeze and much damage is done to the building. Is this consequential damage to the building "physical injury caused by the removal"? We suspect it is. The secured creditor would do well to go slow here. On the other hand, injury to a landlord whose tenants are made uncomfortably hot when the air conditioner is removed in July from a building in Charlotte, North Carolina, would fall outside of the physical injury requirement. The creditor would not be liable for that economic loss. And subsection (d) speaks of the secured party's removal of fixtures that cause damage—when the secured creditor invokes judicial procedures and the sheriff or marshal removes the property and causes damage, there is authority for the proposition that 9–604(d) does not impose liability on the secured creditor. Rather, the owner's action would lie, if at all, against the governmental authorities.[15]

Section 9–604(b)(2) allows a secured creditor who holds a security interest in fixtures to "proceed . . . in accordance with the rights with respect to real property . . . ." Comment 3 to the section tells us that the subsection is intended to "overrule cases holding that

---

[15]   Cla-Mil East Holding Corp. v. Medallion Funding Corp., 6 N.Y.3d 375, 813 N.Y.S.2d 1, 846 N.E.2d 431, 58 U.C.C. Rep. Serv. 2d 748 (2006).

a secured party's only remedy after default is the removal of the fixtures . . . ." The Comment cites Maplewood Bank & Trust v. Sears, Roebuck & Co.[16]

What exactly does subsection 9–604(b)(2) mean for a secured creditor who has a security interest in a fixture? Surely it does *not* mean the secured creditor may sell not only the fixtures but also the property to which the fixtures are attached, for the fixture holder will typically have no interest in any part of the real estate except for the fixture. (In the unusual case where the fixture holder has a real estate mortgage on the entire property, of course, the fixture holder would be able to sell the entire property to satisfy its debt. Such creditors will likely often proceed under the state real property foreclosure laws and sell the entire property as an entire package; in such case, the enforcement provisions of Article 9 need not be followed.)[17] Where the fixture creditor has an interest only in the fixture, presumably the subsection authorizes the fixture holder to claim the lesser of its debt or the value of the fixture out of the proceeds of a sale of the property.

To appreciate some of the complexities that might be presented, consider the facts of *Maplewood Bank & Trust*. A mortgagee sold the real property and Sears kitchen fixtures in a foreclosure sale. When Sears (whose security interest was prior to the mortgagee's security) asked for a share of the proceeds equal to the difference between the value of the property with and without its fixtures, the mortgagee declined to give Sears anything. The New Jersey court held that Sears' only right was to remove the fixtures and to sell them independently. Because of the citation, we know the drafters intended to overrule *Maplewood* which means that Sears would now be entitled to a share of the proceeds, but how much? Depending on the circumstances, the prior perfected fixture lender might ask for the difference in value with and without, as Sears did. Or the fixture claimant might ask for a share of the proceeds equal to the discounted price of the fixtures. One can imagine cases where those two measures would be different; in some cases the discounted price might be greater, and in other cases the reverse could be true. We suspect those questions will have to be worked out under the real estate law in each jurisdiction.

But there are other problems as well. What would Sears' rights be if it were junior to the mortgage lender? Presumably Sears would receive money in that case only after the mortgagee had been fully satisfied. And what are Sears' rights under section 9–604(b)(2) if there is no mortgage foreclosure and yet it wishes to exercise its

---

[16]   265 N.J.Super. 25, 625 A.2d 537, 21 UCC2d 171 (App.Div. 1993).

[17]   In re Vantage Investments, Inc., 385 B.R. 670 (Bankr. W.D. Mo. 2008).

rights under the real estate law? As we suggest above, if Sears has no mortgage and is relying merely on its security interest in the fixtures, we do not see how the subsection helps it at all. If that is the case, and notwithstanding the apparent promises to the contrary in the subsection and the Comment, we suspect that Sears will be left to its rights to remove under section 9–604(c).

PROBLEM

1.   Assume that secured creditor has a security interest in debtor's supply of bricks. Creditor has perfected its security interest by filing a financing statement at the state Capital. The bricks are used to build a commercial building. In a competition with the real estate mortgagee, does the secured creditor prevail?

He does not. The bricks have become real estate just as much as the dirt under the building.

2.   Secured creditor takes a purchase money security interest in the elevators that are being installed in a new building. There is a mortgage on the building held by another lender. Secured creditor files a financing statement at the state capital. Does he also need to do a fixture filing?

The answer is yes and even that might not give him priority. The elevators are not readily removable offices machines so 9–334(2) will not help. If the mortgage is a construction mortgage, even a fixture filing will not do the trick. Why?

A UCC–1 at the state capital is good only against someone who is probably not relying on the fixtures (mortgagees don't care about Xerox machines but they certainly are interested in and would rely on the elevators in a high rise building).

But why won't the creditor win for sure if he does a fixture filing? The "except" clause at the beginning of subsection (d) in effect elevates a construction mortgagee (also a purchase money lender) over the personal property purchase money lender.

4–6   ACCESSIONS AND COMMINGLED GOODS, SECTIONS 9–335, 9–336

Rules having to do with accessions and commingled goods are similar to the rules discussed above with respect to fixtures. Whereas fixtures involve goods attached to land, these concepts deal with goods attached to, or combined with, other goods. As with fixtures, one question is the relative priority between the one who claims the accession and a person who has a claim to the goods to which the accession is attached. In the case of commingled goods, of course, there can be many claimants.

What is an accession and how does it differ from "commingled goods"? "Accession" is defined in section 9–102(a)(1) as goods that are "physically united with other goods in such a manner that the identity of the original goods is not lost." On the other hand, "commingled goods" are defined in section 9–336(a) as goods "that are physically united with other goods in such a manner that their identity is lost in a product or mass." Comment 2 to 9–335 tells us that something does not lose its status as an accession merely because of "the cost or difficulty of removing the accession from the other goods, and regardless of whether the original goods have come to form an integral part of the other goods."[18] Some cases are easy. Installing a new alternator on an automobile engine is clearly attaching an "accession" and putting one's harvested corn crop into a grain elevator is obviously "commingling goods." The official comments to 9–336 also posit that eggs and flour in a bakery would be commingled once cakes were baked.

What if one puts new chips into a computer or bearings into an industrial product? What if one could not, thereafter, distinguish between the chips or bearings that had been later inserted and chips or bearings that had been earlier inserted? Perhaps these are commingled goods because their "identity" has been lost, at least in the sense no one can tell which were first inserted or later inserted. We are sure that some cases live on the indistinct border between these two sections, but we doubt they are significant. Comment 2 to 9–335 directs many of the hard cases into the "accession" category.

a. Accessions

Subsection (c) of 9–335 sends one to the "other provisions" of Article 9 to determine priority. In most cases priority conflicts will be resolved by section 9–324 on purchase money security interests. Typically, the person with the claim on the accession will be a purchase money seller, or one who financed a purchase with a loan, and will so enjoy priority because of the rules discussed above and set out in 9–324.

Note, however, the special rule set out in section 9–335(d) for one who has perfected a security interest in the "whole" by compliance with certificate of title legislation. This rule dictates priority for the secured creditor who perfects by notation on the certificate of title. The drafters have made a decision that one who

---

[18] Some courts (and/or lawyers) overlook this comment, and cite to pre-Article 9 law which imposed these requirements. See, e.g., In re Sweeney, 556 B.R. 208 (Bankr. E.D.N.C. 2016) ("North Carolina courts employ a two-part test to determine whether an accession exists. First, a court must consider whether the good has become an 'integral part of the property to which it was attached.' Second, a court must determine whether the goods then 'could be conveniently detached.' If the first prong is negatively answered, or if the second prong is then affirmatively satisfied, then the item at issue does not constitute an accession.") (citing Goodrich Silvertown Stores v. Caesar, 214 N.C. 85, 87, 197 S.E. 698, 700 (N.C.1938)). But the drafters seemingly intended to dispose of these older requirements.

finances a new engine for an automobile or truck should bear the responsibility of securing a subordination agreement from the lender whose name appears on the certificate of title if the "engine" financier wishes priority over the "car lender." This subsection overrides not only 9–322 but also 9–324. Thus, a seller that finances tires for a car which is also subject to a security interest securing the purchase price of the car, will not generally be in a position to remove the tires upon default.[19]

Consider too, the unlikely case where the accession lender is not a purchase money lender. Assume that Bank has a security interest in a diesel locomotive, and assume that Finance Co. has a non-purchase money security interest in a diesel engine. When the engine is installed in the locomotive, the priority between the two secured creditors is determined by 9–322(a). If Bank made the first filing in the debtor's name, it will argue that it enjoys priority under section 9–322(a)(1) because it filed first. The inference from example 3 in Comment 6 to 9–335 is that Bank would win the argument. On the other hand, Finance Co. could argue that the Bank's financing statement did not qualify as a "filing covering the collateral" until the diesel engine was installed in the locomotive. If that were the first time Bank was considered to have filed, it would lose to Finance Co. who, by hypothesis, had filed earlier as to that collateral. We favor Bank's position and see little room for argument.

Observe that a person holding a security interest in an accession has rights and liabilities on default similar to those of the secured creditor who holds a security interest in a fixture. See Section 9–335(e) and (f).

b.   Commingled Goods

Since "commingled goods" become physically united with other goods so their identity is lost, "a security interest does not exist in commingled goods as such." Subsection 9–336(b) tells us that a security interest in the goods that become commingled attaches to the "product or mass" and that a security interest continues to be perfected if the security interest in the goods was perfected before the commingling.

Subsection 9–336(d) provides that, with the exception of multiple security interests in commingled goods, the "other provisions" of Article 9 apply to priority disputes. Thus, in Comment 7, if Bank A has a perfected security interest in baked goods and Bank B has a subsequently perfected (non-purchase money) security interest in eggs, Bank A will have priority under 9–322. But

---

[19]   See, e.g., In re Brady, 508 B.R. 736 (Bankr. E.D. Wash. 2014).

Subsection 9–336(f)(2) provides that perfected security interests in commingled goods "rank equally in proportion to the value of the collateral" at the time the collateral was commingled. Thus, if Bank One had a perfected security interest in $400,000 of commingled oats and Bank Two had a perfected security interest in $800,000 of commingled oats, Bank Two would be entitled to a share of the commingled products that would be twice as large as Bank One's share. That would be true even if Bank One's debt was $2 million and Bank Two's was only $800,000 (Bank One might get some of Two's oats if Two's debt is less than $800,000). If, on the other hand, one of the competitor's interest is not perfected at the time of the commingling, that person is subordinated by section 9–336(f)(1). To the extent that the secured creditors with claims in commingled goods compete with persons who are not secured creditors, e.g., owners or bailors, other law governs.

4–7 PRIORITIES IN DEPOSIT ACCOUNTS AND INVESTMENT PROPERTY, SECTIONS 9–327, 9–328

Section 9–102(a)(49) defines investment property as "a security, whether certificated or uncertificated, security entitlement, securities accounts, commodity contract, or commodity account." Priority disputes concerning investment property are complicated by the fact that a secured creditor can perfect its security interest by control, filing, and in some cases by possession or delivery. There are similar but less significant complications for security interests in deposit accounts, which are defined in 9–102(a)(29) as "a demand, time, savings, passbook, or similar account maintained with a bank." One can take an original security interest in a deposit account only by control, but where the deposit account is "proceeds," perfection is possible without control; so a secured creditor with control over a deposit account may find itself in conflict with a secured creditor who has perfected an interest in proceeds.

In general, the drafters grant higher status and higher priority to the secured creditor who has control than to one who perfects by other means. Typically, this is true even when the person who claims control achieved control after its competitor filed or otherwise perfected. In fact, a creditor who gets control is often second in time but first in right. It is principally this complication that calls for a separate rule for deposit accounts and for investment property of the kind we see in sections 9–327 and 9–328.

a.   Investment Property

The definition quoted above from 9–102 is not particularly helpful. It deals in the forms of the investment property but not the substance. To understand investment property, you need to study 8–102. It has definitions of "security"—certificated and not—and, more important of "security entitlement." Most secured loans by brokers and others to individual debtors against investment property will use security entitlements as collateral. A security entitlement is what the typical investor has "in" his brokerage account, or, more precisely, the name of the claim that he has against his broker. The local office of Merrill Lynch where the debtor does business is unlikely to have any stock certificates on the premises and the investor is even more unlikely to be the holder of uncertificated shares (except in mutual funds and federal debt instruments). Now is the time to wrestle with the definitions in 8–102 and to read its comments.

Subsection 9–328(1) states the general rule that the person with control has priority, irrespective of the timing. Consider the consequences of this rule. Assume, for example, a debtor grants a bank a security interest in debtor's securities account ("security entitlement") with its stockbroker and that bank then perfects by filing a financing statement. Later debtor borrows from its stockbroker, who, by hypothesis, already has "control" (just by being debtor's stockbroker and secured creditor). The priority rule stated in subsection (1) means that the stockbroker will invariably defeat the bank, even though the bank was first in time. Even if the bank is lucky enough to achieve "control," the stockbroker will still prevail because of the priority rule set forth in subsection 9–328(3). Subsection (2) of 9–328 has a series of complicated rules for other cases in which two parties somehow achieved control. With the exception of the claims of the stockbroker (the "securities intermediary") discussed above, these rules generally follow a first in time, first in right policy.

We do not believe it is possible for a stockbroker and other lenders simultaneously to have control of a certificated security in registered form or a certificated security in bearer form. But clearly it is possible under section 8–106(d) for the stockbroker and another simultaneously to have control of a securities account. For example, the stockbroker could make an agreement under 8–106(d)(2) to "comply with entitlement orders originated by" the bank, so granting "control" to the bank. If the stockbroker then makes a secured loan to the common debtor, the stockbroker will also have control under subsection (e). If that happens, the stockbroker, though later in time, would have priority over the bank (that is the rule from 9–328(3)). Despite the clear grant of priority to the broker, we can imagine the bank would feel aggrieved. Does the bank have a cause of action against the stockbroker? Might it argue that it was implicit in the stockbroker's agreement that the stockbroker would not itself prime the bank? This should be covered in any "control" agreement that the stockbroker grants to the bank. Absent explicit provisions in the control agreement, we anticipate claims by earlier secured creditors against later but superior brokers. Depending upon the circumstances ("they promised not to prime us"), we can imagine some broker losses here too.

If the bank achieved control by causing its own name to be listed as the only customer on the brokerage account, presumably the stockbroker would be foreclosed from achieving control over that account. By hypothesis, the debtor who was formerly listed as the owner of the security entitlement would no longer have the power to grant an interest in that entitlement after it had allowed the bank to be listed as owner of the account. If, on the other hand, the bank is listed merely as a co-owner of the entitlement, a different rule probably applies. In that case the bank may well have achieved control but, absent an agreement to the contrary, it will have left the debtor with the full power to transfer title to all of the assets in the account, including perhaps even the power to grant control to the broker.

b.   Deposit Accounts

The general rule on priority of security interests in deposit accounts is easy to state: almost always the depositary bank with a security interest in the account will have control and will be entitled to priority over competing secured creditors. The most common competition for the bank will come from a secured creditor whose proceeds have been deposited into the account. Invariably the bank will defeat that secured creditor either because of subsection 9–327(1) or (3). Under subsection (1) a security interest perfected by control has priority over one without control; subsection (3) provides the bank with control where the account is housed priority over others. A bank with a security interest in a deposit account perfected by control does not lose such interest simply because it has not yet setoff the account or refused to continue honoring checks on the account.[20]

Subsection (2) provides that, in other cases with multiple security interests perfected by control and not governed by

---

[20]   Fifth Third Bank v. Peoples Nat. Bank, 929 N.E.2d 210 (Ind. App. 2010). Although the competing creditor in this case was a judgment creditor and not another Article 9 secured party, we see no reason the result would be different if such were the case.

subsections (3) and (4), the security interest that is first to control wins. Instances governed by subsection (2) will likely be rare. Subsection (4) of 9–327 states the only significant exception to these general rules. If the competing creditor achieved control over the deposit account (section 9–104(a)(3)) by becoming the "bank's customer," that creditor defeats the bank even if the bank had control of the account before that creditor acquired control. Note too, the third party may be able to achieve this result by making the account a joint account. At least as we read 9–104, the secured creditor need not become the sole holder of the account.

4–8 BUYERS OF GOODS, SECTIONS 9–317, 9–320

In one way or another, many sections of the Code pose the question whether a buyer takes free of a prior security interest. The general rule stated in section 9–201 is that the security agreement "is effective . . . against purchasers of the collateral." The rule of that section is confirmed by 9–315(a)(1) which states that the security interest "continues in collateral notwithstanding sale . . . or other disposition." Thus, the default rule in sales of personal property subject to a security interest (as with real property subject to a mortgage), is that the buyer purchases the property subject to the security interest. Meaning, of course, that in the event of seller's/debtor's default on the secured obligation, the secured party could potentially repossess or otherwise exercise dominion over the collateral in the hands of a disappointed buyer.

However, there are major exceptions to this general rule. Thus, subsection 9–317(b) states that a buyer who gives value and receives delivery of collateral without knowledge of a prior security interest and "before it is perfected" takes free of the security interest. Section 9–320 goes even further—it allows certain buyers to take free even of certain perfected security interests. Moreover, many buyers will take free of a security interest because the secured party has "authorized the disposition free of the security interest," see section 9–315(a)(1). Thus, the starting point for any analysis about the rights of a buyer vis-à-vis a prior secured creditor is the security agreement itself.

a. Buyers vis-à-vis Unperfected Secured Creditors

Section 9–317(b) is essentially unchanged from former 9–301. The section only applies to collateral which is capable of being physically "delivered." The section thus applies to buyers of "tangible chattel paper, tangible documents, goods, instruments, [and] certificated security[ies]." To defeat a prior unperfected secured creditor, the buyer must first give value; section 1–204 states minimal requirements for "value." For example, it is enough that the buyer merely promises to do something in return for the transfer of the goods. The buyer must however receive "delivery"; that term was brought forward in 1999 from the prior Code and has not caused trouble even though the definition of "delivery" in section 1–201 does not apply to "goods." (That definition applies to instruments and several other forms of intangibles, and in that case it means "voluntary transfer of possession.") We do not understand why "goods" have been omitted, but applying the definition by analogy might lead one to conclude that a buyer who did not get "possession" would lose to a prior unperfected secured creditor. The buyer must also be "without knowledge of the security interest" at the time of its purchase. Knowledge is defined in 1–202 as "actual knowledge"; so the transaction can be a little suspicious and still leave the buyer as victorious as one "without knowledge."[21]

b.   Buyers in the Ordinary Course vs. Perfected Secured Creditors

Most of the interesting buyer cases will arise under section 9–320(a) (former 9–307(1)) which reads as follows:

(a) [Buyer in ordinary course of business.] Except as otherwise provided in subsection (e), a buyer in ordinary course of business, other than a person buying farm products from a person engaged in farming operations, takes free of a security interest created by the buyer's seller, even if the security interest is perfected and the buyer knows of its existence.

Consider the classic case of consumer Jones who buys a refrigerator. Even though the refrigerator is subject to a perfected security interest, neither Jones, the public-at-large, nor even the secured creditor would expect Jones to take subject to the security interest. Nor would we expect Jones to search the files to determine whether the seller had granted a security interest in inventory to a third person. Section 9–320(a) bows to that commercial reality.

The cases with which lawyers are concerned will not be as simple as the Jones case. The cases have presented a variety of challenges to the buyer in ordinary course rules. Dissection of this subsection together with 1–201(b)(9) reveals a variety of conditions that one must meet if one is to be free of a prior perfected security interest:

(1) The person must be a buyer in the ordinary course,

---

[21]   Under 9–320(d), a buyer in ordinary course of business buying oil, gas or other minerals at the wellhead takes free not only of Article 9 security interests, but also of interests "arising out of an encumbrance."

(2) who does not buy in bulk and does not take his interest as security for or in total or partial satisfaction of a pre-existing debt (that is, he must give some form of "new" value),

(3) who buys from one in the business of selling goods of that kind (that is, cars from a car dealer, i.e. inventory),

(4) who buys in good faith and without knowledge that his purchase is in violation of others' ownership rights or security interests, and

(5) does not buy farm products from a person engaged in farming operations, and

(6) the competing security interest must be one "created by the buyer's seller."

Several of these conditions come from subsection (9) of 1–201(b) which defines the term "buyer in ordinary course of business." The new value and good faith requirements, and the requirement that the buyer buy out of inventory enter 9–320(a) via 1–201. Let us turn to some of the interpretive difficulties. Only rarely will it be difficult to tell whether the seller was "in the business of selling goods of that kind."[22] The jeweler sells jewels, a haberdasher sells clothes, an automobile dealer sells automobiles, an appliance dealer sells appliances, etc. But what of a buyer who purchases an automobile from a seller whose primary business is renting automobiles, yet who occasionally engages in selling them? In Hempstead Bank v. Andy's Car Rental System, Inc.,[23] the New York Appellate Division refused to find such a car rental agency "in the business of selling goods of that kind," even though its cars were classified as "inventory" under 9–102. And yet, inventory goes beyond goods held by a store for retail sale, such that timber cut and sold to mills was held to result in a buyer in the ordinary course of business in Fordyce Bank and Trust Co. v. Bean Timberland, Inc.[24]

That the buyer must purchase in "good faith" and "without knowledge that the sale to him is in violation of the . . . security interest of a third party" may cause uncertainty. Exactly what the good faith requirement adds is unclear. Also, the requirement that the buyer have no knowledge may seem to conflict with the words of 9–320(a), which permits the buyer to take free even though the buyer "knows of [the security interest's] existence." On careful reading the

---

[22]   See Kusler v. Cipriotti, 221 N.J.Super. 654, 535 A.2d 567, 5 UCC2d 492 (Law Div. 1987) (private owner not in the business of selling yachts, though sold through a broker/dealer who was in that business); American Nat'l Bank v. Cloud, 201 Cal.App.3d 766, 247 Cal.Rptr. 325, 6 UCC2d 8 (1988).

[23]   35 A.D.2d 35, 312 N.Y.S.2d 317, 7 UCC 932 (1970).

[24]   251 S.W.3d 267, 62 U.C.C. Rep. Serv. 2d 133 (2007).

two requirements do not conflict. The buyer fails to qualify under 9–320(a) only if buyer knows that the sale is "in violation" of the security interest.[25] Normally a lender with a security interest in inventory intends the debtor to be able to sell the inventory free and clear. Thus, it is perfectly consistent for a buyer to know of a security interest but to believe the sale is not in violation of that interest.[26] Comment 3 to 9–320 explains:

> Reading the definition together with the rule of law results in the buyer's taking free if the buyer merely knows that a security interest covers the goods but taking subject if the buyer knows, in addition, that the sale violates a term in an agreement with the secured party.

A final requirement of 9–320(a) is that the security interest of which the buyer takes free be "created by the buyer's seller." In the usual case where the buyer purchases an automobile from a dealer's inventory, the dealer created the security interest in the lender. But consider the case of Mrs. Jones who purchases a new automobile and gives a security interest to Rao Bank; then Mrs. Jones trades the automobile in (without revealing the security interest) to Purkayastha Motors, an automobile dealer who in turn sells the automobile to Szot. Ultimately, Rao Bank attempts to recover the automobile from Szot. Because the security interest was not created by Szot's seller (Purkayastha Motors), but by Jones, Szot does not qualify for coverage under 9–320(a), and his interest will be subordinate to the security interest of Rao Bank.[27] The language and the intention of the Code seem clear enough. The difficulty is that the policy of 9–320 would seem to cover Szot. He is neither more nor less than a garden variety purchaser who pays cash and buys out of the inventory of a dealer. Perhaps the drafters intended that as between two innocent parties the ultimate loss should fall on the party who dealt most closely with the bad guy. After Szot buys from

---

[25]   O.M. Scott Credit Corp. v. Apex, Inc., 97 R.I. 442, 198 A.2d 673, 2 UCC 92 (1964) (buyer could not qualify as buyer in ordinary course of business when he knew sale violated terms of security agreement); Producers Cotton Oil Co. v. Amstar Corp., 197 Cal.App.3d 638, 242 Cal.Rptr. 914, 5 UCC2d 32 (1988) (buyer of beets knew farmer required written authorization for sale when its request for subordination was turned down); Transamerica Commercial Finance Corp. v. Union Bank & Trust Co., 584 So.2d 1299, 15 UCC2d 412 (Ala.1991) (purchaser, a leasing company, and seller, a car dealership, were mutually owned, thus purchaser was aware that purchase was in violation of security agreement).

[26]   But see, Davis County Sav. Bank v. Production Credit Ass'n, 419 N.W.2d 384, 5 UCC2d 559 (Iowa 1988) (buyers' knowledge of security agreement prevented them from being buyers in the ordinary course).

[27]   See Martin Bros. Implement Co. v. Diepholz, 109 Ill.App.3d 283, 64 Ill.Dec. 768, 440 N.E.2d 320, 34 UCC 1749 (1982) (9–307(1) does not protect a buyer in ordinary course from a security interest created by a former owner who is not the buyer's seller).

Purkayastha Motors, both he and Rao Bank are innocent parties. Szot will have a cause of action against Purkayastha Motors for breach of warranty of title; Purkayastha Motors will have a similar cause of action against Mrs. Jones who committed the fraud. If Mrs. Jones cannot pay or is otherwise out of the picture but Purkayastha Motors is solvent, the loss will land on Purkayastha.

Prior to the enactment of the Food Security Act, a person buying farm products[28] from a person engaged in farming operations would not take free of a security interest created by the farmer.[29] To illustrate, assume that bank held a perfected security interest in all of Farmer Jones' livestock. Farmer took a load of hogs to the sale barn where the hogs were purchased by a packing house. Although the packing house would be a buyer in the ordinary course of business, the good faith purchase did not cut off the bank's security interest in the hogs under 9–320(a) as originally enacted. Even after the hogs were slaughtered and hanging in the packing house cooler, the bank could repossess them. It could, if it were quick, follow them into the hands of a retail store.[30] In December 1985, Congress invalidated the farm products rule of 9–320(a).[31]

Prior to the federal law, farm buyers often escaped the rule of former 9–307(1) (now 9–320(a)) by arguing that the competing farm lender had "waived" its security interest or was estopped to assert it. Although the federal act referred to above has rendered most of the waiver and estoppel cases moot in the farm context, those cases still

---

[28]   See, e.g., In re Cadwell, Martin Meat Co., 1970 WL 12561, 10 UCC 710 (Bankr.E.D.Cal.1970) (cattle in feedlot are "farm products"). Compare Farmers State Bank v. Webel, 113 Ill.App.3d 87, 68 Ill.Dec. 619, 446 N.E.2d 525, 36 UCC 319 (1983) (where debtor marketed pigs but also held some pigs for fattening, the pigs were "inventory").

[29]   Where the secured party consented to sales (in violation of the security agreement) on the condition that proceeds be remitted, a buyer could not take free of the secured party's interest in proceeds. See, e.g., In re Coast Trading Co., 31 B.R. 670, 36 UCC 1753 (Bankr.D.Or.1983); Southwest Washington Production Credit Ass'n v. Seattle-First Nat'l Bank, 92 Wash.2d 30, 593 P.2d 167, 26 UCC 1346 (1979). Compare with cases in which secured parties had knowledge of the unauthorized sale of secured collateral or of prior sales, but did nothing. Some courts held such inaction to be a waiver of the secured party's rights to the collateral sold. See, e.g., Clovis Nat'l Bank v. Thomas, 77 N.M. 554, 425 P.2d 726, 4 UCC 137 (1967); United States v. Central Livestock Ass'n, 349 F.Supp. 1033, 11 UCC 1054 (D.N.D.1972).

[30]   Several courts have drawn the line at the horse's mouth. Brace v. Farmers Home Administration, 163 B.R. 274, 22 UCC2d 1184 (Bankr.W.D.Pa.1994) (security interest in hay extinguished when eaten by cattle).

[31]   Although many cases will be overruled by the Food Security Act, their reasoning is still relevant to cases outside of the farm products context. See, e.g., In re Darling's Homes, Inc., 46 B.R. 370, 40 UCC 1507 (Bankr.D.Del.1985) (where security agreement expressly authorized sale of collateral, the fact that the debtor failed to remit proceeds was a violation of a condition subsequent and therefore did not invalidate the authorization to sell).

have vitality in other areas.[32] For example, one who buys equipment will not be a buyer in the ordinary course and will therefore not be entitled to the protection of 9–320(a). Nevertheless, such a purchaser may argue, like the purchasers of farm collateral formerly did, that the security creditor waived the security interest or was estopped to assert it.

In any case in which the creditor has given proper notice under the Farm Security Act, or in which the buyer fails to be a buyer in the ordinary course of inventory or other goods for any reason, the old farm products sale cases above may be relevant. If the buyer believes that the debtor seller is selling free of the security interest because it had done so before, or because there were acts implicitly waiving the security interest, those cases may support that argument. They are most likely to be useful and a waiver to be found, of course, where there are repeated opportunities for action as in the periodic sale of cattle or crops. (For a brief discussion of the federal farm product rules, see Chapter 4–9.)

c.   Relationship Between Sections 9–320 and 2–403

Section 2–403 is the Article 2 analog to 9–320. Like 9–320 it is a bona fide purchase provision designed to protect good faith purchasers from certain prior interests. May a subsequent purchaser disappointed under 9–320 fall back on 2–403 and argue that it renders him superior to a prior security interest? We believe the answer is no, and we think that the cases holding to the contrary are in error.[33]

---

[32]   See Citizens Nat'l Bank of Madelia v. Mankato Implement, Inc., 427 N.W.2d 23, 8 UCC2d 233 (Minn.App.1988) (applying farm product waiver cases to security agreement involving equipment), aff'd, 441 N.W.2d 483, 8 UCC2d 874 (Minn.1989).

[33]   We find the New Hampshire court's interpretation on this issue to be persuasive. In National Shawmut Bank v. Jones, 108 N.H. 386, 236 A.2d 484, 4 UCC 1021 (1967) the court held that the buyer did not qualify for the preferred treatment of 9–307(1) because the competing security interest had not been "created by his seller." Buyer also argued that he took free from the security interest under 2–403. The court rejected that argument and found that 2–403 did not apply in part on the basis of the restrictive language in former 9–306(2) referring to Article 9 (emphasis added): "[Section] 9-306(2) provides for the continuance of the security interest '*except when this Article provides otherwise*,' thereby limiting any exceptions to those contained in Article 9." *Id*. at 486. In addition, the court pointed to 2–402 which, along with 2-403, at least intimates that the dispute between purchasers and secured creditors should be governed by Article 9. *Id*.

The outcome of the *Jones* case is also supported by Comment 2 to 2–403. In part, that Comment provides: "As to entrusting by a secured party, subsection (2) is limited by the more specific provisions of section 9–307(1), which deny protection to a person buying farm products from a person engaged in farming operations."

In general the drafters of Revised Article 9 indorse this outcome. Example 1 in Comment 3 to 9–320 follows:

> Manufacturer, who is in the business of manufacturing appliances, owns manufacturing equipment subject to a perfected security interest in favor of Lender. Manufacturer sells the equipment to Dealer, who is in the business of buying and selling used equipment. Buyer buys the equipment from Dealer. Even if Buyer qualifies as a buyer in the ordinary course of business, Buyer does not take free of Lender's security interest under subsection (a), because Dealer did not create the security interest; Manufacturer did.

But the drafters equivocate. For example, Comment 6 to 9–320 recognizes that a secured creditor might waive or "be precluded from asserting its security interest against the buyer. See section 1–103." And, example 2 from Comment 3 recognizes that a secured creditor might have its rights cut-off by section 2–403 if it acquiesced in a dealer's possession of its collateral:

> Manufacturer, who is in the business of manufacturing appliances, owns manufacturing equipment subject to a perfected security interest in favor of Lender. Manufacturer sells the equipment to Dealer, who is in the business of buying and selling used equipment. Lender learns of the sale but does nothing to assert its security interest. Buyer buys the equipment from Dealer. Inasmuch as Lender's acquiescence constitutes an "entrusting" of the goods to Dealer within the meaning of section 2–403(3), Buyer takes free of Lender's security interest under section 2–403(2) if Buyer qualifies as a buyer in ordinary course of business.

So the lines are not quite as bright as one might wish. We suspect that buyers and sympathetic courts may interpret the Comments to 9–320 to be invitations to allow the sacred cows of equity to stomp out the clear line between successful bona fide purchasers and losers now set out in section 9–320. However, in at least one case where section 2–403 was argued by a buyer to avoid a security interest granted by a prior owner (who had then transferred the vehicle to the dealer who then sold to the arguing buyer), the court declined the invitation, instead holding that the buyer did not take free under 9–320(a) because the security interest was not created by the buyer's seller.[34]

---

[34] Walden v. Mercedes Benz Credit Corp., 57 U.C.C. Rep. Serv. 2d 182 (C.P. 2005).

Comment 8 to section 9–320 provides an explanation for subsection (e). It says that the subsection "rejects the holding of Tanbro Fabrics Corp. v. Deering Milliken, Inc., 39 N.Y.2d 632, 350 N.E.2d 590, 19 UCC 385 (1976)[35] and together with 9–317(b) prevents a buyer of goods collateral from taking free of a security interest if the collateral is in the possession of the secured party." Of course, this subsection overlaps to some degree with section 1–201(b)(9)'s provision denying buyer in ordinary course status to a buyer who does not obtain possession or possessory rights.[36] When the secured party retains possession of the goods to the exclusion of the seller or buyer, the case against granting ordinary course status becomes clearer.

d.   Consumer Buyers of Consumer Goods vs. Secured Creditors

Section 9–320(b) restates and clarifies the rules of former 9–307(2):

(b) [Buyer of consumer goods.] Except as otherwise provided in subsection (e), a buyer of goods from a person who used or bought the goods for use primarily for personal, family, or household purposes takes free of a security interest, even if perfected, if the buyer buys:

(1) without knowledge of the security interest;

(2) for value;

(3) primarily for the buyer's personal, family, or household purposes; and

(4) before the filing of a financing statement covering the goods.

One should first understand that this provision is very narrow. In the words of Professor Gilmore, it is intended for sales "by amateurs to amateurs." Note that the seller must have used goods primarily for personal, family or household purposes and the buyer must do the same. Therefore, if the seller is in the business of selling these goods, the section does not apply; like-wise, if the buyer is purchasing the goods for its business, the section does not apply. Note too, the buyer does not take free if the secured creditor has filed a

---

[35]   In *Tanbro*, first seller, pending payment, retained possession of goods sold to protect its interest. Without paying the original seller, the first buyer resold to a second buyer who successfully asserted the right of a BIOCB and took the goods out of the hands of the astonished, unpaid and angry first seller.

[36]   See, e.g., Crestmark Bank v. Electrolux Home Products, Inc., 88 U.C.C. Rep. Serv. 2d 711 (E.D. Mich. 2016) (denying buyer in ordinary course status to buyer of finished component parts from manufacturer, when parts remained in manufacturer's possession, and manufacturer had granted security interest in the parts to it slender).

financing statement (or, in the case of motor vehicles, before the secured creditor has effected its lien on the certificate of title under 9–311(b)).[37] In effect, this section is the antidote for the automatic perfection rules found in 9–309(1). Recall that a seller of a refrigerator to a consumer who retains a purchase money security interest is automatically perfected without filing or any other public act. That means one who wishes to purchase the refrigerator from the original owner will have no way of finding out about the purchase money seller's security interest. Accordingly, it is only fair that the amateur buyer takes free. This rule is sometimes called the "garage sale" exception to the general rule; it is hard to exaggerate its unimportance.

4–9 PROTECTION OF PURCHASERS OF FARM PRODUCTS

In the 1985 Food Security Act, Congress changed the rules concerning ordinary purchase of farm products. Stimulated by auctioneers, representatives of grain elevators, and other purchasers of farm products, Congress provided as follows:

> Except as provided in subsection (e) and notwithstanding any other provision of Federal, State or local law, a buyer who in the ordinary course of business buys a farm product from a seller engaged in farming operations shall take free of a security interest created by the seller, even though the security interest is perfected; and the buyer knows of the existence of such interest.[38]

Unless a buyer in the ordinary course of farm products "from a seller engaged in farming operations" fits within one of the sections provided in the federal law, that buyer is treated as any other buyer in the ordinary course and, therefore, takes free of almost all prior security interests in those products even though those security interests are perfected.

Congress was not impressed with lenders' justification for the anti-bona fide purchaser rule for farm sales. Farm lenders had justified the exception to bona fide purchaser priority in former 9–307 for farm products on the ground that buyers of farm products are much more sophisticated than the typical consumer buyer and can therefore be expected to check the files and to remit proceeds when necessary to the one holding a security interest. Moreover, they

---

[37]   See, e.g., Bank v. Parish, 317 P.3d 750, 82 U.C.C. Rep. Serv. 2d 551 (Kan. 2014) (holding, under § 9–320(b), that consumer did not take free of security interest in vehicle because it had already been perfected via the certificate of title by the time of purchase).

[38]   Food Security Act of 1985, § 1324, 7 U.S.C.A. 1631 (1982 & Supp.).

analogize such sales to bulk sales, for in many cases a farm product sale will constitute the sale of all of the livestock of a farm or of its entire crop in one sale on a single day to a single person.

In a limited recognition of these policies, the Act gave creditors three exceptions to the override; if the creditor fits into any of the three exceptions, its security interest will carry over against the buyer. Two of the exceptions depend upon a state's enactment of a central filing system of a kind specified in the federal act. As of October 1, 2017, 19 states have enacted such a statute.[39]

In the absence of such a federally blessed central filing system enacted by the state,[40] the secured creditor can get protection against an ordinary course buyer only by giving that buyer notice of the creditor's interest in a form specified in the federal law. The notice is much more detailed than a UCC–1, for it requires information such as the debtor's social security number or taxpayer identification number, requires the identification of farm products by type, county, crop year, and amount. Because of the detail required in the notice, it will be easy for the creditor to fail to give proper notice. The names of buyers are typically provided either by the farm debtor or will be procured by the lender itself; the list would include any large-scale bulk purchasers of grain or livestock in the debtor's place of residence or in the adjoining counties. Of course, this system can be easily foiled by the farmer's selling out of his normal trade area, particularly in states which prohibit the bank from sending notice to anyone not on the farmer's list.

Because the federal act contains its own definition of "buyer in ordinary course,"[41] a notice that tells the buyer that a sale to that buyer by a specific farmer is a violation of a security agreement will not keep the buyer from being a purchaser in the ordinary course under the federal definition. Under the UCC, however, one who has notice that the sale to him is in "violation of the ownership right or security interest" is not a buyer in the ordinary course. Under the

---

[39]   19 states have central filing systems certified by the U.S. Department of Agriculture: AL, CO, ID, LA, ME, MN, MS, MT, NE, NH, NM, ND, OK, OR, SD, UT, VT, WV, and WY. See, Erickson, The Federal Farm Products Statute: What do Buyers and Agricultural Lenders Think After Eight Years of Living With It, 18 Hamline L. Rev. 363, 380 n.39 (1995) (citing 20 states with certified central filing systems, however, certification of Arkansas' filing system was withdrawn in 1989); U.S. Department of Agriculture. https://www.gipsa.usda.gov/laws/cleartitle.aspx (providing regularly updated information).

[40]   Even in states that create a central filing system, direct notice in accordance with the federal statute is sufficient by itself to protect a secured creditor. See Lisco State Bank v. McCombs Ranches, Inc., 752 F.Supp. 329, 13 UCC2d 927 (D.Neb.1990).

[41]   Section 1631(c)(1) defines "buyer in the ordinary course of business" as: a person who, in the ordinary course of business, buys farm products from a person engaged in farming operations who is in the business of selling farm products.

federal law, that person can be a buyer in the ordinary course because there is no similar knowledge exclusion.

One studying the federal law should not throw out all old learning, however. In the first place, a secured creditor who provides potential buyers with notice under the Farm Food Security Act does not thereby perfect an Article 9 security interest. The federal notice protects the creditor against the buyer to whom notice is given (even when the security interest is unperfected), but it will not protect an unperfected security interest against an attack by the trustee in bankruptcy. Even if the secured creditor gives a proper notice to the buyer, the buyer may still argue that the terms prohibiting sale in the security agreement and the note were waived by the secured party or that the secured party is estopped to assert them. This argument will arise in exactly the same circumstances and be based upon the same scenario as cases decided under former 9–307(1). Notwithstanding these arguments in common, a practitioner in this area must study the Food Security Act carefully, as landmines await in the form of differences with the structure of Article 9.[42]

4–10 BUYERS OF INTANGIBLES

a. Buyers of Chattel Paper and Instruments

1. Chattel Paper

The classic case under Section 9–330 involves a secured creditor with a floating lien on inventory who includes a proceeds claim in chattel paper whose interest conflicts with that of a "purchaser" of this very chattel paper. In some cases the secured creditor may have expected the debtor to sell the chattel paper and to remit the proceeds as payment on its secured debt. When the debtor sells the chattel paper but fails to use the proceeds to reduce the inventory loan, the inventory lender and the purchaser of the chattel paper may assert conflicting claims to that paper. In other cases, the original secured creditor may have lent money against specific items of chattel paper and may therefore assert a more credible claim against that paper in competition with the purchaser of the paper.

Section 9–330 states rules—similar to those in former 9–308—that allow a buyer of the chattel paper to take free of such an earlier

---

[42]   See, e.g., State Bank of Cherry v. CGB Enterprises, Inc., 964 N.E.2d 604, 76 U.C.C. Rep. Serv. 2d 468 (Ill. App. Ct. 3d Dist. 2012), aff'd, 984 N.E.2d 449 (Ill. 2013) (applying a "strict compliance" test to secured party's notices to buyer under Food Security Act, whereas cases applying Article 9 in Illinois had applied a more lenient "substantial compliance" test to notices given under Article 9); In re Printz, 478 B.R. 876, 78 U.C.C. Rep. Serv. 2d 782 (Bankr. C.D. Ill. 2012) (noting that the Food Security Act's definition of "security interest" does not apply to proceeds).

claim if the buyer meets a certain set of conditions. Specifically, section 9–330 provides in pertinent part as follows:

(a) [Purchaser's priority: security interest claimed merely as proceeds.] A purchaser of chattel paper has priority over a security interest in the chattel paper which is claimed merely as proceeds of inventory subject to a security interest if:

(1) in good faith and in the ordinary course of the purchaser's business, the purchaser gives new value and takes possession of the chattel paper or obtains control of the chattel paper under section 9–105; and

(2) the chattel paper does not indicate that it has been assigned to an identified assignee other than the purchaser.

(b) [Purchaser's priority: other security interests.] A purchaser of chattel paper has priority over a security interest in the chattel paper which is claimed other than merely as proceeds of inventory subject to a security interest if the purchaser gives new value and takes possession of the chattel paper or obtains control of the chattel paper under Section 9–105 in good faith, in the ordinary course of the purchaser's business, and without knowledge that the purchase violates the rights of the secured party.[43]

Subsection (a) deals with the case where the original secured creditor claims chattel paper "merely as proceeds." Subsection (b) covers the case where the original secured creditor claims something more than "proceeds." In the latter case, the original secured creditor has loaned money to the debtor somehow in reliance upon the chattel paper. The 1999 revision does not elaborate on "merely as proceeds," rather it directs one to PEB Commentary No. 8:

A lender who agrees to lend up to a specified percentage of the cost of inventory and receivables, has more than a mere proceeds interest in the chattel paper which is a part of the receivables covered by the security agreement.

In other words, if the value of the chattel paper was included in the formula to determine the amount of the loan, the Commentary suggests that a person making the loan is asserting a claim greater

---

[43] Section 9–330(b)'s reference to section 9–105 pertains to perfection by obtaining "control" of chattel paper in electronic form. In 2010, 9–105 was amended to add new subsection (a), which provides that the security party effects control of electronic chattel paper if "a system employed for evidencing the transfer of interests in the chattel paper reliably establishes the secured party as the person to which the chattel paper was assigned." This is in addition to the more specific means by which to obtain control which are now set forth in subsection (b) of 9–105.

than a "proceeds" claim in the chattel paper and, therefore, is entitled to the greater protection of subsection (b).

Assume an original secured creditor lent principally against inventory. That is, assume its claim to the chattel paper was *merely* a proceeds claim. Under former section 9–308, a buyer took free of the original secured creditor's interest only if it gave new value and took possession in the ordinary course of business—even if the buyer knew "the specific paper" was "subject to a security interest." If, on the other hand, the claim of the original secured creditor was considered to be something *more than a mere* proceeds claim, the buyer had to act "without knowledge that the specific paper" was "subject to a security interest."

The rules in section 9–330 are similar but different. Under 9–330(a) the secured creditor beats the buyer of chattel paper if the chattel paper itself "indicates that it has been assigned." Thus, a stamp on chattel paper showing ownership in an assignee-secured creditor will protect a secured creditor even though that creditor has only a proceeds claim. Unlike former 9–308, new subsection (a) makes no mention of the knowledge of the buyer, in the priority dispute between the buyer and the inventory lender claiming the chattel paper as proceeds. Thus, by subordinating the buyer where there is a legend on the face of the paper, the new law cuts back on the buyer's rights and concomitantly gives the inventory lender a means to protect its interest in the paper from such buyers. On the other hand, it expands the buyer's rights by allowing the buyer to take free even if the buyer knows that its purchase may violate the rights of the prior secured creditor. (The only restriction on buyer's knowledge is the requirement that it act in good faith.)

Section 9–330(b) allows a buyer of chattel paper to take free of a prior perfected security interest claimed "other than merely as proceeds" if that buyer meets the usual conditions (new value, possession, ordinary course) and is "without knowledge that the purchase violates the rights of the secured party." The change from the former law (which subordinated the buyer when the buyer had "knowledge that the *specific paper*" was "subject to a security interest") is to conform to what the drafters believe to be the current practice. In Comment 6 the drafters note that it is insufficient to subordinate a purchaser of chattel paper simply because that purchaser has "seen a financing statement covering the chattel paper" (and so knows it is probably subject to a security interest). The Comment goes on to state that a purchaser who has seen a statement in a financing statement with an indication that a purchase "would violate the rights of the filed party" has the kind of knowledge that would and should subordinate the purchaser.

Subsection (f) states that if "chattel paper . . . indicates that it has been assigned to an identified secured party," this will be conclusive proof of the purchaser's knowledge that its purchase "violates the rights of the secured party." So a legend on the face of the paper protects a secured creditor whether that creditor claims "merely as proceeds" or otherwise.

Section 9–102(a)(57) provides the definition of "new value" relevant to buyers under 9–330. It states that "new value" means "(i) money, (ii) money's worth in property, services, or new credit, or (iii) release by a transferee of an interest in property previously transferred to the transferee. The term does not include an obligation substituted for another obligation."

The changes in section 9–330 point in opposite directions. They give safe harbor to the inventory lender who wishes to insure that no buyer of chattel paper will gain priority. If the inventory lender stamps the chattel paper to show that the paper has been assigned to the inventory lender, the purchaser's claim is subordinated, see 9–330(a) and (f). The changes also expand the rights of a purchaser, somewhat. First, subsection (b) allows the purchaser to take free of a prior perfected security interest even though the purchaser knows of the existence of a security interest in the particular paper as long as the purchaser does not know that its purchase will "violate" the rights of the prior secured party. Second, subsection (a) omits any reference to the knowledge of the purchaser.

2. *Instruments*

Although 9–330 deals mostly with chattel paper, it also covers instruments. Subsection 9–102(a)(47) defines an "instrument" as:

> . . . a negotiable instrument or any other writing that evidences a right to the payment of a monetary obligation, is not itself a security agreement or lease, and is of a type that in ordinary course of business is transferred by delivery with any necessary indorsement or assignment. The term does not include (i) investment property, (ii) letters of credit, or (iii) writings that evidence a right to payment arising out of the use of a credit or charge card or information contained on or for use with the card[.]

Of course, the purchaser of a negotiable instrument might qualify as a holder in due course under Article 3 and so take free of a prior security interest (a possibility made explicit in section 9–331 and discussed below). But even if the purchaser fails to be a holder in due course, the purchaser will frequently win under subsection 9–330(d) over a prior perfected security interest (perfected by any method other than "possession") where the purchaser "gives value and takes possession of the instrument in good faith and without knowledge that the purchase violates the rights of the secured party." Ordinarily, to prevail under 9–330(d) the purchaser will need to take actual possession of the instrument as provided by the text. However, in a proper case, constructive possession of the instrument (as when it is physically possessed by an escrow agent on behalf of the purchaser) has been held to suffice under 9–330(d).[44]

So how does 9–330(d) add anything to the holder in due course status that the purchaser enjoys anyway? Consider what Comment 7 shows, that takers whose "notice" might deprive them of holder in due course status may still prevail here:

> Generally, to the extent subsection (d) conflicts with section 3–306, subsection (d) governs, see section 3–102(b). For example, notice of a conflicting security interest precludes a purchaser from becoming a holder in due course under section 3–302 and thereby taking free of all claims to the instrument under section 3–306. However, a purchaser who takes even with knowledge of the security interest qualifies for priority under subsection (d) if it takes without knowledge that the purchase violates the rights of the holder of the security interest. Likewise, a purchaser qualifies for priority under subsection (d) if it takes for "value" as defined in section 1–201, even if it does not take for "value" as defined in section 3–303.

An additional difference arises from the definition of "instruments": "instruments" in Article 9 are a larger class than negotiable instruments. As a result, one may fail to be a holder in due course because he does not hold a "negotiable" instrument and yet win out under 9–330 as a bona fide purchaser of an Article 9 "instrument."

The rules in section 9–330 are complicated, but clear. Both the original version (9–308) and its successor (9–330) are attempts to conform the law to practice. Presumably the drafters of 1999 knew the practice better than the drafters of 1962.

---

[44]   Wakefield Kennedy, LLC v. State Capital Holdings, LLC, 614 Fed.Appx. 929, 86 UCC Rep.Serv.2d 869 (10th Cir. 2015). The court also noted that:

> "[c]onstructive possession of an instrument has been recognized in cases involving the UCC's related 'holder in due course' principle." *Id.* (citing Georg v. Metro Fixtures Contractors, Inc., 178 P.3d 1209, 1214 (Colo.2008)).

b.   Priority Rights of Other Purchasers and Transferees, Sections 9–331, 9–332

Section 9–331 is the successor to 9–309 of the pre-1999 Code. The new section, even more than the old, states what would probably have been assumed in any case: that one who enjoys the rights of a holder in due course (or has similar rights under Articles 7 or 8) enjoys those rights vis-à-vis the secured creditor and, if the rights of that secured creditor would be cut off under Article 3, nothing in Article 9 would change the outcome. Subsection (c) states that filing of a financing statement or the like does not constitute "notice of a claim or defense." Subsection 9–332(a) tells us what every drug dealer and fence knows: possession gives one good title to cash— except in quite extraordinary circumstances and in criminal law. More interesting is the rule in subsection (b) that the "transferee of funds from a deposit account takes free of a security interest in the deposit account unless the transferee acts in collusion." Consider example 1 in Comment 2:

> Debtor maintains a deposit account with Bank A. The deposit account is subject to a perfected security interest in favor of Lender. Debtor draws a check on the account, payable to Payee. Inasmuch as the check is not the proceeds of the deposit account (it is an order to pay funds from the deposit account), Lender's security interest in the deposit account does not give rise to a security interest in the check. Payee deposits the check into its own deposit account, and Bank A pays it. Unless Payee acted in collusion with Debtor in violating Lender's rights, Payee takes the funds (the credits running in favor of Payee) free of Lender's security interest. This is true regardless of whether Payee is a holder in due course of the check and even if Payee gave no value for the check.

While the check itself may not be "proceeds," presumably the credit which the payor bank forwards to the depositary bank is "proceeds" and would be subject to a claim under section 9–315 but for section 9–332(b).

An important case for sections 9–331 and 9–332 involves the rights of junior secured creditors who have been paid, see Comment 5 to section 9–331. Assume that Secured Creditor One has a prior perfected security interest in debtor's inventory and in the receivables from the inventory. Assume that Secured Creditor Two has a subordinate security interest in the same assets. By hypothesis, all of the checks, cash and other payments that come into the hands of debtor are subject to Secured Creditor One's security interest as identifiable proceeds. Assume the common debtor pays Secured Creditor Two in three different ways: 1) by check from debtor's bank account, 2) by indorsement of checks received from debtor's customers, and 3) by direct transfer of cash from the till. Secured Creditor Two is probably protected as to the cash by 9–332(a),[45] and as to the checks drawn on the debtor's account, by 9–332(b).[46] Secured Creditor Two fails under these two sections only if it acts "in collusion with the debtor in violating the rights" of Secured Creditor One. Comment 4 to 9–332 emphasizes that Secured Creditor Two must truly be a "bad actor" to be "in collusion." Normally knowledge that the payment violates Secured Creditor One's security interest is not enough for "collusion." After all, we are hypothesizing a junior creditor that has a right to payment and a senior creditor that has failed to take the actions that might protect its proceeds (e.g., requiring a "lockbox"). Although, as an aside, much depends on the language of the lockbox agreement. In one case, a court held that a senior creditor's rights to customer payments on collateral accounts (i.e., proceeds) was not affected by the payments being directed to a lockbox account at the instruction of a junior creditor. The reason was that the owner of the lockbox account was specified to be the debtor, and not the junior creditor—thus, the debtor, and not the junior creditor, was the transferee of the funds.[47]

The second form of payment, direct indorsement, looks to 9–330(d) or to the holder in due course rules in Article 3 (as brought here by 9–331). Does a transferee who knows that the transferor has a contractual obligation to give that very instrument to a third party lack good faith or have knowledge of a defense? In this case section 9–330(d) will not be helpful because our transferee knows his transfer "violates the rights of the secured party." Comment 5 to 9–331 has an interesting but somewhat equivocal discussion of these issues. We take particular note of the following part of the Comment:

> Generally, the senior secured party would not be prejudiced because the practical effect of such payment to the junior secured party is little different than if the debtor itself had made the collections and subsequently paid the secured party from the debtor's general funds. Absent collusion, the junior secured party would take the funds free of the senior

---

[45]   "(a) [Transferee of money.] A transferee of money takes the money free of a security interest unless the transferee acts in collusion with the debtor in violating the rights of the secured party."

[46]   "(b) [Transferee of funds from deposit account.] A transferee of funds from a deposit account takes the funds free of a security interest in the deposit account unless the transferee acts in collusion with the debtor in violating the rights of the secured party."

[47]   In re Tusa-Expo Holdings, Inc., 811 F.3d 786, 88 U.C.C. Rep. Serv. 2d 990 (5th Cir. 2016).

security interests, see section 9–332. In contrast, the senior secured party is likely to be prejudiced if the debtor is going out of business and the junior secured party collects the accounts by notifying the account debtors to make payments directly to the junior. Those collections may not be consistent with "reasonable commercial standards of fair dealing."

Collusion is a high standard and justly so. Perhaps the courts should be a little more willing to find good faith here than in some other cases, for we regard cases under 9–331 (where good faith is the test) as little different from cases under 9–332 (where collusion is the test).

c. Returns and Repossessed Goods

A less frequent conflict between chattel paper purchasers and inventory lenders arises when goods that have been sold are returned (usually through repossession) to the original dealer. In that case, the inventory lender's security interest will reattach pursuant to an after-acquired property clause. On the other hand, the chattel paper purchaser will not have a security interest in the inventory in the hands of the seller as such. Rather, the chattel paper purchaser, even one who achieved priority under 9–330, will have to rely on its proceeds claim, i.e., that the repossessed goods are proceeds of its chattel paper. First, one needs to inquire into the title of the dealer in the goods returned. Until there has been either foreclosure by sale, or strict foreclosure, the dealer is likely to be a non-owner who is merely the bailee for the chattel paper owner. On the other hand, goods might be returned because the buyer rejects or in the other circumstances in which the buyer purports to transfer title back to the dealer. These cases were covered by section 9–306(5) in pre-1999 law. In the current Code, section 9–330(c) generally grants priority to the purchaser of the chattel paper if that purchaser had a prior right to the chattel paper under subsections 9–330(a) or (b) discussed above. This is true in certain cases even if the chattel paper purchaser's interest is not perfected. Section 9–330(c)(2) reads as follows:

> (a purchaser having priority in chattel paper . . . also has priority . . . to the extent that) the proceeds consist of the specific goods covered by the chattel paper or cash proceeds of the specific goods, even if the purchaser's security interest in the proceeds is unperfected.

4–11　"DOUBLE DEBTOR" AND OTHER WEIRD CASES

a.　Double Debtors

Generally, priority rules in Article 9 assume a debtor with good title to the collateral. Most of the priority sections deal with the conflict between two parties, each of whom takes from or through that common debtor. Sections like 9–322 then provide which of two or more parties dealing with the common debtor has a better right to the collateral when the debtor defaults. To the extent the debtor's title to the collateral is defective because the debtor is merely a lessee or because the conveyance to the debtor from a prior party did not give the debtor free and clear title (but rather, for example, a title already encumbered by another security interest), the priority rules do not work. Put another way, the general priority rules in Article 9 do not allow a subsequent party to take free of a defect in the debtor's title, but only to profit from the failure of other creditors who deal with the same debtor.

A particular variant can occur as follows: Debtor One grants a security interest to Creditor One who properly perfects. Debtor Two grants a security interest to Creditor Two who properly perfects. Then the two debtors merge or consolidate. At that point Creditor One, Creditor Two, or both, might claim priority as to all of the assets of the merged company on the ground that *its* after-acquired property caused its security interest to attach to those assets upon the merger and that its priority related back to the time of its filing, which was before the filing of its competitor. This is the case of Bank of the West v. Commercial Credit Financial Services.[48] Another variant occurs when a partnership grants a security interest in property, and then transfers that property to individual partners (the second debtors) who then grant a security interest to their own lenders. The operation of 9–325 is that the secured creditor of the second debtor loses.[49]

Before 1999, no provision of Article 9 dealt directly with this issue. Now, section 9–325 explicitly rejects the view that the priority between the two creditors is determined by 9–322. Assuming the debtor took the collateral subject to a security interest, section 9–325 generally subordinates the rights of the secured creditor who claims through the debtor buyer to the rights of the secured creditor that

---

[48]　852 F.2d 1162, 6 UCC2d 602 (9th Cir.1988).

[49]　U.S. ex rel. Farm Service Agency v. Harvey Fertilizer and Gas Co., 80 U.C.C. Rep. Serv. 2d 216 (E.D. N.C. 2013).

attached prior to the debtor's purchase. Example 1 in Comment 3 to 9–325 makes the point as follows:

> A owns an item of equipment subject to a perfected security interest in favor of SP-A. A sells the equipment to B, not in the ordinary course of business. B acquires its interest subject to SP-A's security interest, see sections 9–201, 9–315(a)(1). Under this section, if B creates a security interest in the equipment in favor of SP-B, SP-B's security interest is subordinate to SP-A's security interest, even if SP-B filed against B before SP-A filed against A, and even if SP-B took a purchase-money security interest. Normally, SP-B could have investigated the source of the equipment and discovered SP-A's filing before making an advance against the equipment, whereas SP-A had no reason to search the filings against someone other than its debtor, A.

The drafters recognized they were treading on uncertain ground here. Accordingly, they applied the rule only to a security interest that was perfected at the time when the debtor acquired the collateral. They also acknowledged the possibility of cases that might not fit within the rule; cases that should be dealt with in the court's own discretion (see Comment 6).

One should understand how this rule is interrelated with the rules of a bona fide purchase from Article 2 and those, such as 9–320, in Article 9. Section 9–325 applies if and only if the debtor acquired the collateral "subject to the security interest created by" another. Thus, if the debtor cut off the prior perfected security interest because the debtor was a buyer in the ordinary course protected by 9–320 or if, somehow, the debtor cut off the prior claim as a buyer protected by section 2–403, the original secured creditor loses and the later secured creditor is protected. This is but a version of the familiar "shelter principle," namely, that subsequent takers are "sheltered" by the good title of their transferors.

b.   Priority of Security Interests Created by a New Debtor

Section 9–326 deals with a set of cases that may be of such microscopic insignificance that they are not even visible to the naked eye. The section applies only to a security interest created by a "new debtor." A "new debtor" is defined by section 9–102(a)(56) as a person who becomes bound under 9–203(d) "by a security agreement previously entered into by another person." Who is this "new debtor"? More often than not, it is a company that succeeds a debtor by merger or consolidation. Under the terms of the typical state corporation law, a successor corporation is bound by the contracts including any security agreements entered into by its predecessor.

In language that is not comprehensible unless one can simultaneously remember not only the identity of "new debtor," but also the rules contained in sections 9–316(i) and 9–508, subsection 9–326(a) tells us that the perfected security interest which the successor or buyer achieves by becoming bound by the target company's security interest and by enjoying the benefits of a prior perfection by filing (under sections 9–508 or 9–316(i))—and without which such special Article 9 provisions would not be perfected in the new debtor scenario—is subordinate to a security interest in the same collateral if that security interest is perfected "other than by such a filed financing statement." Not so clear, huh?

PROBLEM

To get a grip on the issue, consider a variation on one of the examples in the Comments to 9–326. Assume that Acquire Corporation has granted a perfected security interest in inventory and after-acquired property to Bank A. Target Corporation has granted a security interest in inventory and after-acquired property to Bank T. Acquire then purchases Target Corporation. Under corporation law, Acquire will be bound by Target's security agreement and will qualify under 9–102 and 9–203 as a "new debtor." Section 9–508 will make Bank T's financing statement effective against the new corporation, Acquire. (Note that the financing statement will be effective only for assets held at the merger, or acquired within four months, unless Acquire has or adopts the name of Target or a name like Target's.)

Now we return to section 9–326(a) and find that the security interest of Bank T is subordinate—as to the collateral in which the "new debtor has or acquires rights"—to the security interest of Bank A. Presumably, "new debtor's rights" refers only to collateral acquired after merger and to collateral owned by Acquire prior to that time. Bank T will still retain priority over the assets that belonged to Target at the time of the merger. This may seem a wretched excess! We suspect the only users of section 9–326 will be law professors and bar examiners. Beware, we only examined the first, not the most complex, set of rules buried in these sections. Moreover, we have left alone the 2010 addition of the reference to section 9–316(i) and multistate scenarios involving new debtors.

c. Good Faith

The general rule under sections 9–322 and 9–323 is that knowledge is irrelevant in determining priorities; thus, knowledge of a preexisting unperfected security interest by a subsequent security interest holder is not itself bad faith. This is a sensible general principle because priorities *generally* ought not to depend on such disputatious inquiries. Nevertheless, in cases where something more than knowledge on the part of the subsequent creditor is involved, courts have modified the priority rules, sometimes they resort to section 1–304 (formerly 1–203). For example, in General Insurance Co. v. Lowry,[50] General had an unperfected security interest in Lowry's stock. With knowledge of the security agreement between General and Lowry, Lowry's attorney took a security interest in the same stock and perfected the interest. Emphasizing that the case involved an attorney for one of the parties, not a disinterested creditor attempting to protect his commercial interests, the court held that the priority provision in former 9–312 did not preclude the imposition of an equitable lien under the circumstances because the obligations of good faith under 1–203 had not been met. Similarly, in Thompson v. United States,[51] the court held that 1–203 permits the consideration of lack of good faith to alter priorities that would otherwise be determined under Article 9.[52] Perhaps such decisions can be limited to their facts without doing much damage to the first to file rule.

The same cannot be said for the decision in In re Davidoff.[53] In that case two banks had improperly filed financing statements. Subsequently a seller of goods took and properly perfected a security interest in the same assets. The supplier knew that the banks claimed a security interest in the same goods, but neither saw nor knew of an improperly filed financing statement. Relying on the *Thompson* case cited above, Judge Brieant reversed Judge Schwartzberg's finding that the banks were subordinated to the subsequent creditor, holding instead, that under the circumstances "it was not good faith to impose a security interest on assets which a debtor had already said were secured to two named banks." The case does disservice to the first to file rule by inviting every creditor who makes an improper filing to assert that each subsequent and properly filed creditor acted in bad faith.

A recent case denied that a secured creditor had acted in bad faith. The lender had a security interest in all the debtor's cattle, including after-acquired. A seller sold debtor cattle on unperfected credit; unfortunately, the debtor's checks were dishonored by the payor bank (which was also the lender). The seller claimed that the bank's security interest did not attach, because it's failure to volunteer the debtor's potential lack of creditworthiness meant that it was not a "good faith purchaser" under 2–403 and thus its security

---

[50]   570 F.2d 120, 23 UCC 1058 (6th Cir.1978).

[51]   408 F.2d 1075, 6 UCC 20 (8th Cir.1969).

[52]   See also Limor Diamonds, Inc. v. D'Oro by Christopher Michael, Inc., 558 F.Supp. 709, 35 UCC 1509 (S.D.N.Y.1983) (bad faith on the part of a secured party may subordinate its rights in the collateral to that of an unpaid seller).

[53]   351 F.Supp. 440, 11 UCC 609 (S.D.N.Y.1972).

interest did not attach. The court denied the claim, holding the facts were not enough for bad faith to deny priority, and also that the bank's duty of good faith was owed to its debtor, not the seller-third party. A vigorous dissent disagreed, citing cases where the duty of good faith was held to be owed to third parties in certain instances. These cases, seemingly, are quire fact-dependent in their resolution.[54]

d. Estoppel

In specific circumstances courts may apply the equitable doctrine of promissory estoppel, pursuant to section 1–103, to alter priorities that would otherwise be governed by Article 9. For example, in Citizens State Bank v. Peoples Bank,[55] Peoples had a security interest in debtor's equipment but made oral and written representations to Citizens that it would release its interest. Acting in reliance on People's representations, Citizens renewed its loan to the debtor and took a security interest in his equipment. Applying the doctrine of promissory estoppel, the court found that Citizens (1) reasonably relied on People's representations, (2) substantially changed its position by renewing its loan to the debtor, and (3) would suffer substantial economic loss if People's were permitted to reassert its prior right to the equipment. Thus, the court awarded priority to Citizens.[56]

e. Subrogation

In French Lumber Co. v. Commercial Realty & Finance Co.,[57] Creditor One lent to the debtor pursuant to a good security agreement and duly filed. Creditor Two later did the same as to the same collateral. Meanwhile the debtor defaulted on his loan from Creditor One. Creditor Three refinanced that loan but failed to take an assignment of Creditor One's security interest and instead paid off Creditor One and filed pursuant to its security interest in the collateral. If determined by order of filing, the priorities in the collateral would have been: Creditor One, Creditor Two, Creditor Three. The court held that Creditor Three was subrogated to the rights of Creditor One and was therefore entitled to priority in the proceeds of the collateral. The court cited 1–103 and reasoned that

---

[54]   Bank of Beaver City v. Barretts' Livestock, Inc., 295 P.3d 1088, 78 UCC Rep.Serv.2d 1029 (Okla. 2012).

[55]   475 N.E.2d 324, 40 UCC 1549 (Ind.App.1985).

[56]   The government as creditor is also subject to the equitable doctrine of promissory estoppel. See, United States v. Gleaners & Farmers Co-op. Elevator Co., 314 F.Supp. 1148, 8 UCC 16 (N.D.Ind.1970), aff'd, 481 F.2d 104, 12 UCC 1232 (7th Cir.1973).

[57]   346 Mass. 716, 195 N.E.2d 507, 2 UCC 3 (1964).

no provision in the UCC purports to affect the equitable doctrine of subrogation.[58]

Is the case correct? White has his doubts. Why should the court not insist that Creditor Three follow the avenue open to it, and by assuming Creditor One's position with formality, enjoy the rights of Creditor One? Article 9 does have a rule that governs this case, 9–322: the first to file wins. Here Creditor Two filed before Creditor Three and would therefore defeat Creditor Three if section 9–322 were applied.

---

[58] But see Chadron Energy Corp. v. First Nat'l Bank, 221 Neb. 590, 379 N.W.2d 742, 42 UCC 1519 (1986) (superior lien of bank was extinguished upon novation, thus previously junior lien became first lien).

Chapter 5

DEFAULT AND ITS CONSEQUENCES

Analysis

5–1 INTRODUCTION

The point of a security interest, as we have seen, is to protect the creditor in the event that the debtor fails to perform its obligations. That failure is what Article 9 calls a "default." As we note in more detail below, there are many ways in which a debtor can fail to perform—not making payments, destroying or disposing of the collateral, failing to keep insurance in force, providing the creditor with false statements, creating additional security interests in the collateral, filing for bankruptcy, even (in some cases) dying. Few debtors and creditors enter into transactions expecting that there will be a default. It is the lawyers' job to worry about default and deal with it when it happens.

Much of the first four parts of this volume deal with planning for and preparing against the possibility of a default. But the lawyer's work is far from over when the dreaded event occurs. On the contrary, good legal work is critical in protecting secured clients *after* default, as secured parties must tread a narrow and often perilous path to satisfy their claims. Not only are there significant risks that the secured party will not get the protections it bargained for, but there are looming possibilities of tort and statutory liability—up to and including punitive damages—if things are not done correctly. The books are full of cases where creditors suffered severe self-inflicted wounds when seeking to collect their debts. On the other side of the coin, good lawyering is also the key to helping debtors avoid the potential consequences of their actions.

Part 6 of Article 9—the subject of the chapters that follow—defines the rights and remedies of the secured party and its debtor on default. It is important to realize, however, that Article 9 rights make up only part of the default scenario. Part 6 gives creditors certain statutory rights, but the individual security agreement signed by the parties (which is, of course, a contract) can give the secured creditor even more. The parties also can (within some limits) supplement or vary Part 6 by the terms of their agreement.

The critical provisions of Part 6 give the secured party the right to (1) take possession of the collateral upon the debtor's default and (2) dispose of it in satisfaction of its claim, all without (in most cases) setting foot in court. But in doing so, the creditor must comply with the rules (9–610 et seq.). If it deviates, the Code affords remedies to the debtor and others having an interest in the collateral. The principal legal problems of Part 6 concern the propriety of the secured party's conduct in repossessing and reselling the collateral, and the debtor's remedies for illegal or improper acts by the secured party. Although the creditor may, on default, resort to other methods to satisfy its claim, such as "strict foreclosure" under 9–620 (Chapter 5–9 infra), or judgment and execution on the debt under 9–601, we will begin by focusing on the usual method of realizing value to replay the debt, "foreclosure by sale."

From the beginning of time, the creditor's seizure and sale of the debtor's collateral has created disputes. Almost invariably, the debtor—who usually both loses the collateral and still faces a deficiency judgment for the remainder of the debt—believes that the collateral is worth more than the creditor sold it for. Meanwhile, the creditor believes it made all proper efforts to sell the collateral, but there was simply no good market for it. With respect to consumer goods, for example, the debtor will tend to attach high retail value to the goods, but the creditor is likely to sell them in a low wholesale used-products market. Thus a two-year-old automobile that might bring $25,000 if it were polished up and put on a dealer's lot for retail sale by motivated commission sales people, may bring only $15,000 or $17,000 at a dealer's auction.

There is a great deal of history here. The problem of high debtor expectations and low resale prices was a prominent feature of American real property security law during the 1920s and 1930s. The issue of properties being knocked down at courthouse auctions for pennies on the dollar was a stark fact of the Depression. Over decades, state legislatures enacted many detailed rules in attempts deal with the issues and satisfy the dispossessed owners who still faced big deficiencies. Most of their attempts were fruitless.

Article 9 of the UCC was informed by those failures. The original drafters of Article 9 were intimately familiar with all of the debtor-protection legislation of that era. In certain circumstances, they consciously chose to depart from real property practice. For example, it is still common in the real property arena for the sheriff to conduct a public sale at the courthouse, even though such sales routinely bring low prices. The winning bidder in such sales is usually the secured creditor who "bids in" its debt.[1] The drafters of article 9 decided not to require Article 9 secured creditors to do public sales. The sheriff is not always the best auctioneer; the courthouse steps are not necessarily the best forum to sell goods. Thus, Article 9 tries to be much more flexible, while still protecting the interests of debtors to the extent possible.

---

[1] Several features of these sales have probably helped keep prices down. Among these are the statutory equity of redemption, which means that buyers cannot be sure that they will actually get the property the bid on, the requirement that the sales be conducted for cash, and the relatively limited amount of information buyers can get about the property in advance.

Collectively, the rules in Part 6 of Article 9 can be regarded as a conscious rejection of the detailed rules about modes of sale and foreclosure that have attended real estate security.

5–2 DEFINING "DEFAULT"

The rights of the secured creditor are triggered by "default." So what is "default?" Article 9 does not define the word. Instead, it leaves the meaning to the agreement of the parties and to any scraps of common law lying around. Apart from the modest limitations imposed by the unconscionability doctrine (2–302) and the requirement of good faith (1–304), default is "whatever the security agreement says it is."[2] Security agreements often include default clauses as long as the creditor's arm and as wide as the counsel's imagination. A provision which stipulates that debtor's nonpayment constitutes default is only the starting point for a well-drawn default clause. A default clause should also take into account the possibility that the debtor will suffer financial reverses (i.e., bankruptcy or assignment for benefit of creditors). When the collateral is goods, the default clause commonly includes provisions on the loss, damage, destruction or removal of the goods and a debtor's breach of covenant to maintain insurance on them. Of course, the content of these clauses varies with the facts of each transaction and with the foresight of the lawyers doing the drafting. In each case, the careful lawyer will study the transaction at hand and insert provisions necessary to protect the secured creditor against those risks which might adversely affect its interest in the collateral.

There are limitations on the creditor, however. Section 9–602 contains a list of sections that "give rights to a debtor . . . and impose duties on a secured party." There are thirteen subsections to 9–602, which cross-reference twenty-one separate provisions, most of which relate to protections for debtors in the seizure and sale of their property. The debtor may not waive or vary any of those sections in the security agreement. They come out of a deeply rooted attitude that debtors need protection from their creditors when it comes to the drafting of default rules. Thus, creditors cannot in advance require debtors to waive the rules that govern how creditors must behave when seizing and selling property.

---

[2]   2 G. Gilmore, Security Interests in Personal Property § 43.3 at 1193 (1965). See First Nat'l Bank v. Beug, 400 N.W.2d 893, 3 UCC2d 856 (S.D.1987) (parties' contract defines default); Cofield v. Randolph County Comm'n, 90 F.3d 468, 30 UCC2d 374 (11th Cir.1996) (where parties fail to define default, the ordinary meaning of default—failure to pay—is applied; debtor misrepresented value of trade-in camper when purchasing new car and secured creditor rightfully repossessed because debtor's failure of consideration was a failure to pay).

There is some flexibility, however, in specifying the precise *ways* in which secured parties carry out their obligations. Section 9–603(a) authorizes the parties to agree on "the standards measuring the fulfillment of the duties of a secured party . . . if the standards are not manifestly unreasonable." Thus, for example, where the Code requires the secured party to take a "reasonable" action, the security agreement can specify in advance what counts as reasonable, so long as it is not "manifestly unreasonable." The debtor, for example, cannot waive its right to notice of the sale, but the agreement might provide reasonable details regarding how and when the notice may be provided. Not surprisingly, the dividing line is not clear between prohibited "agreements" that waive rights, on the one hand, and "agreed standards" that appropriately modify rights, on the other. Nor is there statutory guidance as to when a merely unreasonable standard crosses the line into being *manifestly* unreasonable.[3] As a practical matter, the most common "standards" that one sees in security agreements have to do with the ways in which a creditor must give notice, the time that must intervene between the notice and the foreclosure sale and, in some cases, even a statement of what is a "commercially reasonable" resale. None of these ordinarily will create a problem.

There is an important exception to 9–603 flexibility, however. Under section 9–609, for example, creditors can seize collateral if it can be done without a "breach of the peace." Can the parties in advance agree to what counts as a "breach of the peace"? No. Section 9–603(b) expressly bars the parties even from establishing any standards concerning what amounts to a "breach of the peace." Given that such breaches may create public safety issues, this is unsurprising.

Part 6 rights exist for the benefit of the creditor, and the creditor is under no obligation to pursue them. Creditors are free to waive their Article 9 rights on default—they are not *required* to repossess property—and are free to waive their contract rights under the security agreement. Creditors, for example, frequently do not bring foreclose actions based on the first late payment. But if the creditor accepts a late payment or fails to take action after another default, has the creditor waived its rights to foreclose? The answer is unclear. Ordinarily, a creditor who accepts a single late payment will not be held to have waived its rights, but a creditor who has accepted several late payments without demur may be found to have waived its right

---

[3] The drafters, who are frequently lavish in their use of illustrations on many provisions of Article 9, do not do so for 9–603.

to foreclose, at least without additional notice to the debtor.[4] A creditor that forecloses and is later found to have waived its rights can find itself facing liability to its debtor.

This raises the question whether a creditor can avoid such inadvertent waivers by appropriate language in the original security agreement. Creditors, after all, are often willing to give debtors a little more time to perform, and debtors ordinarily appreciate that. But if the creditor will be penalized for that discretion, it is less likely to do so. Can a creditor who wants to maintain that flexibility do so by providing in the security agreement that such actions do not constitute waivers? Again, the answer is unclear. In Cobb v. Midwest Recovery Bureau Co.,[5] the Minnesota Supreme Court held that despite the no-waiver clause, the secured party's actions constituted a waiver in light of acceptance of habitually late payments. The court imposed a duty on the secured party to notify the debtor of their intent to require strict compliance with the original agreement after having accepted habitually late payments. The court reasoned:

> The basis for imposing this duty on the secured party is that the secured party is estopped from asserting his contract rights because his conduct has induced the justified reliance of the debtor in believing that late payments were acceptable.[6]

Other decisions point to the unequal bargaining power of the debtor and creditor as further support for such a rule.[7]

Other courts hold that a no-waiver clause is enforceable.[8] Thus, in Wells Fargo Bank v. Smith,[9] the court concluded that even where the creditor's conduct in accepting late payments would have created an estoppel, an explicit "No Waiver By Loan Holder" clause in the security agreement meant that the bank's various forbearances did not amount to waivers.

In general, while we are sympathetic to debtors, we are doubtful of cases like *Cobb* that effectively punish creditor for accepting late payments. There is a danger that those cases, in which the creditor's

---

[4]   See, e.g., Slusser v. Wyrick, 28 Ohio App. 3d 96, 502 N.E.2d 259 (1986) (accepting late payments without objection estops the creditor from repossessing the collateral without giving warning to the debtor).

[5]   295 N.W.2d 232, 28 UCC 941 (Minn.1980). See also, Nevada Nat'l Bank v. Huff, 94 Nev. 506, 582 P.2d 364, 24 UCC 1044 (1978).

[6]   295 N.W.2d at 236, 28 UCC at 949.

[7]   Steichen v. First Bank Grand, 372 N.W.2d 768, 41 UCC 1866 (Minn.App.1985).

[8]   Monarch Coaches, Inc. v. ITT Indus. Credit, 818 F.2d 11, 3 UCC2d 1274 (7th Cir.1987) (applying Illinois law); K.B. Oil Co. v. Ford Motor Credit Co., 811 F.2d 310, 3 UCC2d 417 (6th Cir.1987) (applying Ohio law).

[9]   2013 WL 5230615 (Ohio Ct. App. Sept. 11, 2013).

earlier good deeds are held against it, may encourage creditors to sue or seek repossession earlier than they otherwise would, instead of giving debtors time to work things out. In our view, voluntary workouts and grace periods should be preferred to lawsuits and bankruptcy, and the law should not actively discourage that behavior.

5–3   DEFINING "DEFAULT," ACCELERATION CLAUSES

Security agreements nearly always provide that the secured party may "accelerate" the maturity of the debt and so cause all payments to become immediately due and payable. Acceleration is not an Article 9 remedy, it comes from contract, but such clauses routinely are included in security agreements. They are not necessarily designed to be punitive; rather, they allow the creditor to avoid an expensive series of lawsuits. If, on an installment loan, all installments did not come due on the debtor's default on one installment, the creditor would have to wait for each successive default in order to sue for that particular missed payment. That perfectly reasonable justification, however, does not mean that the creditor does not also enjoy the leverage that an acceleration clause gives. Generally, courts uphold and enforce acceleration clauses.

One type of acceleration clause, known as an "insecurity clause," provides that the creditor may accelerate the maturity of the entire debt whenever the creditor "deems itself insecure." The ostensible reason for such clauses is that when the creditor has serious reason to believe that the debtor is about to default, it may legitimately want to take action before the default and avoid potentially damaging acts by the debtor. The need for the insecurity acceleration clause is less clear than the need for a general acceleration clause, in which there has been an actual default. It is, moreover, subject to possible abuse (deliberate or not) by trigger-happy creditors.[10] Nevertheless, courts have generally upheld insecurity clauses.

What does "insecurity" mean? Different courts have taken different approaches. Some courts read them to permit acceleration

---

[10]   Mistrust of such clauses is manifested in various retail installment sales acts which prohibit or restrict the operation of insecurity clauses. See, e.g., Mich.Stat.Ann. 19.416(114)(a) (1981): "A retail installment contract or retail charge agreement shall not contain provisions by which: a) In the absence of buyer's default in the performance of any of the buyer's obligations, the holder may accelerate the maturity of part or all of the amount owing thereunder." N.Y.Pers.Prop. Law § 403(3)(b) (1977) prohibits a clause by which "[i]n the absence of buyer's default, the holder may, arbitrarily and without reasonable cause, accelerate the maturity of any part or all of the amount owing thereunder."

at the creditor's whim, while others deny acceleration unless a reasonable, prudent creditor would consider itself insecure.

We should note that not all acceleration clauses involve Article 9 security interests. Article 1 has its own acceleration provision in 1–309, which (per Comment 1) applies to "clauses in many transactions governed by the Uniform Commercial Code, including sales of goods on credit, notes payable at a definite time, and secured transactions." Under 1–309, such clauses are enforceable so long as the party "believes in good faith that the prospect of payment or performance is impaired."

Article 9 has its own good faith standard. Originally, it required only subjective good faith on the part of the secured creditor. As Professor Gilmore described it, "a creditor has the right to accelerate if, under all circumstances a reasonable man, motivated by good faith, would have done so." But the 1999 revisions added an objective component to the test. Section 9–102(a)(43) now defines the term as follows:[11]

> "Good faith" means honesty in fact and the observance of reasonable commercial standards of fair dealing.

By making explicit reference to "commercial standards of fair dealing," the drafters apparently intended to establish a somewhat more objective standard of good faith than formerly prevailed.

The practical differences between an "objective" and a "subjective" test of good faith are not clear. Two cases illustrate the difficulties in applying the Code's standard of "good faith." In the first case, Fort Knox National Bank v. Gustafson,[12] the Kentucky Court of Appeals speaks almost exclusively in subjective language, but it would certainly have been decided the same way under an objective test. The debtor was eight months behind on rent payments and had consulted an attorney about the possibility of filing bankruptcy. However, he had also arranged with the secured party for a pay-off settlement and introduced evidence at trial that another agency had notified the secured party that funds were available for paying off the debt. The appellate court reversed the trial court and concluded that the creditor was sufficiently justified in accelerating the debt that the trial court should direct a verdict in his favor: "It must be

---

[11] Broader than former Article 9's incorporation of "good faith" under 1–201(19) (defining "good faith" as "honesty in fact in the conduct or transaction concerned"), "good faith" under Revised Article 9–102(a)(43) is now in accord with the definition used in Articles 2, 2A, 3, 4, 4A and 8. Comment 19 to 1–201 suggests the definition of "good faith" found in subsection (19) serves merely as a minimum standard. Articles may, by specific provision, apply additional requirements to the definition of "good faith."

[12] 385 S.W.2d 196, 2 UCC 336 (Ky.1964).

remembered that here we are dealing with the 'good faith' belief of the bank—that is, its state of mind."[13]

In the second case, Sheppard Federal Credit Union v. Palmer,[14] the Court of Appeals for the Fifth Circuit paid homage to the objective nature of the 1–309 (then 1–208) test, but reversed a lower court decision in favor of the debtor, and remanded with an instruction to the trial court to impose the burden of proving bad faith upon the debtor. In that case, an Air Force lieutenant obtained a loan from the base credit union to purchase an automobile. When he told the creditor of his intent to resign from the Air Force, the creditor repossessed the car under a clause which said he could repossess at any time he "shall ... deem ... said security unsafe or insecure ...."[15] The repossession was accomplished over the debtor's protestations that he had made all the payments promptly and could easily obtain higher wages outside of the Air Force because of his training as a registered nurse. In fact, he did obtain a better paying job and continued to make his payments after repossession. He then sued the secured party and sought punitive as well as compensatory damages on the ground that the creditor repossessed "maliciously." The trial court instructed the jury that the debtor was "entitled to damages unless Credit Union proves by a preponderance of the evidence that it had reasonable grounds to believe ... the debt involved herein or said security was unsafe or insecure ...."[16] Although the Court of Appeals, quoting Professor Gilmore, acknowledged that the Code enacts an objective test, it reversed because the trial judge had erroneously imposed the burden of proof upon the secured party. On the good faith test, the court remarked:

> [T]he Credit Union's determination that it was insecure was certainly erroneous; it could hardly have asked for a more conscientious and responsible debtor. However, it takes more than mere error to show unreasonableness or bad faith, not to mention malice.[17]

These two cases indicate that the objective-subjective dispute may not be important in many cases. In the *Gustafson* case, it appears that the court would have reached the same result irrespective of the test applied. Presumably, a creditor does not act in bad faith on either version of the test when it repossesses from a debtor in default who has gone so far as to consult a lawyer about the possibility of filing for bankruptcy. While the Court of Appeals in

---

[13]   *Id.* at 200, 2 UCC at 341.
[14]   408 F.2d 1369, 6 UCC 30 (5th Cir.1969).
[15]   *Id.* at 1370, 6 UCC at 31.
[16]   *Id.* at 1371, 6 UCC at 31.
[17]   *Id.* at 1373, 6 UCC at 34.

Palmer explicitly applied an objective standard, one supposedly more favorable to the debtor, it openly invited the court below on remand to find the creditor in good faith, even though the debtor had not defaulted on his payments, held a responsible position in the armed forces and, because of his technical training, could easily obtain a high paying civilian job. He was, as the court suggests, the model debtor.

In the final analysis, the operational effect of the standard applied must be measured by the results reached rather than the particular incantations uttered by the priests. An examination of pre-Code cases reveals that although many courts required "good faith," "reasonable grounds" or both for insecurity, in only a handful did the courts decide that acceleration was unreasonable and thus improper. Therefore, it appears the courts, both before and after enactment of the Code, are loath to find acceleration of a debt under an "insecurity clause" to be unreasonable.

Even the most reasonable creditor might justifiably consider itself insecure when the debtor's financial condition changes radically or the debtor endangers the collateral through his own misconduct or lack of care. But not all cases are easy. A 1982 case, Clayton v. Crossroads Equipment Co.,[18] shows how section 1–309 might protect a debtor. There the seller of a combine had included a "deem insecure" clause in the parties' agreement that read: "This note shall be in default . . . if for any reason the holder of this note deems the debt or security unsafe . . . ." Although the buyer was not behind on his payments, the secured party deemed himself insecure and repossessed largely because of credit information it had acquired subsequent to the sale. The Utah Supreme Court upheld a finding that the declaration of default was in bad faith under 1–309 (then 1–208). The court stated that:

> [I]t would be highly inequitable to allow . . . [the secured party] to change its mind once it had accepted the contract simply because it subsequently conducted a more thorough investigation; it is unfair to put the buyer in default based upon information which was apparently available in one of . . . [secured party's] own branch offices at the time that it had accepted plaintiff.

5–4 CREDITOR'S ALTERNATIVES UPON DEFAULT

Consider the alternatives available to the creditor when the debtor defaults. Almost invariably, the parties will seek to work out

---

[18] 655 P.2d 1125, 34 UCC 1448 (Utah 1982).

the problem. In that case creditor's possible repossession may give the debtor considerable incentive to negotiate. The *threat* of repossession may, in fact, be better for the creditor than actual repossession. For example, the asset may have considerable value to the debtor but relatively little market value—special tools used only to make the debtor's product, for example, for those in which the debtor has some special personal interest. In some cases, the threat of repossession may be enough to get the debtor to pay. But assuming it isn't, what can the secured creditor do? There are two basic options.

First, the creditor can repossess the goods subject to the security interest. The creditor can either (with some limitations) keep the goods itself in satisfaction of the debt, or resell them and apply the proceeds to the debt. The basic policies of the resale provisions are twofold: to allow realization on the collateral with a minimum resort to judicial proceedings and to encourage higher yields upon disposition by allowing private as well as public sale of collateral. Even when done correctly, however, a resale will often result in a "deficiency" for which the debtor is usually liable,[19] which will lead to a "deficiency judgment suit."

Alternatively, the creditor can ignore its security interest and (like an unsecured creditor) obtain a judgment on the underlying obligation. The creditor will then proceed by execution and levy. The Code itself does not govern what the creditor must do to obtain judgment and execution on the debt—statutes and common law in each state (some of it ancient) specify the precise steps to take. Generally, the creditor first brings suit and obtains a judgment for the debt owed. After judgment, the clerk of the court will, on request, issue a "writ of execution," or the like. This writ recites that a judgment has been obtained, and directs the sheriff or other appropriate officer to seize the property of the debtor and sell it to satisfy the judgment debt. With the writ in hand, the officer will "levy" against the debtor's property at home or place of business— that is, will exercise dominion over the property such that it is safely

---

[19]   A deficiency, as the name implies, is the amount by which the net sum obtained from resale of the collateral falls short of the debt outstanding at the time of default. Thus if the net proceeds from resale of a repossessed automobile are $900 and the amount still owed by the debtor is $1400, then the deficiency is $1400 less $900 or $500. Note, however, that 9–615(a) stipulates that:

A secured party shall apply or pay over for application the cash proceeds of disposition in the following order to:

(1) the reasonable expenses of retaking, holding, preparing for disposition, processing, and disposing, and, to the extent provided for by agreement and not prohibited by law, reasonable attorney's fees and legal expenses incurred by the secured party;

(2) the satisfaction of obligations secured by the security interest or agricultural lien under which the disposition is made.

preserved for satisfaction of the debt. Finally, after giving public notice, the officer will sell the property at a public auction to the highest bidder and turn over proceeds necessary to satisfy the debt to the creditor. The surplus, if any, goes to the debtor. For debtors who have an ongoing stream of income, such as wages, an attractive alternative to levy is garnishment. Although various statutory consumer provisions, such as the Truth-in-Lending Act,[20] provide important limitations, wages remain an inviting asset for satisfaction of a consumer debtor's obligation.

Why would a secured party ever go through all the judicial rigmarole of this second approach to get its money when it could simply repossess the collateral and sell it under 9–610? There are, in fact, several reasons. First, a creditor cannot carry out an extra-judicial repossession when it can be carried out without breach of the peace, and debtors may be stubborn. Second, the value of the collateral may have become diminished that the proceeds will not begin to satisfy the debt, and thus the creditor will end up having to sue anyway. In such cases, suing first simply avoids a two-step process. Third, creditors who proceed with the judicial action can eliminate their own liability risk for potential violations of the repossession and resale rules of 9–609 and 9–610, because all of the actions in a judicial proceeding are undertaken by officers of the court. (Creditors must act "reasonably," but judicial officials need not.)[21] Fourth, 9–601(f) allows a creditor at a sheriff's sale to purchase the collateral, something it cannot usually do under 9–610(c) in a private sale of property it has repossessed.

Those are relatively rare situations, however, and in practice few creditors will want to follow that path. Lawsuits are expensive; they can take years to litigate; and searching for other non-exempt assets of the debtor—who is, after all, in trouble for not being able to pay—can be difficult. Thus, most secured creditors opt for seizure and sale of the collateral under 9–610.

Does the secured creditor have to choose between the two? Under pre-Code law, courts often held that the secured creditor who sued on the debt irrevocably elected to seek its sole remedy by that method. But section 9–601(c) states that the creditor's rights—those under Article 9, those under individual state creditors' rights laws, and those under the parties' own security agreement—are "cumulative and may be exercised simultaneously." Moreover, if the

---

[20]   The Consumer Credit Protection Act of 1968, Pub.L.No. 90–321, Title III § 303, 82 Stat. 163, 15 U.S.C.A. § 1673 (1982), restricts the amount which may be garnished.

[21]   Dakota Bank & Trust Co. v. Reed, 402 N.W.2d 887, 3 UCC2d 1976 (N.D.1987) (post-judgment execution procedures are not subject to the same standards of commercial reasonableness that apply in non-judicial sales and may not require notice; judicial or sheriff sales are outside Article 9).

creditor proceeds to judgment under the state law, subsection (e) provides that its judicial lien dates back as far as the date of filing of its financing statement, or perhaps even earlier if the state law so provides.[22]

Although the Code forces no election of remedies on the secured creditor, other state law may displace the Code and require election.[23] Interpreting California's Unruh Act,[24] for example, the Ninth Circuit Bankruptcy Appeal Panel in In re Maldonado[25] held that creditors of retail buyers must elect remedies under the Act even though the UCC would not compel election. In the absence of such displacing state law, however, courts are unlikely to hold that a secured party has elected remedies or that the security agreement requires an election.

5–5   COLLECTION RIGHTS OF THE SECURED PARTY, SECTIONS 9–606, 9–607

When the creditor's collateral consists of rights to payments owed to the debtor by a third party, "foreclosure" normally means to collecting the amounts due from the debtor's own debtors—from the third party "account debtors." These account debtors owe money to the debtor, who in turn owes money to the secured creditor. Assume, for example, Consumer buys a car from Dealer, and gives Dealer a security interest. Dealer borrows money from Bank and gives Bank a security interest in his chattel paper.[26] If Dealer goes into bankruptcy, Bank does not have to wait for Dealer to first collect payments from Consumer before it can seize them, but can exercise its rights under 9–607 to collect the amounts due directly from

---

[22]   Courts split on the question whether former section 9–501 authorized a "double-barreled" attack upon the debtor. In Ayares-Eisenberg Perrine Datsun, Inc. v. Sun Bank, 455 So.2d 525, 39 UCC 360 (Fla.App.1984), the court held that a secured party who repossessed must first dispose of the collateral before suing on the note. The court reasoned that this prevents the creditor from harassing the debtor. Several jurisdictions have accepted this rationale. The court in Coones v. FDIC, 848 P.2d 783, 21 UCC2d 414 (Wyo.1993) vacated on remand, held that "cumulative" does not mean "simultaneous," holding that it means "individual, sequential actions." The dissent argued that that secured party does not have to elect, although it recognized that ultimately the creditor would have to choose between inconsistent remedies. However, a number of jurisdictions do allow secured parties to pursue multiple remedies simultaneously. Under the former Code, most of these courts reasoned that 9–507(1) and general obligations of good faith provided debtors with adequate protection against harassment.

[23]   For example, the Washington state legislature, by amendment of the Official UCC Text, forces election of remedies for purchase money secured creditors in consumer goods. Wash.Rev.Code § 62A.9–501(1) (1966). See also, Cal.Civ.Code § 2983.8 (West 1985) (limiting remedy to repossession and sale, while disallowing deficiency judgment whenever collateral is mobile home).

[24]   Cal.Civ.Code §§ 1801 et seq. (West 1985).

[25]   46 B.R. 497, 40 UCC 1151 (B.A.P. 9th Cir.1984).

[26]   "Chattel paper" under 9–102(11) is the combination of the security agreement signed by the debtor and the debtor's note or other promise to pay.

Consumer. (While this example uses chattel paper, the same principle would apply to such things as accounts, instruments, and general intangibles.)

With respect to collections, there are two significant questions, one easy and one difficult. The first (easy) question is, what rights does the secured creditor have and when do they arise under 9–607 and 9–608? The second (difficult) question is, when may the account debtor or others raise defenses against payment to the secured creditor and thus prevent the creditor from receiving all or part of what it is owed? This second question is complicated and involves interpretation of 9–404 and 9–406, along with a substantial body of not-always-consistent case law. Sorting through it is beyond our present scope.

Turning to the first question, if the security agreement so provides, the secured creditor will have a right to collect amounts from the account debtor even *before* default by the secured creditor's own debtor. This is thus sometimes called "notification lending" because the creditor merely must notify the account debtor and direct the account debtor to make payments directly to the creditor. When that has been done, there is little for sections 9–607 or 9–608 to do at default because collection is already being made directly by the secured creditor.

In the case of non-notification lending—as where the creditor's right to directly obtain payment depends on a prior default—section 9–607 gives the secured creditor the right to notify the account debtor upon default, and section 9–406 then obliges the account debtor to pay the secured creditor. The account debtor, of course, needs to make sure that payment made to the secured creditor will discharge its own liability to the debtor. As for the debtor itself, if the account debtor's payments are insufficient to satisfy the debtor's liability to the secured creditor, the debtor may or may not have liability for the deficiency. This depends entirely upon the terms of the agreement between the secured creditor and its debtor, and absent specific terms, on the form of the transaction. According to subsection 9–608(b):

> (b) [No surplus or deficiency in sales of certain rights to payment.] If the underlying transaction is a sale of accounts, chattel paper, payment intangibles, or promissory notes, the debtor is not entitled to any surplus, and the obligor is not liable for any deficiency.

In this context the word "sale" presumably means some form of a nonrecourse transfer from the debtor to its secured creditor.

To understand how a "security agreement" in chattel paper, entitling the debtor to a surplus and obliging the debtor on a deficiency, might differ from a "sale" leading to the opposite legal conclusion, consider the following case. Dealer has $50,000 of chattel paper and Bank agrees to "lend" to Dealer against that chattel paper. If Dealer signs a note promising to repay the Bank's $50,000 loan and a document titled "security agreement," we have a secured loan, not a sale of chattel paper. If the chattel paper, on default, brings less than the loan due, Bank has a right to a deficiency judgment against Dealer.

Assume, on the other hand, Dealer "sells" the chattel paper to the bank for a fixed sum, say $45,000, Bank probably has no right to a deficiency, yet is entitled to any surplus above the $45,000.[27] Bank in this second case has bargained for both the risk and the benefit.

As we have seen in other contexts, one should understand that the line between a "sale" and a "secured loan" is indistinct. Nevertheless, different legal rules attach to each transaction under section 9–608, unless the parties agree otherwise. If the transaction is a loan with some form of recourse and not merely a sale, section 9–607(c) obliges the secured party "to proceed in a commercially reasonable manner" to collect its money. If there is no recourse, by hypothesis, the secured creditor will be spending its own money and can suit itself in the way it goes about collecting the money.

With respect to buyers of intangibles, section 9–607(a) is more explicit about the rights of the creditor who is a buyer of intangibles than its former version, the old 9–502. For example, subsection (a)(3) authorizes the secured party to "exercise the rights of the debtor," not only on the underlying obligation of the account debtor, but also "with respect to any property that secures the obligations of the account debtor." Subsections (a)(4) and (a)(5) authorize a secured party to "apply the balance" in a deposit account to the secured obligation or to instruct the depositary bank to pay over the balance (when the secured creditor has a security interest in the bank account perfected by control). These sections, in effect, authorize set-off.

To reiterate, we omit the hard questions involving 9–404 and 9–406. One seeking guidance on those questions should look to the practitioners' edition. Once one understands the difference between

---

[27]   Careful lawyers can help cut down the risk inherent in "probably" by specifying clearly in the agreement that the bank is assuming the credit risk associated with the consumers' obligation to pay, and provides that the bank may not recover any amounts that remain unpaid upon default by the consumer purchasers.

a sale and a secured loan, the application of 9–607 and 9–608 are relatively straightforward.[28]

5–6 REPOSSESSION IN GENERAL, SECTION 9–609

In many cases, the creditor's ultimate threat is to repossess the collateral and turn it into money, either by taking it in satisfaction of the debt or selling it. Before it can either, however, it must somehow get possession. Sometimes this is easy; debtors may turn over the collateral voluntarily. In other cases, such as the enforcement of security interests in automobiles, self-help repossession is common. Section 9–609 authorizes the debtor to obtain possession as follows:

(a) [Possession; rendering equipment unusable; disposition on debtor's premises.] After default, a secured party:

(1) may take possession of the collateral; and

(2) without removal, may render equipment unusable and dispose of collateral on a debtor's premises under section 9–610.

(b) [Judicial and nonjudicial process.] A secured party may proceed under subsection (a):

(1) pursuant to judicial process; or

(2) without judicial process, if it proceeds without breach of the peace.

(c) [Assembly of collateral.] If so agreed, and in any event after default, a secured party may require the debtor to assemble the collateral and make it available to the secured party at a place to be designated by the secured party which is reasonably convenient to both parties.

The two options for the creditor are thus to repossess the collateral (§ 9–609(a)(1)) or to "render" it unusable in situ (§ 9–609(a)(2)). In either case, the creditor has two more choices—either to do so pursuant to judicial process (subsection (b)(1)) or by self-help (subsection (b)(2)).

5–7 REPOSSESSION, SELF-HELP

The creditor who opts to use self-help—whether in repossessing or in rendering the collateral unusable—may do so only if it can

---

28   The 1999 revisions of former § 9–502 (9–607, 9–608) add certain additional details that were not covered by former 9–502. For example, 9–607(b) allows the transferee of a payment secured by mortgage to record that mortgage. Subsection (d) specifically authorizes deduction of collection costs and subsection (e) disavows any intention to establish any duty by an account debtor or other person to a secured party.

accomplish it "without breach of the peace." This restriction is extremely important. If the creditor or its representative breaches the peace when engaging in self-help, the creditor may face (1) tort liability, including punitive damages;[29] (2) criminal penalties;[30] and (3) liability under 9–625. In a consumer case it may also cost the creditor the right to a deficiency judgment. Lawyers for both the creditor and the debtor will thus pay careful attention to the circumstances under which the creditor takes possession—one with an eye to avoiding potential liability and the other with an eye to discovering a fatal departure from "peaceful" repossession.

The meaning "breach of the peace" has been the subject of countless judicial opinions over the years. The drafters did not try to define it, but knowingly adopted the well-worn phrase with all its history in each adopting state. Accordingly, the numerous pre-Code cases, as well as those under the 1962 and 1972 Codes, are still good law.

Ordinarily, if the collateral is taken from a public place (such as when a car has been parked on a public street) and if the debtor or his representative is not present to object, there is no breach of the peace. The result is the same if the property is taken from the debtor's own premises, but the debtor consented to the entry and the taking. But there are two broad situations where a breach of the peace may be found even though no actual violence flares: (1) where the creditor entered the debtor's premises without permission; and (2) where the debtor (or someone acting on his behalf) objected to taking of possession.

As to entry, the general rule is that the creditor may not enter the debtor's home or garage without permission, even if the debtor is not present to object. Thus, in Girard v. Anderson,[31] the creditor repossessed a piano from the debtor's home while the debtor was absent. The security agreement ostensibly allowed the creditor to enter the debtor's home to take the property, and the creditor argued that its agents had entered through an unlocked door. The court nevertheless found that the entry was a breach of the peace. The great majority of cases dealing with entry into debtor's residence are

---

[29]   The secured creditor cannot avoid liability by entrusting the repossession to an independent contract. The creditor generally is liable not only for breaches of its own agents, but for those committed by independent contractors in its employ. General Finance Corp. v. Smith, 505 So.2d 1045, 3 UCC2d 1278 (Ala.1987); Sanchez v. Mbank of El Paso, 792 S.W.2d 530, 12 UCC2d 1169 (Tex.App.1990), aff'd, 836 S.W.2d 151, 17 UCC2d 1358 (Tex.1992) (independent contractor repossessed car with debtor inside and towed car to fenced lot with loose guard dog).

[30]   See, e.g., Md.Ann.Code Art. 27 § 243 (1988).

[31]   219 Iowa 142, 257 N.W. 400 (1934).

in agreement with *Girard*. To the same effect are cases dealing with entry into enclosed spaces, such as closed garages.

As one moves away from the interior of the residence, things get more tenuous. Courts generally have recognized a limited privilege to enter some portions of the debtor's property to seize property that is in plain sight.[32] We have found no case which holds that the repossession of an automobile from a driveway itself constitutes a breach of the peace, and many cases explicitly uphold such repossessions.[33] The expectation of privacy in the given location seems to play a role, courts have tended not to find breaches of the peace when the car was taken from a garage whose door was open,[34] or from under unenclosed carports.[35]

But even if the creditor is properly at the location, such as when the collateral is on a public street, the debtor's opposition—however slight and even if merely oral—normally makes any entry or seizure a breach of the peace.[36] While there are cases to the contrary,[37] we believe the rule makes sense. The goal is to avoid violence, so requiring the debtor actually to physically confront or threaten the repossessor would be counterproductive. Repossessors should not be encouraged to make shows of overawing force, nor should debtors have to brandish Bowie knives or shotguns. The law should be *discouraging* breaches of the piece, not offering incentives to the debtor to provoke them.

Other factors also may come into play. For example, what about the situation where creditors enter the property under false pretenses? Where the creditor's representatives pose as police

---

[32]   See, e.g., Callaway v. Whittenton, 892 So.2d 852, 52 UCC2d 525 (Ala. 2003).

[33]   Ragde v. Peoples Bank, 53 Wash.App. 173, 767 P.2d 949, 7 UCC2d 1314 (1989) (repossession of car from driveway at 5 AM not breach of peace). See also Salisbury Livestock Co. v. Colorado Central Credit Union, 793 P.2d 470, 12 UCC2d 894 (Wyo.1990) (question for jury whether breach of peace when vehicles which were not visible from public place were repossessed from a secluded yard on an isolated ranch).

[34]   Pierce v. Leasing Int'l, Inc., 142 Ga.App. 371, 235 S.E.2d 752, 22 UCC 269 (1977).

[35]   Raffa v. Dania Bank, 321 So.2d 83, 18 UCC 263 (Fla.Ct.App. 1975).

[36]   See, e.g., Hester v. Bandy, 627 So.2d 833, 24 UCC2d 1344 (Miss.1993) (breach of the peace found where debtor awakens to vehicle repossession during early morning hours, yells at and pursues repossessing party on foot). But see, Chrysler Credit Corp. v. Koontz, 277 Ill.App.3d 1078, 214 Ill.Dec. 726, 661 N.E.2d 1171, 29 UCC2d 1 (1996) (no breach of the peace occurs when debtor yells "don't take it" to secured creditor as it repossesses debtor's car; "breach of the peace connotes conduct which incites or is likely to incite an immediate loss of public order and tranquility"); Clark v. Auto Recovery Bureau Conn., Inc., 889 F.Supp. 543, 27 UCC2d 649 (D.Conn.1994) (no breach of the peace occurs when debtor protests repossession to an unconnected third party, particularly when debtor's objection occurs after the creditor has sufficient dominion over the collateral to control it).

[37]   See, e.g., Chrysler Credit Corp. v. Koontz, 277 Ill.App.3d 1078, 661 N.E.2d 1171, 214 Ill.Dec. 726, 29 UCC 1 (1996).

officers, they are likely to have broken the peace, even though the hoodwinked debtor has not objected.

What about creditors who bring along off-duty police officers to their repossessions? Creditors under the pre-1999 Code discovered that debtors tended to be much more compliant if a uniformed but off-duty police officer was paid to come along. Comment 3 to 9–609 of the 1999 Article 9 notes a number of cases had found that to be a "failure to comply" with the older provisions, and states that the revised section "does not authorize a secured party who repossesses without judicial process to utilize the assistance of a law enforcement officer." While this language could have been clearer, it seems like the Comment endorses the older cases. Perhaps that is due to the idea that presence of a police officer will cow the debtor into failing to object. Yet at least some of the present authors doubt the wisdom of those cases. If the goal is to prevent breaches of the pace, why is it wrong for the person who is entitled to possession to take along a "peace officer" to ensure that it gets possession "peacefully"?

Assuming the debtor consents, the timing is important. Any consent to entry or seizure must be contemporaneous with the repossession, or nearly so. Putting such "consent" in the security agreement itself is expressly forbidden by 9–602(6). The rules relating to breach of the peace are rooted in concerns of public safety, and a prospective agreement to consent should be given no more weight than a prospective agreement to tolerate a violent misdemeanor or felony. On the other hand, no particular formalities for consent are required. Even an oral consent to repossession is enough if it is contemporaneous. After all, the debtor in default has a duty to give up possession under section 9–609. Consent also must be voluntary, at least to the extent it is not being made in response to an improper threat.

The courts generally have reached sound conclusions in defining "breach of the peace." In the absence of consent, entry into a debtor's house is not permitted whether he is there or not. For the most part, courts ignore clauses purporting to authorize a repossession which results in a breach of the peace, and they will not usually permit a creditor to repossess in the face of unequivocal oral protests. Conversely, courts do permit the repossession of cars from private driveways. Simple trespass does not vitiate an otherwise valid repossession.

5–8 REPOSSESSION, JUDICIAL ACTION

A secured party who wishes to repossess by judicial action, has several means available. For instance, it can bring an action in replevin, originally a common-law action, now largely codified. In other jurisdictions, it can proceed under the statutory successor to replevin, an action of claim and delivery. Naturally, repossession by judicial action is more expensive than repossession by self-help. In addition to attorneys' fees, such costs normally include the cost of posting a bond and fees for the sheriff who actually repossesses the goods. Subsections (a) and (d) of 9–615 make the debtor liable for those costs. If the debtor will not part with the goods without a fight, and if the debtor's pockets are deep enough that they will cover the costs of repossession, the secured creditor is well advised to proceed by judicial action. Of course, it will be the unusual debtor that has enough money to both make good the deficiency and pay the attorneys' fees involved in collecting it.

The secured party's cause of action in repossessing rests on its right to possession under 9–609. Under a typical replevin or claim-and-delivery statute, after the plaintiff files a complaint and an affidavit and posts the required bond, the sheriff may seize the property. Unless the defendant objects within a specified period, the property may be delivered to the plaintiff pending final judgment. At common law, the plaintiff in a replevin action sought only to recover the property in specie; however, under the modern form of the action and under some claim and delivery statutes, the plaintiff may recover the property or its value.

There is no mystery about a straightforward judicial foreclosure against the debtor. Complications arise when a third party has purchased the collateral or a competing lien creditor has procured a lien on the collateral. Whether purchase cuts off the secured creditor's rights is a question we deal with elsewhere. Assuming the competitor has not cut off the secured creditor's claim, the secured creditor can repossess from the purchaser, or alternatively, recover in conversion from that person. Where a judicial foreclosure by a secured creditor coincides with a lien creditor's attempt to foreclose, there may be a dispute about who controls the disposition. Courts have disagreed on this question. Some favor the secured creditor; others allow the sheriff to proceed on behalf of a junior lien creditor but require the sale to be subject to the secured creditor's interest. We doubt the wisdom of the latter procedure; a sale subject to a prior security interest seems likely to restrict the market for the collateral. We consider questions of third party competitors more extensively in the practitioner's edition.

5–9　"STRICT FORECLOSURE," SECTIONS 9–620, 9–621, 9–622

Sometimes the secured creditor will wish to accept the collateral in complete or partial satisfaction of its debt. This is known as a "strict foreclosure." For a number of reasons, the creditor may decide that repossession, resale, and suit for a deficiency are not feasible or not productive. The debtor may not have enough assets that a deficiency would be collectable in any event. Moreover, taking the collateral in full or partial satisfaction enables the creditor to avoid any challenge to its notice or conduct of sale. It also enables the creditor to avoid the cost of a formal notice and sale. The strict foreclosing creditor may also thereafter sell the goods wherever and however it wishes. Indeed, if the creditor believes the collateral will bring a better price several months hence, it may want to go through a strict foreclosure to avoid the claim that its delay was unreasonable.

Strict foreclosure has a long history. It was known to the common law, and was available a century ago under the Uniform Conditional Sales Act of 1917. Prior to 1999, section 9–505 authorized it. Strict foreclosure rights and procedures were elaborated in the 1999 revision and now reside in three sections: 9–620, 9–621, and 9–622. The revision describes the general change from the prior law and the general policy of the rule in Comment 2 to 9–620 as follows:

> Although these provisions derive from former section 9–505, they have been entirely reorganized and substantially rewritten. The more straightforward approach taken in this Article eliminates the fiction that the secured party always will present a "proposal" for the retention of collateral and the debtor will have a fixed period to respond. By eliminating the need (but preserving the possibility) for proceeding in that fashion, this section eliminates much of the awkwardness of former section 9–505. It reflects the belief that strict foreclosures should be encouraged and often will produce better results than a disposition for all concerned.

The procedures and the protection inherent in those procedures are set out in subsections 9–620(a), (b) and (c):

> (a) [Conditions to acceptance in satisfaction.] Except as otherwise provided in subsection (g), a secured party may accept collateral in full or partial satisfaction of the obligation it secures only if:
>
> > (1) the debtor consents to the acceptance under subsection (c);

(2) the secured party does not receive, within the time set forth in subsection (d), a notification of objection to the proposal authenticated by:

(A) a person to which the secured party was required to send a proposal under section 9–621; or

(B) any other person, other than the debtor, holding an interest in the collateral subordinate to the security interest that is the subject of the proposal;

(3) if the collateral is consumer goods, the collateral is not in the possession of the debtor when the debtor consents to the acceptance; and

(4) subsection (e) does not require the secured party to dispose of the collateral or the debtor waives the requirement pursuant to section 9–624.

(b) [Purported acceptance ineffective.] A purported or apparent acceptance of collateral under this section is ineffective unless:

(1) the secured party consents to the acceptance in an authenticated record or sends a proposal to the debtor; and

(2) the conditions of subsection (a) are met.

(c) [Debtor's consent.] For purposes of this section:

(1) a debtor consents to an acceptance of collateral in partial satisfaction of the obligation it secures only if the debtor agrees to the terms of the acceptance in a record authenticated after default; and

(2) a debtor consents to an acceptance of collateral in full satisfaction of the obligation it secures only if the debtor agrees to the terms of the acceptance in a record authenticated after default or the secured party:

(A) sends to the debtor after default a proposal that is unconditional or subject only to a condition that collateral not in the possession of the secured party be preserved or maintained;

(B) in the proposal, proposes to accept collateral in full satisfaction of the obligation it secures; and

(C) does not receive a notification of objection authenticated by the debtor within 20 days after the proposal is sent.

Putting aside consumers, and ignoring for the moment partial strict foreclosure, the procedure for a secured creditor is quite simple.

If the creditor sends a proper proposal to accept the collateral in full satisfaction, the debtor's silence for 20 days seals the deal. If, on the other hand, the debtor objects before the end of 20 days, the creditor may not proceed.

If the creditor wishes to take the collateral in *partial* satisfaction, the debtor's silence is not enough; the creditor must procure the debtor's actual agreement "in a record authenticated after default." This is due to the increased risk of overreaching by the creditor. In full satisfaction cases, it will be an unusual situation in which the collateral is worth considerably more than the debt owed, and thus it is reasonable to presume that a debtor who does not object is willing to simply wipe out its existing debt in exchange for giving up the collateral. But a creditor who is owed $10,000 might be tempted to propose taking collateral worth $10,000 in satisfaction of only $1,000 of the debt—leaving the debtor still owing $9,000 after the creditor sells the collateral, reaping a very nice windfall.

By granting explicit recognition to partial strict foreclosure and providing the details on how the debtor can be bound, Article 9 provides a significant remedy for creditors. If the creditor follows the rules carefully, and complies with the notice provisions of 9–621, section 9–622 confirms the secured creditor's title, the termination of subordinate interests, and the discharge of the debtor's obligation.

Subsections (e) and (f) have special rules for consumers. First, if more than 60% of the principal amount or the cash price has been paid, the creditor may not use strict foreclosure at all. The rule is likely based upon the hope, however faint, that the consumer will have some equity in the collateral after more than 60% has been paid. Second, subsection (g) prohibits taking in *partial* satisfaction in a consumer transaction. Third, subsection (a)(3) bars strict foreclosure in consumer cases if the collateral is still in the possession of the debtor at the time of debtor's consent. Presumably this last rule is to make sure an inattentive consumer, who has not been put on absolutely unequivocal notice by having the property repossessed, will not overlook mail from his creditor.

The debtor is always entitled to notice of foreclosure. But the creditor is further obliged to give notice to certain other persons, such as any other person who has filed a financing statement against the collateral at issue in the debtor's name, and any other person who has given the secured creditor an "authenticated notification of a claim . . . in the collateral." Note that the failure to notify these parties does not invalidate the foreclosure. Their consent—unlike that of the debtor under section 9–620(a)—is not a condition on which the effectiveness of the foreclosure depends. Comment 2 to section 9–622 makes that point as follows:

> Subsection (b) makes clear that subordinate interests are discharged under subsection (a) regardless of whether the secured party complies with this Article. Thus, subordinate interests are discharged regardless of whether a proposal was required to be sent or, if required, was sent. However, a secured party's failure to send a proposal or otherwise to comply with this Article may subject the secured party to liability under section 9–625.

Section 9–625 carries a list of remedies for those parties who were harmed by the creditor's failure and also provides for statutory damages.

We should emphasize that under section 9–601 the creditor has *discretion* to (1) ignore the collateral, (2) repossess the collateral and sell it, or (3) take the collateral in full or partial satisfaction of the debt. The choice is the creditor's, not the debtor's.[38]

Section 9–602(10) explicitly prohibits advanced waiver by the debtor of the rules stated in 9–620, 9–621, and 9–622. Under 9–620(c), the debtor is free to waive his rights *after* default, but at that point the debtor is simply consenting to the creditor's proposal. The debtor cannot in advance contract away hope that a resale will produce more than the amount of the indebtedness and entitle him to a surplus.

---

[38]   In some cases under the pre-1999 law, debtors attempted to force strict foreclosure on unwilling secured creditors. In nearly all of these cases, the secured creditor had taken possession of the collateral, had not disposed of it, and yet had not served formal notice of a proposal to it, retain the collateral as required for strict foreclosure. In the absence of a modifying agreement, some appeared to hold that the case automatically fell in to strict foreclosure that barred any further recovery by the secured creditors. See the opinion of the dissenters in S.M. Flickinger Co. v. 18 Genesee Corp., 71 A.D.2d 382, 423 N.Y.S.2d 73, 27 UCC 1232 (1979). Other courts held that while the there is no such automatic strict foreclosure, the creditors' actions might be construed as elections to retain the collateral, assuming the court found sufficient evidence of implied elections by the secured creditors to retain the collateral in satisfaction of the debt. See, e.g., In re Boyd, 73 B.R. 122, 3 UCC2d 1993 (Bankr.N.D.Tex.1987) (use by creditor was election); Nelson v. Armstrong, 99 Idaho 422, 582 P.2d 1100, 24 UCC 1378 (1978) (mere failure to resell for long period not election); Service Chevrolet, Inc. v. Sparks, 99 Wash.2d 199, 660 P.2d 760, 35 UCC 1371 (1983); Wang v. Wang, 440 N.W.2d 740, 8 UCC2d 1262 (S.D.1989) (de facto election of strict foreclosure); General Electric Capital Corp. v. Vashi, 480 N.W.2d 880, 18 UCC2d 988 (Iowa 1992) (retention of hotel telephone system for which there was no market was not strict foreclosure); Comer v. Green Tree Acceptance, Inc., 858 P.2d 560, 21 UCC2d 457 (Wyo.1993) (transfer of title of mobile home to secured party was election).Those cases tended to turn on the specific conduct of the creditors in each case. And still other courts appeared to hold that such implied elections could not occur, but that debtors might have remedies for failure to comply with the sales provisions.

5–10 FORECLOSURE BY SALE OR OTHER DISPOSITION AFTER DEFAULT, SECTIONS 9–610 AND 9–627

Although creditors seek deficiency judgments in only a minority of all cases in which there is a default—relatively few debtors have the assets to make it worthwhile—deficiency judgment cases produce most of the law under this part of Article 9. (Where the creditor is not pursuing a deficiency judgment, the debtor likely cares little how much the creditor received.) These cases show an ancient and irrepressible conflict between the interests and perceptions of debtors and creditors. Invariably the debtor believes the collateral's value greatly exceeds the price at which the creditor sold it in a foreclosure sale and that the creditor must have made an unreasonable or collusive resale. The creditor, on the other hand, believes the collateral's value has declined below the amount of the debt because the debtor has maintained it badly, has misused it, or (in the case of inventory and the like) selected inferior material from the start. Needless to say, the creditor will maintain that it achieved the best possible price under the circumstances. This difference of perception prevails whether the collateral is farm land in North Dakota during the Great Depression, inventory from a failed department store in Los Angeles in the 1930's, or a repossessed Mercedes in Miami in 2017. Part of the difference in views arises from the parties differing views of the collateral. Debtors tend to overestimate the value of the things they possess, and they assume that a crowd of willing, interested, and motivated buyers will be there to pay what the debtor believes to be the full retail value of the collateral. Creditors, on the other hand, know that sales may need to be done quickly, usually in wholesale markets, and often in markets that are plainly inefficient, such as the courthouse steps.

Appreciating the dismal history of public sales of personal and real property in that last-named forum, the drafters of Article 9, from explicitly authorized "private" sales. Today the idea is commonplace, but it was an important innovation in its day. The original draft required additional tinkering in subsequent amendments. Prior to 1999, almost all of the important rules on resales and deficiencies were contained in former section 9–504. Those rules now appear in half a dozen sections of Article 9.

The core rules are today stated in the first three subsections of section 9–610:

(a) [Disposition after default.] After default, a secured party may sell, lease, license, or otherwise dispose of any or all of the collateral in its present condition or following any commercially reasonable preparation or processing.

(b) [Commercially reasonable disposition.] Every aspect of a disposition of collateral, including the method, manner, time, place, and other terms, must be commercially reasonable. If commercially reasonable, a secured party may dispose of collateral by public or private proceedings, by one or more contracts, as a unit or in parcels, and at any time and place and on any terms.

(c) [Purchase by secured party.] A secured party may purchase collateral:

(1) at a public disposition; or

(2) at a private disposition only if the collateral is of a kind that is customarily sold on a recognized market or the subject of widely distributed standard price quotations.

The language in the first sentence of subsection (b) comes directly from former 9–504, and thus most of the cases that were decided under that section are still good law under the 1999 revision. But lawyers must be careful—the commentary to section 9–610 and the text of 9–627 modify the prior case law in certain limited ways.

As for section 9–627, its first subsection reads as follows:

[Greater amount obtainable under other circumstances; no preclusion of commercial reasonableness.] The fact that a greater amount could have been obtained by a collection, enforcement, disposition, or acceptance at a different time or in a different method from that selected by the secured party is not of itself sufficient to preclude the secured party from establishing that the collection, enforcement, disposition, or acceptance was made in a commercially reasonable manner.

Despite the disclaimer ("that a greater amount could have been obtained . . . at a different time or in a different method . . . is not of itself sufficient to preclude" a finding of commercial reasonableness), in our view the price received will ultimately be, in fact, the talisman.

Bear in mind that the standard for conducting a disposition is that it be "commercially reasonable." That means disputes can arise over virtually every aspect of the sale. If the seller sells the goods quickly, the buyer can argue that it should have waited for a better price. If the seller waits, the buyer can argue that it should have acted more promptly. If the goods are sold privately, the debtor will argue that there should have been an auction; if there was an auction, the debtor will claim that a private sale would have obtained a better price. If the creditor spent money furbishing up the goods for sale (money which will be charged to the debtor), the debtor will claim that the goods should have been sold as-is. If they are sold as-is, the buyer will claim that a little refurbishing would have vastly increased the price obtained.

Given these diametrically opposed views—all of which may be "reasonable" depending on one's view of the facts—our review of commercial practice and the cases suggest that all of the factors used in determining "commercial reasonableness" are actually proxies for "reasonable price." Comment 2 to 9–627 does an interesting waltz around this apparent inconsistency between the Code's language and real life. The Comment notes that price is not the key, but that "a low price suggests that a court should scrutinize carefully all aspects of a disposition to ensure that each aspect was commercially reasonable." It sounds as if the drafters in fact concede that price is a very important indicator.

The commentary to 9–610 seems to offer a great many suggestions for courts. Comment 3 notes it may be "prudent not to dispose of goods when the market has collapsed. Or, it might be more appropriate to sell a large inventory in parcels over a period of time instead of in bulk." The drafters seem to be telling courts that they should give the secured creditor a little more time to dispose of repossessed collateral than they have sometimes been allowed. And while subsection (a) allows the creditor to dispose of the collateral "in its present condition," Comment 4 walks that back, advising creditors to take into account the "costs and probable benefits of preparation or processing and of the fact that [it] would be advancing the costs at its risk." According to the Comment, it seems that at least some secured creditors, in some cases, might be obliged to expend their own funds to clean up, prepare, or process the collateral.

Comment 8 relates to secured creditors who have possession of investment property. Under federal securities law, disposition of some types of investment property may require filings with the Securities and Exchange Commission. But while federal law might require such filings, Article 9 does not. The Comment notes that a disposition that would be a "private placement" under securities law might well be a "public" disposition for the purpose of the Code. It suggests that a reasonable foreclosure sale might be valid *for purposes of Article 9* even if it fails to comply with federal registration requirements.

Under Article 2, sales of goods commonly come with warranties. Comment 11 recognizes that a transferee of goods under an Article 9 disposition gets the same warranties that they would get in a voluntary purchase from the debtor. Non-Article 9 law governs the extent to which statutory or implied warranties beyond those envisioned by subsection (d) (relating to title, possession, and quiet enjoyment) are applicable to disposition under Article 9. Subsection (e) permits parties to disclaim these warranties, but the disclaimer must take the form of a record, as defined by 9–102. Hence, an oral agreement would not suffice.

The Comments also contain a discussion of the rights of junior secured parties. They even discuss and invite the use of the "marshalling" principle. This is the situation in which secured creditor *A* has an interest in two pieces of collateral, while competing creditor *B* has an interest only in one. If marshalling is required, *A* would have to first dispose of the property in which *B* has no interest, and satisfy as far as possible its interests out of that, before proceeding against the property in which *B* also has an interest. The Comments, of course, are not part of the statute, but it is fair to say that many potentially serious issues lurk in them.

a.   Safe Harbors

Given the uncertainty involved in dispositions, creditors look for ways to minimize their risk. Section 9–627(b) seems to give them three "safe harbors" into which they may try to sail. These provisions are neither "required nor exclusive," according to Comment 3, but if they are followed, it would seem that creditor would be protected:

[Dispositions that are commercially reasonable.] A disposition of collateral is made in a commercially reasonable manner if the disposition is made:

(1) in the usual manner on any recognized market;

(2) at the price current in any recognized market at the time of the disposition; or

(3) otherwise in conformity with reasonable commercial practices among dealers in the type of property that was the subject of the disposition.

The language suggests that following one of these methods means that the sale will, in fact, be commercial reasonable. But it is not that simple.

The first of these actions, "disposition" in the "usual manner on any recognized market," helps, but not much. Comment 4 tells us that the concept of a "recognized market" is "quite limited." It applies only where "there are standardized price quotations for property that is essentially fungible, such as [those on] stock exchanges." Presumably, the drafters concur with the cases which hold that special auctions and other markets where used cars are sold do *not* qualify as "recognized markets." Nor, according to Comment 9 to section 9–610, do any other markets where "prices are . . . subject to individual negotiation."

The second is perhaps even more restricted. Most repossessed collateral involves used goods which almost never have "current prices" on recognized markets. Some collateral may fit into this provision—gold bullion, shares of publicly traded stocks, commodities in ordinary commercial units—but these will usually be exceptions. A *Bluebook* price for a used automobile or the catalog price of a baseball card does not qualify.

That means that by far the most important category is the third, subsection (b)(3). It protects all dispositions that conform to "reasonable commercial practices among dealers in the type of property" involved. Yet there is a huge question left hanging. The statute does not refer to commercial practices among "secured creditors" who are disposing of repossessed property, but rather to practices of "dealers in [that] type of property." An automobile dealer, for example, may routinely dispose of cars in many ways—through direct sales to customers, through public auctions, and through more limited dealer wholesale auctions. We do not believe that the drafters intended to hold creditors to the standards of retail dealers—they lack the expertise and resources to do so. We believe that the provision requires only that the sale conform to the usual practices involved in selling *repossessed* property. But it is not entirely clear from the language.

b.   Case Law

Section 9–610(b) is the central rule on disposition and provides that "[e]very aspect of a disposition of collateral, including the method, manner, time, place, and other terms, must be commercially reasonable." Hundreds of reported opinions—many of which date to before the 1999 revisions but are still good authority—interpret the words in the quoted sentence. These cases make dismal reading for the secured creditor; they seem to be an endless repetition of Murphy's Law: Anything that *can* go wrong, *will* go wrong.

What normally triggers the dispute? Despite the language of 9–610(b), the actual dispute between debtor and creditor is almost never over some "aspect of the disposition"—it is over the price. The debtor thinks the price was too low. A low price is not itself a reason to find a disposition unreasonable. Subsection 9–627(a) states:

> (a) [t]he fact that a greater amount could have been obtained by a collection, enforcement, disposition, or acceptance at a different time or in a different method from that selected by the secured party is not of itself sufficient

to preclude the secured party from establishing that the collection, enforcement, disposition, or acceptance was made in a commercially reasonable manner.

But from the debtor's point of view, price is what really matters. In fact, realizing a satisfactory price is the reason—the *only* reason—why we force secured creditors to act in a commercially reasonable manner.

Yet the price is not an "aspect" of the sale and a low price does not show that any "aspect" was commercially unreasonable. Reasoning backward from a low price to a conclusion that the sale was not commercially reasonable is incorrect.[39] On the other hand, we suspect that low price (lower than the court thinks right) is in fact the single most important fact in most of these cases—even in cases where it is not identified as the basis for the court's finding of noncompliance.[40] Even though the court may not mention price, a high price for the collateral will likely save the creditor no matter what it has done, while a low price may put the most scrupulous creditor in trouble.

What are the "aspects" of the disposition that are important? While these are many and varied, the cases focus mainly on six things. First, the *timing* of the disposition. Did the sale occur "too quickly" after the notice, or "too long" after the repossession? If the goods depreciate and the creditor waits any appreciable time, the sale will be attacked for not being timely. For that reason, a creditor who repossesses an automobile in the winter dares not await the spring season for a better market. A creditor who sells the inventory of a business where similar sales would normally occur only with two weeks or three weeks of advertising and notice, will be in trouble if the creditor advertises for a public sale to be held five days later. If timing is important, the creditor can be outside the bounds of commercial reasonableness either by being too quick or too slow.[41]

---

[39] When a creditor submits evidence as to the commercial reasonableness of a sale (e.g., notice to the debtors, advertising the sale in the country paper), a debtor must demonstrate that the process was flawed, beyond an assertion that a better price could have been obtained elsewhere, in order to establish commercial unreasonableness. Prince v. R & T Motors, Inc., 59 Ark.App. 16, 953 S.W.2d 62, 34 UCC 2d 261 (1997).

[40] See, e.g., Associates Capital Services Corp. v. Riccardi, 454 F.Supp. 832, 24 UCC 1359 (D.R.I. 1978).

[41] See, e.g., Bloomington Nat'l Bank v. Goodman Distrib., Inc., 482 N.E.2d 727, 41 UCC 1874 (Ind.App.1985); Leasing Service Corp. v. Frey, 735 F.2d 1370, 38 UCC 1414 (9th Cir.1984) (more than 17 months); In re Johnson, 116 B.R. 863, 14 UCC2d 341 (Bankr.M.D.Ga.1990) (value of collateral decreased because of delay). But see, Interfirst Bank Clifton v. Fernandez, 844 F.2d 279, 6 UCC2d 302 (5th Cir.1988) (not commercially unreasonable simply because 2 year delay).

Second, the *publicity* surrounding the sale. The creditor must properly advertise or employ other proper measures for finding the best market and the best buyers.[42] Advertising a drilling rig in the county newspaper will not do where all others would advertise in trade journals. Here the creditors should consult the debtor—if they are on speaking terms—or should ask an expert about the market. How does one find the market? How should one advertise in this market? If, for example, the best advertising medium is published only biweekly or monthly, the creditor has a problem because the first requirement of speedy sale may conflict with the need to advertise. If delay is justified by the need to advertise in infrequently published journals or for other good reasons, those reasons for the delay should be memorialized so that they can be proved later at a deficiency judgment trial.

Third, the *location* of the disposition. The sale should be held in the proper place. If the collateral is repossessed in Nashville and the most appropriate market is in Chicago, the creditor should think about selling in Chicago if that is possible. Conceivably, different geographic locations are better or worse at different times of the year.[43] For example, the automobile market might be better in the south in the winter and in the north in summer. The price of farm equipment undoubtedly fluctuates on a seasonal basis, and demand might vary in different places in different seasons.

Fourth, *access by prospective buyers*. Arrangements should normally be made for prospective bidders to inspect the repossessed goods. If it is normal for buyers to bring their mechanics to inspect automobiles, for example, that should be allowed. If it is common for purchasers of grain to take a sample and test it, that too should be permitted. The creditor dare not bar inspection except in the rare case where the relevant market prohibits inspection.

Fifth, *cleaning and refurbishment*. The creditor should consider limited cleanup and maintenance. Section 9–610 authorizes sale in its "present" condition or "following any commercially reasonable preparation or processing." Notwithstanding the absence of a statutory duty to clean or repair, some courts have held sales to be commercially unreasonable because the seller failed to clean, paint,

---

[42]   Ford & Vlahos v. ITT Commercial Fin. Corp., 8 Cal.4th 1220, 36 Cal.Rptr.2d 464, 885 P.2d 877, 25 UCC2d 630 (1994) (advertising must be reasonably aimed at informing potential buyers, provided such outlets exist; failure to direct advertisements to potential buyers is commercially unreasonable).

[43]   In First Interstate Credit Alliance, Inc. v. Clark, 1990 WL 14688, 11 UCC2d 1017 (S.D.N.Y.1990), the court held that an outdoor sale of a backhoe in Massachusetts in early January was not commercially reasonable. Notices of the sale circulated during the Christmas season, the sale included only two pieces of equipment, and buyers were unlikely to have use for the equipment until spring.

or otherwise repair goods. We doubt that a creditor should be made to do much cleaning or repair. Especially where the debtor has allowed the collateral to deteriorate, we see no justification for generally requiring a creditor to put good money after bad and to, in effect, take the risk that this new money will not be recovered either in the sale price or from the debtor. On the other hand, if sellers in the market generally believe that the cost of minimal repairs or cleaning always raise the sale price by more than the cost—as may be the case with washing and waxing a used car—the creditor may well be obliged to undertake that minimal work. Comment 4 to 2–610 strengthens the claim that there is sometimes a duty to clean or repair if the preparation is not unduly expensive and if it would be considered unreasonable to fail to prepare the goods. Where the line falls between selling "as is" and a duty to clean, we are uncertain. We would give creditors a great deal of leeway on this point, but the careful creditor will get advice on this and should be prepared to perform at least minimal repair and cleaning functions, especially if that is the general practice. It should at least be prepared to explain why it did not consider such actions to be necessary.

Sixth, *conformity to the advertisement*. This should be obvious, but once the creditor has specified the time and place in the notice and advertising, it should conduct the sale at that time and place. Failure to do so—even if the actual time and place would itself have been perfectly reasonable if it had in fact been specified—is probably not commercially reasonable.[44]

There are many, many cases belaboring these points. They involve almost every conceivable fact pattern. Those who are faced with questions on particular facts should consult the practitioners' edition for a discussion of the frequently dull and repetitious cases on what is, and what is not, commercially reasonable.

Finally, an increasing number of situations are arising in which creditors seek to dispose of property by internet auctions. The attractiveness of such a procedure is obvious: online auctions avoid many of the problems of time, place, and notice, and vastly increase the number of potential bidders. The 1999 revisions came just before the enormous boom in online sales, and thus did not directly address the issue. The 2010 amendments did not elect to deal directly with the problem, but the revised Comment 2 to 9–610 now reads, with the added language italicized, "Although subsection (b) permits both public and private dispositions, *including public and private dispositions conducted over the Internet*, 'every aspect of a disposition . . . must be commercially reasonable.'" The new language suggests

---

[44]   C.I.T. Corp. v. Anwright Corp., 191 Cal.App.3d 1420, 237 Cal.Rptr. 108, 3 UCC2d 1638 (1987) (sale held at different place).

that online sales are at least not disfavored. The choice of language also finesses a nice question—whether an internet auction over a site that requires bidders to become members of the site (such as the popular eBay auction site) counts as "public" or "private." The language also appears broad enough to cover both actual auctions and the type of "buy it now" direct sales one finds on many such sites.

As the Comment suggests, internet auctions are not inherently unreasonable, and therefore creditors may want to seek to specify such procedures in their security agreements under 9–603(a). Such agreements will be valid unless "manifestly unreasonable."

c.   Price

A word of caution about price. In many of these cases, the courts should be slow to accept the debtor's *ex post* assertions about how a better price could have been achieved. Assuming a debtor has received notice of the proposed method of disposition, there is nothing that prevents it from objecting to the proposed procedures, or even suggesting its own. Debtors, after all, may have much better information about the market for their property than creditors who are not in the business themselves. While some creditors may elect to give the cold shoulder to the debtor, sophisticated creditors worried about potential challenges may be quite willing to hear these suggestions. After all, both the creditor and the debtor want to get as high a price as possible. Courts may quite reasonably wonder why the debtor waited until after the sale if it thought a much better price could have been obtained elsewhere.

Courts have often faced the situation in which a creditor has sold collateral at wholesale rather than at retail prices. In such cases the debtor may claim that a retail price would have been higher, and it is quite likely that the debtor is correct. It is thus tempting for the court to second-guess the decision and hold that the sale was unreasonable.[45] But it is important to remember that repossessing creditors are not retail sellers. To be able to command retail prices, retail sellers must incur higher costs than wholesalers, including such things as storage, insurance, sales commissions, and so on. Those higher costs must be taken into account when evaluating a sale price. When we account for these differences, as the Seventh Circuit has noted, we cannot presume that the debtor would have received more from a retail sale.[46]

---

[45]   See, e.g., Ford Motor Credit Co. v. Jackson, 126 Ill.App.3d 124, 466 N.E.2d 1330, 81 Ill.Dec. 528, 39 UCC Rep.Serv. 743 (1984).

[46]   Contrail Leasing Partners, Ltd. v. Consolidated Airways, Inc., 742 F.2d 1095, 1101, 39 UCC 9 (7th Cir. 1984).

Finally, courts should remember that the secured creditor is selling not only in the wholesale market, but usually at the low end of that market. No matter how accessible or well-publicized a sale is, there will always be only a limited number of persons willing to purchase at that place and time. These buyers realize that repossessed goods may not have been well maintained in the last days of a debtor's financial crisis. Buyers who are willing to pay full price can get goods from reputable dealers who will stand behind them, rather than at foreclosure auctions where the seller makes no warranties. Moreover, the low value of some goods after repossession (such as inventory) may be directly related to the reasons why the debtor failed. If the debtor could not sell its inventory at a profit while it was in business, it is entirely possible that a low sale price for the repossessed inventory is the fault of the inventory itself, not the creditor.

d.   Disposition to Related Parties

Dispositions are usually made to unrelated third party buyers, but they are sometimes made to parties related to either the creditor or thee debtor. Particular problems come up when the disposition is made to a person or entity connected to the secured creditor. It is fair to suspect, for example, that when a secured creditor sells the assets to a close relative or a wholly owned subsidiary, the transaction may not be entirely fair and disinterested. Thus, for dispositions to "persons related to the secured party" or secondary obligors, section 9–615(f) has a special rule that reduces the deficiency in any case in which the debtor proves that the "value of the proceeds of the disposition is significantly below the range of proceeds that a complying disposition . . . would have brought." Unlike the usual deficiency case, here the closeness of the parties and the low price is enough—the debtor need not go through the normal ritual of attacking notice and other aspects of the sale. Note that this rule in 9–615(f) assumes that the disposition was effective as a disposition under 9–610 (even if it was unreasonable).

But when we turn to "secondary obligors," such as guarantors, we see that some dispositions are not recognized as effective under 9–610 at all. Issues associated with the sale or other disposition of collateral to "secondary obligors" have recurred as long as there has been secured credit in modern commercial transactions. There were a number of problems under former section 9–504(5) that were dealt with in the 1999 Amendments, which resulted in the more elaborate section 9–618:

(a) [Rights and duties of secondary obligor.] A secondary obligor acquires the rights and becomes obligated to perform the duties of the secured party after the secondary obligor:

(1) receives an assignment of a secured obligation from the secured party;

(2) receives a transfer of collateral from the secured party and agrees to accept the rights and assume the duties of the secured party; or

(3) is subrogated to the rights of a secured party with respect to collateral.

(b) [Effect of assignment, transfer, or subrogation.] An assignment, transfer, or subrogation described in subsection (a):

(1) is not a disposition of collateral under Section 9–610; and

(2) relieves the secured party of further duties under this article.

To appreciate the subtleties in 9–618, we must first understand the definitions of "obligor" and "secondary obligor," in sections 9–102(a)(59) and (71) respectively.[47] An "obligor" will ordinarily include the debtor, but in addition it will include a guarantor or other surety—that is, a third person who has put up collateral to secure the debtor's payment—along with any others who are "otherwise accountable . . . for payment or other performance of the obligation." Who falls into the third ("otherwise accountable") category is not completely clear to us.

The definition of "secondary obligor" is not the drafters' best work. Subsection (a)(71)(A) is a mere tautology: one is a secondary obligor if his obligation is "secondary." Subsection (B) is more helpful;

---

[47]   Section 9–102(a)(59) provides:

"Obligor" means a person that, with respect to an obligation secured by a security interest in or an agricultural lien on the collateral, (i) owes payment or other performance of the obligation, (ii) has provided property other than the collateral to secure payment or other performance of the obligation, or (iii) is otherwise accountable in whole or in part for payment or other performance of the obligation. The term does not include issuers or nominated persons under a letter of credit.

Subsection (71) provides:

"Secondary obligor means an obligor to the extent that:

(A) the obligor's obligation is secondary; or

(B) the obligor has a right of recourse with respect to an obligation secured by collateral against the debtor, another obligor, or property of either."

it identifies those with rights of "recourse" against certain other persons to be secondary obligors.

Return now to section 9–618. If a person is a secondary obligor and fits within any of the subsections in 9–618(a), the transfer of repossessed collateral to that person is *not* a disposition under 9–610 and cannot be used to establish a deficiency against the debtor. An example may be helpful. Assume, for example, that Bank makes a $1 million secured loan to Manufacturer and that Purchaser guarantees the repayment of the loan. Bank repossesses the collateral and sells it to Purchaser who buys it for $100,000 and who then repays Bank the remaining $900,000 deficiency. Purchaser would be subrogated to Bank's rights to pursue Manufacturer, but the sale of the collateral to Purchaser for $100,000 would not be a disposition under 9–610 and would not establish Manufacturer's liability for a deficiency. In this case, Purchaser would clearly be a secondary obligor and would have received "an assignment of secured obligation from the secured party" or have been "subrogated" to the secured party's rights, so satisfying 9–618(a). If Purchaser wishes to sue Manufacturer for a deficiency, it will itself have to do a resale of the collateral that satisfies section 9–610. Why is this? The drafters believed, with some reason, that a sale to a person with essentially the same interest as that of the secured creditor was not a reliable measure of the value of the collateral.

Consider an alternative where the sale to the related party probably *does* qualify as a disposition under section 9–610. Assume some different facts. Bank is making a loan to Distributor, who routinely buys goods from Manufacturer. Manufacturer is willing to help Distributor get the loan, but is not willing to act as a guarantor. Instead, Manufacturer agrees that in the event Distributor defaults on the Bank loan, Manufacturer will repurchase (at wholesale invoiced cost) any inventory in the hands of Distributor at the time of default. Assume Bank repossesses and sells the remaining inventory to Large Manufacturer at invoice cost. Has Bank done a "disposition" under 9–610 so that it may now sue the debtor for the deficiency? We believe so. In this case Manufacturer is probably an "obligor" because it is "accountable . . . in part for payment or other performance of the obligation." Whether it is also a "secondary obligor" depends upon the mysterious tautology in 9–102(a)(71)(A). However, it seems clear to us that Manufacturer does not meet any of the three tests in 9–618(a), for it does not receive an assignment of the secured obligation, it is not subrogated to the secured party's rights, and it does not assume the duties of the secured party. Standing back from the transaction, it is clear that a resale at the wholesale invoice value is at least is good as could ever be expected in a foreclosure sale, thus policy also suggests that this sale should be recognized as a proper disposition under section 9–610. We believe our conclusion is supported by the following commentary to section 9–618:

> As discussed more fully in Comment 3, a secondary obligor may receive a transfer of collateral in a disposition under section 9–610 in exchange for a payment that is applied against the secured obligation. However, a secondary obligor who pays and receives a transfer of collateral does not necessarily become subrogated to the rights of the secured party as contemplated by subsection (a)(3). Only to the extent the secondary obligor makes a payment in satisfaction of its secondary obligation would it become subrogated. To the extent its payment constitutes the price of the collateral in a section 9–610 disposition by the secured party, the secondary obligor would not be subrogated. Thus, if the amount paid by the secondary obligor for the collateral in a section 9–610 disposition is itself insufficient to discharge the secured obligation, but the secondary obligor makes an additional payment that satisfies the remaining balance, the secondary obligor would be subrogated to the secured party's deficiency claim. However, the duties of the secured party *as such* would have come to an end with respect to that collateral. In some situations the capacity in which the payment is made may be unclear. Accordingly, the parties should in their relationship provide clear evidence of the nature and circumstances of the payment by the secondary obligor.

We suspect the exhortation in the last sentence of the Comment will not be widely followed. Accordingly, it will be the job of lawyers and courts to determine whether parties are in fact "secondary obligors" and whether they satisfy any of the conditions in 9–618(a). As a starting point, we suggest one should examine the incentives of the person who has purchased the collateral. If, in these circumstances, that person appears to have incentives similar to those of the secured debtor itself (i.e., to lowball the price when a deficiency might be collectible), that is a good start toward the conclusion that the sale should not be regarded as satisfying 9–610.

5–11 NOTICE, SECTIONS 9–611, 9–612, 9–614, 9–615

a. In General

Section 9–611(b) requires the secured party to send "a reasonable authenticated notification of disposition." This notice must be sent to the debtor,[48] to any secondary obligor (e.g., a guarantor), and, if the collateral is not consumer goods, to certain other persons who claim an interest or who have filed financing statements in the debtor's name that cover the same collateral. Observe that the creditor's obligation is merely to "send," not to ensure receipt of the notice. The creditor must check the relevant records to discover financing statements before sending the notice. There inevitably will be a time lag between the search and the notice, so subsection (e), by giving the secured creditor a window of time to check filings, protects it against the possibility that a third person will file a financing statement after the creditor has checked the files but before it has sent notice.

Section 9–612 makes the timeliness of notice a "question of fact." However, subsection (b) gives creditors in non-consumer transactions a safe harbor; notices sent 10 days or more before the "earliest time of disposition set forth in the notification" are timely as a matter of law. Section 9–613 spells out the form and contents of the notification as follows:

(1) The contents of a notification of disposition are sufficient if the notification:

(A) describes the debtor and the secured party;

(B) describes the collateral that is the subject of the intended disposition;

(C) states the method of intended disposition;

(D) states that the debtor is entitled to an accounting of the unpaid indebtedness and states the charge, if any, for an accounting; and

(E) states the time and place of a public sale or the time after which any other disposition is to be made.

(2) Whether the contents of a notification that lacks any of the information specified in paragraph (1) are nevertheless sufficient is a question of fact.

(3) The contents of a notification providing substantially the information specified in paragraph (1) are sufficient, even if the notification includes:

---

[48]   FDIC v. Jahner, 506 N.W.2d 57, 24 UCC2d 692 (N.D.1993) (though debtor was not given formal written notice, it had actual knowledge of the terms of the sale prior to sale; actual knowledge is sufficient under 1–201(25) and 1–201(38)); Medallion Funding Corp. v. Helen Laundromat, Inc., 1997 WL 835420, 34 UCC2d 250 (N.Y.Sup.1997) (oral notice of sale may be sufficient if the fact-finder determines that the debtor was made sufficiently aware of the sale through such oral communication).

(A) information not specified by that paragraph; or

(B) minor errors that are not seriously misleading.

(4) A particular phrasing of the notification is not required.

(5) The following form of notification and the form appearing in section 9–614(3), when completed, each provides sufficient information.

Subsections (2) through (4) alleviate creditor anxiety. Minor errors are okay, and slight deviations from the rules are fine if it is "substantially" the same as what was required. Subsection (5) provides a simple form that creditors should have no trouble following. Even where the information given does not follow the subsection (5) form and does not comply with the requirements of subsection (1), the creditor is not doomed—whether the notice was proper will then simply be a "question of fact."

In consumer goods transactions, section 9–614 adds the following three requirements to the list in section 9–613(1):

(B) a description of any liability for a deficiency of the person to which the notification is sent;

(C) a telephone number from which the amount that must be paid to the secured party to redeem the collateral under section 9–623 is available; and

(D) a telephone number or mailing address from which additional information concerning the disposition and the obligation secured is available.

In consumer cases, section 9–614 gives somewhat different assurances to the secured creditor than does 9–613. Subsection 9–613(2) disclaims the need for particular phrasing, subsection (5) says the notification is okay even if it has errors, as long as those errors are not in the information required by paragraph (1), and subsection (4) explicitly authorizes "additional information" at the end of the form. The rules in section 9–614 are not quite as generous to the creditor as those in 9–613, and it is hard to predict the consequence of the statement in 9–613 that makes it a "question of fact" whether a form lacking information specified in subsection (1) can be acceptable. For consumer notifications there is no such assurance, but we see no reason why a creditor should be held to a significantly higher standard in consumer cases.

The current version of the Code resolves in favor of creditors some issues that were troublesome in the earlier cases. For example, the plain safe harbor 9–613(1) eliminates most claims that the notice was insufficient, since most of those earlier insufficiencies related to relatively minor issues that did not serious affect the outcome of the procedure. The assurances discussed above in 9–613(3) reduces maneuvering over immaterial misstatements in the notice. The presence of forms expressly blessed by the statute will, if correctly filled out, give creditors protection. And the error rule in 9–614(5) will allow creditors to include additional non-required information without worrying that minor errors will be held against them.

b.   Public or Private Notice

Section 9–613(1)(E) provides that for a public sale the creditor must give notice of the "time and place" of the sale, whereas for a private sale it need only state the "time after which" the sale is to occur. In most cases the distinction is not troublesome, but the issue of adequate notice has arisen in cases involving auctions which are held at a specific time and place but are not open to the general public, such as regular automobile dealer auctions. Do these count as *public* sales (in which case the debtor gets notice of the time and place) or *private* ones (in which only gets the "time after which")? The question has been around since the Code's earliest days, and as we noted earlier arises in online auctions where bidders have to register for accounts in order to bidi. The drafters still have not addressed it. Cases tend to hold that such sales are "private" and thus debtors are not required to get the same notice they would for public auctions.[49] The rule has been criticized. While there are good and practical reasons why the debtor in a purely private sale—which will often involve negotiations over time—need not be given notice of every potential sale, there seems no reason why the debtor should not get notice of a dealer or online auction. On the other hand, if the debtor cannot go to the auction and bid, it is difficult to see that it suffers much harm.

c.   Summary

In general, we are unsympathetic to debtor claims that they have been injured by the creditor's failure to give adequate notice. When the debtor wakes up in the morning and finds his car gone, he should be galvanized into action. After a fruitless call to the police (who will direct him to his secured creditor), the diligent debtor will quickly find out what he needs to do in order to get his car back. Creditors normally *want* debtors to redeem the property and resume payments, and they normally want to maximize the amount of money they get on resale. The debtor's claim that he failed to understand

---

[49]   See, e.g., John Deery Motors, Inc. v. Steinbronn, 383 N.W.2d 553, 42 UCC 1855 (Iowa 1986); Beard v. Ford Motor Credit Co., 41 Ark.App. 174, 850 S.W.2d 23, 20 UCC2d 1158 (1993).

that his car was going to be sold and that he did not understand how he could redeem it, is not credible to us in that scenario.

We are always skeptical of debtor claims that with slightly improved notices they would have sprung to action and produced many aggressive bidders at the sale of the collateral. If our belief about debtor behavior is correct, denial of a deficiency or the imposition of damages for failure to give proper notice is really the award of punitive damages. If the drafters of the 1999 revision had had more intestinal fortitude, they would have substantially reduced the notice requirements and the penalties for failure to give "adequate" notice.

5–12 LEGAL CONSEQUENCES OF SALE AND APPLICATION OF PROCEEDS, SECTIONS 9–615, 9–617, 9–619

What about the people who purchase property at foreclosure sales? Section 9–617(a) protects a good faith transferee at a foreclosure sale from claims to title by the debtor and by subordinate secured parties and lienors. This provision is designed to maximize the payment a buyer is willing to make. Section 9–619, on the transfer of "record or legal title" ties up loose ends in certificate of title cases and other cases where the collateral is subject to a registration system.

Once the creditor has the money, it follows the steps under section 9–615. First, it pays "reasonable attorney's fees" and other costs of repossessing and disposing of the collateral out of the proceeds of the foreclosure sale. These come off the top. Second, it applies the remaining money to satisfy its own secured obligation. Third, in the event there is money left over, it applies the money to satisfy the obligations of subordinate parties who made their claims know. Fourth, if there is any remaining surplus, it is turned over to the debtor. If there is not enough money to pay the secured debt, the debtor normally is "liable for any deficiency." If the loan is "nonrecourse" by agreement or because it is a "sale," the creditor (buyer of the receivable) keeps any surplus and the debtor (seller of the receivable) is not liable for any deficiency.

Given that debtors ordinarily will try to avoid default on collateral that is substantially more valuable than the amount they still owe, and that prices in foreclosure are likely to lower than what can be obtained in ordinary retail sales, surpluses are unusual. In the words of Professor Gilmore, a surplus is the "shimmering mirage," a deficiency, the "grim reality." In most cases, the deficiency is the amount that remains due on the secured debt after the fees of seizure and sale have been paid and after the debt has been reduced by the remaining amount.

Subsection 9–615(f) has a special rule for the case where the collateral is transferred to a person "related to the secured party." In that case, if the proceeds of the disposition are "significantly below the range of proceeds" that a proper sale to a third party would have produced, the deficiency is calculated as though there had been a "complying disposition" to an unrelated party.

5–13 REMEDIES FOR SECURED CREDITOR'S FAILURE TO COMPLY WITH PART SIX OF ARTICLE 9

The remedies of debtors for creditor failures have a rather tortured history under the Code. Before 1999, the former section 9–507 set forth the debtor's remedies for the secured party's failure to comply with its obligations. Creditors long argued that those remedies were exclusive, but courts—looking back at a long history of pre-Code law—adopted many rules that restricted or completely denied a deficiency judgment to a secured creditor found to have violated the rules of Article 9. There were at least three different approaches. Some states found that a creditor who had violated its obligations should be barred from any deficiency as a matter of law. This position was known as the "absolute bar" rule. Other courts adopted the "rebuttable presumption" rule: unless the misbehaving secured creditor proved otherwise (thus rebutting the presumption), the value of the collateral was presumed to equal the amount of the debtor's liability, so no deficiency. In effect, the burden was on the creditor to show reasonableness. The third position was to subtract whatever actual damages the debtor could prove from the deficiency, thus putting the burden on the debtor to show harm.

a.   Denial or Reduction of Deficiency

The 1999 version of Article 9 sought to clear things up, and it did so in part. It changed the rules in several ways. Most important, it explicitly adopted the rebuttable presumption rule for *business transactions* and so, for the first time, recognized that a reduction or a denial of a deficiency judgment is an appropriate remedy. But understanding what was done requires some history relating to the amendments.

During the revision process, the drafters of the 1999 Amendments quickly decided that the rebuttable presumption rule was the proper outcome in business transactions. That conclusion was relatively uncontroversial. The Reporters on the 1999 Amendments had further recommended the same rule be used in consumer transactions, but this was rejected after substantial arguments between lawyers for debtors and creditor. Consumer lawyers were unwilling to withdraw from their advocacy of the absolute bar rule.

This led to arduous negotiations. There was no agreement on using the absolute bar for consumer transactions, and there was a potential problem with simply remaining silent on that topic. Creditor lawyers were worried (and debtor lawyers hopeful) that mere silence would create am implication that the absolute bar rule should apply to consumers. The language ultimately adopted, subsection 9–626(b), explicitly tells courts that while it addresses business but not consumer transactions, courts should draw no inference one way or the other from the fact that consumer transactions were not addressed. Instead, courts were left to resolve the issue themselves:

> The limitation of the rules in subsection (a) to transactions other than consumer transactions is intended to leave to the court the determination of the proper rules in consumer transactions. The court may not infer from that limitation the nature of the proper rule in consumer transactions and may continue to apply established approaches.

In our view, the rebuttable presumption test should have been adopted even for consumer transactions. The absolute bar rule in effect awards punitive damages to debtors in situations that may be unrelated to the amount of their actual losses. Where the creditor has failed in its duties, it seems perfectly reasonable to put on it the burden of demonstrating that the sale was reasonable, but leaving the creditor to absorb the deficiency—without any means of showing that its default caused no damage—is a very crude measure of harm.

A casual reader examining section 9–626 may have trouble finding the rebuttable presumption rule. It is buried in 9–626(a)(4). To see how it works, we start under (a)(1)—the secured party does not need to prove compliance with Part 6 unless its compliance is "placed in issue." The creditor presumably need only prove the amount received on the sale of the collateral, and the amount the debtor owes. The difference between these numbers equals the "deficiency." In many cases, the debtor will not raise an issue. But if the debtor puts the creditor's compliance in issue, the creditor has the burden of showing that the "collection, enforcement, disposition, or acceptance was conducted in accordance with this part." If the secured creditor fails to prove its compliance with Part 6, it suffers the consequence stated in 9–626(a)(4), namely, a presumption that "the amount of proceeds that would have been realized [if the secured creditor had complied] is equal to the sum of the secured obligation, expenses, and attorney's fees." Of course, if the amount that would have been realized equals the amount owed, there is no deficiency.

The creditor then may rebut the presumption. How does it do so? The last clause in subsection 9–626(a)(4) (unless the secured party proves that the amount received on compliance would be less than that sum) offers redemption to the misbehaving secured creditor. If it proves that a complying sale or other disposition would have brought an amount less than the amount due from the debtor, the secured creditor rebuts the presumption and earns a right to a deficiency judgment measured by the amount that would have been recovered in a complying disposition. In other words, the creditor obtains the difference between the amount owed and the amount that *would have been recovered* in a proper disposition.

To understand all this, consider an example. Assume the debtor's total obligation (including costs of sale, etc.) to the creditor is $100,000. Assume also that the foreclosure sale produces $10,000 and the debtor attacks creditor's notice or conduct of the sale. If the creditor proves it complied with Part 6 of Article 9, it recovers the full $90,000. If the creditor fails to prove it complied, and does not prove what a complying foreclosure sale would have brought, the amount produced by a complying sale is presumed to be $100,000 and the creditor recovers nothing. If the creditor is found to have violated Part 6 but proves, for example, that a complying sale would have produced only $15,000, it recovers the difference between its debt and $15,000, $85,000.

The structure of this lawsuit can present some tactical questions for the creditor's lawyer. If a lawyer is unable to convince the court that the creditor complied with Article 9, the lawyer will wish to have evidence in the record to rebut the presumption. Of course, putting such evidence (of what a complying sale would have produced) in the record inevitably weakens the basic argument that the creditor *did* comply with Article 9 and that the amount obtained in the sale was reasonable.

With respect to business transactions, the changes have done much to clarify the law and make it uniform. Section 9–626 provides a clear roadmap for judges and lawyers. As to consumers, courts will continue to work things out. We would hope that they would move toward adopting the rebuttable presumption rule for all transactions, but some courts have continued to follow the absolute bar rule in consumer cases.[50]

---

[50]   See, e.g., Hicklin v. Onyx Acceptance Corp., 970 A.2d 244, 68 UCC2d 413 (Del. 2009).

b.   Other Statutory Remedies

Section 9–625 is the successor to section 9–507. Like the former section, section 9–625 explicitly authorizes both equitable relief ("the court may order or restrain") and damages ("a person is liable for damages in the amount of any loss caused by a failure to comply with this Article").

For several reasons, the actual damages suffered by a debtor are likely to be quite limited. In the first place, it is in the creditor's interest to sell the collateral at the highest price. After all, the creditor usually has no assurance that the debtor—by hypothesis someone already in default—will be able to pay a deficiency judgment. In the second place, and notwithstanding the claims of the debtor, many of the ways in which a creditor may fail to comply with Part 6 of Article 9 will have little impact on the price actually obtained at the foreclosure sale. Assume, for example, the creditor did not send appropriate notice to the debtor of the time and place of the foreclosure sale. If the debtor would not have acted on the notice in any way, such as by trying to drum up bidders, no actual loss could have resulted from the failure to give the debtor notice.

Nor do these cases make particularly good candidates for class actions. Each case typically rests upon its own facts, its own mode of sale, its own notice, and its own circumstances of resale. Thus, it is hard to make a case for a class action, for such an action must involve the same or similar circumstances with respect to each member of the class.

c.   Punitive Damages

Section 9–625(c)(2) carries forward the 10% punitive damage rule from the former Article 9. This applies if the collateral is "consumer goods." Conceivably it could apply to a business transaction where the debtor is using consumer goods as collateral, but the rule chiefly applies to pure "consumer transactions," typically those where the consumer has granted a purchase money security interest to buy consumer goods. The argument in favor of punitive damages is that the dollar amounts are so small in consumer transactions that an unscrupulous creditor might find it economically sensible to violate Part 6 in consumer cases. The punitive damages in (c)(2) make that behavior costlier, and thus *may* deter such a creditor.

The damages are to be "not less than" the credit service charge plus 10% of the principal amount of the obligation or the time-price differential plus 10% of the cash price. We interpret that sentence to grant damages equal to the total interest charge (irrespective of the amount that has been paid) in addition to 10% of the original principal amount of the debt, irrespective of how much of the principal has been repaid. Assume the sale of a mobile home for $50,000, financed at 10% over 10 years. In round figures the total interest (credit service charge) would be somewhere in excess of $20,000. To that, one must add $5,000 (10% of the principal amount). At least with respect to expensive consumer goods such as luxury automobiles, boats, and mobile homes, section 9–625(c)(2) has teeth.

Subsections 9–625(e) and (f) have additional, but more limited, punitive damage rules.[51] Under subsection (e), a creditor will have to pay $500 each time it violates its duty concerning collateral in its possession (9–208), fails to notify an account debtor (9–209), makes an abusive filing (9–509), fails to file or send a termination statement (9–513), fails repeatedly to explain the calculation of a deficiency (9–616), or, without reasonable cause, fails to respond to a request for an accounting (9–210).

As it happens, the punitive damage provisions seem to have been infrequently invoked. Except for large-ticket items (such as the mobile home, above), perhaps the dollar amounts involved are too small to make it worthwhile to pursue them.

d. Torts

In addition to the commission of the conventional torts of trespass, conversion, assault and battery, a person who qualifies as a debt collector under the Consumer Protection Act may be guilty of

---

[51]   The relevant provisions of 9–625 include:

(e) [Statutory damages: noncompliance with specified provisions.] In addition to any damages recoverable under subsection (b), the debtor, consumer obligor, or person named as a debtor in a filed record, as applicable, may recover $500 in each case from a person that:

(1) fails to comply with section 9–208;

(2) fails to comply with section 9–209;

(3) files a record that the person is not entitled to file under section 9–509(a);

(4) fails to cause the secured party of record to file or send a termination statement as required by § 9–513(a) or (c);

(5) fails to comply with § 9–616(b)(1) and whose failure is part of a pattern, or consistent with a practice, of noncompliance; or

(6) fails to comply with § 9–616(b)(2).

(f) [Statutory damages: noncompliance with § 9–210.] A debtor or consumer obligor may recover damages under subsection (b) and, in addition, $500 in each case from a person that, without reasonable cause, fails to comply with a request under § 9–210. A recipient of a request under § 9–210 which never claimed an interest in the collateral or obligations that are the subject of a request under that section has a reasonable excuse for failure to comply with the request within the meaning of this subsection.

"extortionate collection practice." The Federal Consumer Protection Act[52] names these practices as follows:

> An extortionate means is any means which involves the use, or an express or implicit threat of use, of violence or other criminal means to cause harm to the person, reputation, or property of any person.[53]

In the rare case where a secured creditor proceeds all the way to repossession and sale, even though the debtor is not in default, the creditor is likely to be liable for conversion as well. In that case the conversion damages may equal the value of the debtor's "equity." Of course, in aggravated circumstances punitive damages may attend any of these torts.

e.   Relationship Between Damages and Denial or Restriction of a Deficiency

Under section 9–625(d), where a proper disposition would have produced a surplus, the debtor gets to reduce the deficiency to zero plus recover damages for "loss of any surplus." This is unlikely—in our experience they exist in theory but are never actually observed. The real cases will arise under the second sentence of subsection (d): a debtor whose deficiency "is eliminated or reduced *under 9–626* may not otherwise recover under subsection (b) for noncompliance with the provisions of this part" (emphasis added). It appears that any reduction of a deficiency or denial, however small, eliminates the possibility of actual damages under (b).

Subsection 9–625(d) does not prevent the consumer from recovering punitive damages under (c) nor a business debtor from recovering statutory (punitive) damages under (e). Because 9–626 itself does not state a rule for consumer transactions (remember it specifically declines to take a position on the absolute bar/rebuttable presumption debate), in the words of the Comment, "the statute is silent as to whether a double recovery" is permitted in a consumer transaction. We see no reason to treat consumer debtors differently from business debtors, so we would argue that "double recoveries" should be denied in consumer cases too.

---

[52]   Act of 1968, Pub.L. No. 90–321, Title II § 202a et seq., 82 Stat. 160, 18 U.S.C.A. § 891–96 (1976).

[53]   18 U.S.C.A. § 891(7).

Table of Cases

Index

References are to Sections

WAIVERS
Default events, 5–2

WORKOUTS
Generally, 5–4